TRANSFORMING THE ROUGH PLACES

THE MINISTRY OF SUPERVISION

KENNETH H. POHLY

First Edition

Published in the United States of America
Whaleprints™
1405 Cornell Drive
Dayton, Ohio 45406-4727

ISBN: 1-882122-02-X

A voice cries out: "In the wilderness prepare the way of the Lord, make straight in the desert a highway for our God. Every valley shall be lifted up, and every mountain and hill be made low; the uneven ground shall become level, and the rough places a plain. Then the glory of the Lord shall be revealed, and all people shall see it together . . . ."

Isaiah 40:3-5

CONTENTS

BIBLIOGRAPHY

FOREWORD

Ken Pohly has made another significant contribution to the discipline of supervised ministries. Those who had the privilege of reading his first book (*Pastoral Supervision*, 1977) will find his new book a helpful renewal and expansion of his pioneering work. Those who come afresh to his work by reading **Transforming the Rough Places: The Ministry of Supervision** will find it a thought-provoking volume that opens many doors of inquiry and points the way to further exploration. Indeed, these are the marks of a good book.

Pohly's treatment of the history of supervision takes the form of an overview. Its genius is in this survey approach, because in this way the reader can grasp both the scope and depth of the discipline, and is provided with the pegs on which other research and new developments can be based. Particularly helpful is the much expanded bibliography which has now been subdivided. Its breadth, established by the inclusion of texts from other fields, greatly enhances its usefulness.

In one sense the discipline of pastoral supervision is at least as old as the Christian church. Yet in another sense it is a relatively new discipline in theological education. Pohly looks at both history and the contemporary scene, thereby helping the reader to know and experience vicariously the rootedness of the discipline in Biblical word, experience, and injunction as well as in the Judeo/Christian tradition. At the same time, for him the discipline is in contemporary formation—perhaps as few disciplines have been challenged to be.

The ministry of supervision has amassed years of experience and material. Although not always recognized as a discrete discipline, Pohly demonstrates how it is a discipline to be critiqued, compared, developed, and loved. He does each with skill and style.

Pastoral supervision has learned from other professional fields, as Pohly's review of the literature shows. Yet as he draws from them certain common threads, he puts into clear relief the credibility of supervision as a fundamental component of theological education. His work also suggests the great promise that supervision holds for the church's many institutional expressions.

Chapter IV (significantly expanded from his previous work) presents a model for supervised ministry that gives detail and is useful for the evaluation of an established program or the development of a new one. While it is obvious that his home base is the seminary, it is also clear that Pohly's presentation is relevant to parish life. It sets useful guidelines that are easily adapted for enriching the program of any congregation looking for some form of organized supervision.

In Chapter V the reader is brought into the author's current musings. This invitational approach to the theology behind pastoral supervision is marked by its profound, simple, and direct tone. It is here that pastoral supervision establishes its own uniqueness. It not only provides a framework for reflection and growth for a person being formed for professional ministry, but it also outlines an approach by which persons of faith no matter what their vocation can be aided and strengthened in their journey. While the context may differ from calling to calling, the "Signposts Along the Way" that Pohly so carefully sets forth form guidelines for transference to any of life's experiences and issues.

His discussion of Narrative Theology as one method (of three that he offers) for theological reflection is Kenneth Pohly's particular gift to the field. His valuable bibliography invites further exploration. We who have worked in the ministry of supervision will immediately recognize the importance of this approach for the formation of persons for ministry, especially, of those who now come to seminary from a variety of other involvements and at an older age. Drama and trauma often characterizes their family, work and educational background; faith has been strongly tested. Because many have only recently entered upon a course of events that brought them to a theological school, it seems to this writer that Pohly's approach allows, and even encourages, the plumbing of these "pasts" for the values and learning they bring to ministry.

Whether in the halls of academia or the local church, Supervised Ministry looks to improve ministry and to expand the potential for the spiritual growth of everyone. Pohly's book contributes richly to this very old, yet very new, discipline. It is a text which will remain a reference. All of us in the ministry of supervision, believing in its worth for the church's enrichment, give thanks that Pohly disciplined himself to do the research necessary for the development of the book and for his commitment to set it forth for the rest of us.

Pohly's stated reason for writing the text was to "show that supervision offers an historic and effective means for equipping persons for ministry," and to "show how supervision can be a transformative experience for both individuals and the Church." He has admirably fulfilled his task.

George H. Sinclair, Jr.
Andover Newton Theological School
Newton Centre, Massachusetts

PREFACE

This book is the product of many influences that have played upon my life, beginning with a seventeen-year pastorate and a four-year college chaplaincy where the patterns of ministry reflected here were formed. Particularly, it grows out of twenty years of teaching, including two, year-long sabbatical leaves from my teaching responsibilities at United Theological Seminary, Dayton, Ohio. Those responsibilities combined the interests of pastoral care and field education (supervised ministry) within the general discipline of pastoral theology. The move into pastoral supervision has been a natural one.

It had its formal beginning in the writing of my dissertation at Vanderbilt University on "The Clinical Method in Theological Education." During that process one of the members of my committee challenged me to give special attention to the role of supervision. To be sure, supervision had appeared in that study as the critical element, but it loomed as too extensive a subject to be addressed in that document. During the years since, as I have attempted to expand clinical methods in the ministering situation of theological students at United, supervision has occupied more and more of my attention. Its emergence as a critical element in our field education and Doctor of Ministry programs has aroused my interest in its role in the church at large. The formation of the Center for Supervisory Studies (CSS) as part of United Seminary's programs has served to demonstrate its importance and to focus my teaching.

The first edition of this book, *Pastoral Supervision*, appeared in 1977 as a publication of The Institute of Religion, Texas Medical Center, Houston, Texas. At the time of its publication it was, to my knowledge, the first book to be devoted specifically to pastoral supervision. Since that time, there has been a blossoming of literature in the field. Even so, this revision and expansion of my original work continues to draw more widely than others upon multiple disciplines and occupations for theory and practice regarding supervision as a pastoral art.

Most of the original research and writing was done while I was in residence for five months at The Institute of Religion in Houston. Chapter V on theology and supervision was developed during a four-month residency at the Urban Theology Unit, Sheffield, England. Those two locations contributed in vastly different ways to my original thought—with Houston providing the stimulation of a clinical setting where pastoral supervision is a highly developed competency, and Sheffield, with its alternative church concerns, challenging whether pastoral supervision is at all an appropriate subject for pursuit.

The revisions and the new final Chapter VI on theological reflection have grown out of the second sabbatical, a nine-month residency at Andover Newton Theological School, Newton Centre, Massachusetts. That setting with its rich theological tradition and extensive supervisory education program, provided the opportunity to reflect on my experience during the intervening years and to correlate ideas which had been generated through numerous papers, speeches, workshops, courses, supervisory conversations, and discussions about supervision. The result is this book which many people have encouraged me to have republished since the 1977 edition went out of print.

What makes this book distinctive from the earlier edition is its inclusion of the insights and methods growing out of the more recent experiences. I can attest to the fact that what I suggest here works in actual practice. It also, of course, reflects the thought that has been generated in other circles in the intervening years, including the updating of my original research.

A word about format. I have written in first person terms because this material grows out of my experience; I count myself among all those who are always moving between being supervisor and supervisee, teacher and learner. Biblical quotations are from the New Revised Standard Version of the Bible (1989) unless otherwise indicated. The attempt to be inclusive is interrupted only when direct quotations from early sources seems necessary.

There are some people whom I find joy in thanking for their part in making this book possible: my colleagues at United Theological Seminary who shared the task of supervision with me in the field education program and President Leonard I. Sweet who made republication possible; the members of the ecumenical and inter-professional Advisory Board of CSS who have encouraged me to get on with this task (Richard Carson, Marilyn Evans, Pamela Fenn, Mary Olson, David Ramey, Phyllis Schaefer, Richard Schaefer, John Wagner, Robert Walker,) and particularly, Dean Newell Wert who provided the time and space in which to do it; the people with whom I was associated at my sabbatical locations, whose courtesy, assistance, and guidance supported me during those critical blocks of time; and the many people who have participated in study and research at CSS and who continue to share in the excitement of supervision. Their number is too large to name them individually.

I am grateful to George H. Sinclair, Jr., my host and mentor at Andover Newton during my last sabbatical years, for accepting the invitation to write the Foreword. He has been a gracious friend and colleague.

Finally, there are three people who have been the closest to me in this project for whom I am especially grateful. Marti Anderson, with her usual good humor in the midst of her other responsibilities as a faculty secretary typed my revised and heavily annotated copy onto word processor disc; it was a second-mile effort. Marilyn Evans, whose reading and critiquing of the manuscript was a labor of love, was my "sounding board" throughout the project; she continues to share her expertise in supervision as Education Associate at CSS where she is my colleague, teacher, and friend. And my wife, Marge, who had typed the original first-edition manuscript from handwritten copy, was present and patient this second time around during all those moments when she wondered (as did I) why I had gotten myself into this. They have been the inner circle in a community of covenant, relationship incarnation, judgment, and grace in which I live and from which I continue to find nourishment.

Kenneth H. Pohly
Dayton, Ohio

INTRODUCTION

ROUGH ROAD AHEAD:
A WAY TO HERE

Near the end of his book focusing on career development in ministry, Charles Stewart writes:

> In the decades ahead, the ministry will be less associated with the vice-president of a business and more closely associated with the foreman of a group of workers or the teacher of a night school class. Servanthood (ministry) will be understood not as taking care of an institution, but as overseeing a caring community which is in mission. The parish will be defined as the core of committed disciples who find a network of interest and concern within a highly mobile functional group.[1]

Stewart identifies five primary roles that ministers will need to fulfill in order to function effectively within this understanding of the emerging church: (1) **communicator** of the Gospel through the various mediums available to people; (2) **counselor** to persons with genuine needs through caring personal relationships; (3) **change agent** within both the church and the larger community in which the church's ministry takes place; (4) **consultant** to the laity in their church organizational responsibilities and in their mission to the world; and (5) **celebrator** of the significant events in the life of the congregation. While emphasis is placed upon these roles as professional competencies, it is clear that Stewart sees ministry as belonging to all the People of God among whom there are to be "creative, flexible, yet faithful persons" working "in concert" with laity "to generate creative communities."[2]

Stewart's choice of words in describing the ministry of the future suggests two different images to express a single important idea. One image is that of the "shepherd," suggested by the word "overseeing," when he says that ministry will be understood as overseeing a caring community which is in mission. The other image is "enabler," suggested by the word "generate," when he speaks of working in concert with laity to generate creative communities. Both images are pastoral and supervisory in nature. This raises the possibility, though he does not use the term in this connection, that one of the most useful dimensions of ministry in the church's long history may be coming into its day, namely the ministry of supervision.

It seems accurate to project, as Stewart does, that the congregation will continue to be the primary locus for the church's work. It is also clear that the church is on firm biblical ground whenever it makes its combined caring and missional tasks its central concern. The author of Ephesians writes that the purpose of God's gifts to the church is to equip the saints for ministry (Eph. 4:11-12). But the question of **how** the saints are to be equipped for the responsibility of ministry in and through the core of committed disciples, to and on behalf of the world, remains a critical one for the church.

SOME BACKGROUND

My purpose in writing this book is to show that supervision offers a historic and effective means for equipping persons for ministry. I recognize that in doing so I invite resistance, because **supervision** is a term that is loaded with baggage. It carries an image of "bossism," of someone in authority looking over one's shoulder and controlling every move, rewarding or punishing at will. It suggests a hierarchy of superiority/inferiority and dredges up threatening associations with the past. For this reason some people suggest abandoning the term and substituting something more palatable, but that is a false solution because it fails to deal with the condition that produces the resistance.

It is not new to speak of supervision as a necessary occupational function. The shop foreman in a factory, the head nurse on a hospital ward, and the office manager in a financial institution are frequently referred to as supervisors, meaning that in these settings they are responsible for the job performance of other persons who work "under" them. They in turn are ordinarily accountable to others who are "above" them in the hierarchical order of business, industrial, and professional life. No matter how high they are in the pecking order, they earn their living within the authority of somebody's supervision, whether that "somebody" is an individual or board of managers.

The language of hierarchy and management is used above because that is the common frame of reference in which we have usually placed the supervisory role. A bank president with whom I had lunch to discuss my research project responded, "Oh, you're talking about management"; while a clergy person with whom I carried on a similar discussion said, "You're referring to administrative matters." Both were partially correct; there are those components in supervision, and they are the ones that have traditionally been emphasized. The objective has been the production of goods or services, and the approach has been essentially a superior/inferior, assignment/reporting model with the degree of authoritarianism depending upon the particular supervisor involved.

Traditionally, supervision has been viewed as "overseeing"; one person who is skilled, knowledgeable, and experienced in a particular occupation or responsibility superintends (manages, guides) the work of another. Job oversight may be based on the belief that this is the only way the work will get done, or that it will be done more efficiently or, perhaps, that it will be done with better quality. There is one view of supervision which insists that people must be kept under constant surveillance; there is another view which holds that supervision is a temporary means of helping people achieve the ability to supervise themselves. There are some supervisors who run tight ships and others who keep hands off. (Of course, some workers cannot function without direction, while others insist on doing their own thing.) There are views which fall between these extremes, as well as still another which rejects supervision as necessary at all. Since these have been our models, most of us assume that these are the only alternatives.

This is a particular problem for those of us who work in the professions. While there are some people who have the freedom of working without **formal** supervision by someone else, the fact is that most of us carry out our duties within a supervisory relationship. We are tempted to rely on the common assumption that one advantage in being a professional is the freedom (and ability) to act independently as well as responsibly and competently. While this is true, it fails to take into account the fact that:

- every worker, regardless of occupation, is expected to be responsible, competent, and frequently independent; the plumber who tracks down and repairs a water leak in my house must be responsible, competent, and efficiently capable of diagnosing a problem and taking corrective action;
- most professionals do not work independently, at least not completely; a physician who has a private practice, nevertheless is subject finally to the approval of colleagues whose reputation and professional standards she/he either upholds or diminishes; and,
- there are many non-professionals who function more independently than some professionals; having grown up on a farm but having spent all of my professional life as a clergy person, I know that my father was more independent than I am, though his independence was lived out under the constant reality of governmental regulations.

All of this is to say that supervision is a fact of life that all people experience to some degree. For us who participate actively in the life of the church it is an ever-present reality.

Through the years, supervision has been an imprecise practice ranging from one available model to another. The New Testament does not use the term, but it does describe an early provision for offices and functions which were intended to provide pastoral oversight of congregations. However, while supervision has been practiced in the church from its earliest days, its purpose and function has been largely misunderstood and frequently misused. Complicating the situation is the fact that the church has lagged behind other institutions and professional groups in giving attention to this common and important human experience.

The first systematic attempt to correct this came when Anton Boisen invited four theological students to engage in clinical pastoral education in a mental hospital in 1925 under his supervision as a way of studying theology. Across the last three quarters of a century Clinical Pastoral Education (CPE) has developed supervision into a refined art. This is having an influence on the church as more pastors and lay persons engage in clinical training. Increasingly church judicatories are encouraging or requiring such training for their theological students (though the reasons for this relate to the potential for personal change in the participants, not because of an interest in supervision as a ministering responsibility). Concurrent with this development, most theological schools have developed field education (supervised ministry) programs as an integral part of their curricula, and a growing number of denominations are giving attention to supervision for ministerial candidates and/or beginning pastors. Therefore, more and more persons are engaging in ministry with the knowledge and expectation of faithful supervisory relationships.

In spite of this, there is a long way still to go before supervision becomes a pastoral priority in the life of the church. Up to this point we have looked to other occupational and professional groups for our patterns, and these have molded both our theory and our practice. In 1969, Thomas Klink, a CPE chaplain/supervisor, in an address to the Association for Theological Field Education, referred to the impact that supervisory methods in other professions have had on the development of pastoral supervision, but he was not specific about the characteristics involved.[3] About the same time the Association of Theological Schools devoted an issue of its journal to a discussion of educational patterns (including the role of supervised clinical experience) in a variety of professional curricula, but no systematized comparison of supervisory practice was made.[4] There have been other similar attempts to utilize interprofessional experience to shape supervisory practice in relation to CPE and seminary curricula.[5] In the meantime, supervision in the church has been a hit-and-miss affair.

SOME FOREGROUND

It was these influences that led me to devote two sabbatical years to a better understanding of the nature and meaning of supervision as a pastoral responsibility. These studies, combined with my pastoral and teaching experience, have convinced me that the supervisory function which was present in the early church, and which has been used in various ways by not only the church but by other helping institutions, has a new potential in our day for enabling the church to do its ministry. In the first chapter, I seek to establish a basis for capitalizing on this potential by looking at the experiential and biblical precedents we have for such a claim. In that connection I discuss both its opportunity and its neglect in the church's appropriation of its tradition by describing how one denomination, The United Methodist Church, has approached the supervisory question. The concerns raised by that discussion serve to illustrate the issues which are applicable to other denominational traditions.

As a way of gaining new perspective on the issues surrounding supervision in the church, I have pursued a resource to which only limited attention has been given by others. I have investigated the theory and practice of supervision in several professional fields closely allied with the church: business/industry, public education, psychotherapy, social work, and clinical pastoral education. I could have chosen more fields to investigate, but five are manageable; I might have chosen others, but each of these has had a particular influence upon the way supervision is viewed in the church. This investigation is reviewed in Chapter II. Some readers may become impatient with the detail of this review, but I include it because it is basic to the book's thesis and there is no other place where the serious student of supervision can turn for such a correlation of information.

Growing out of the investigation of other professional practices, ten basic characteristics of supervision have been identified in Chapter III. They are discussed in terms of their relevance for pastoral supervision, with reference particularly to theological education and the local church. Building on this foundation, a definition and a model for pastoral supervision are proposed in Chapter IV, along with guidelines for engaging in supervisory conversation, alternative supervisory instruments, characteristics of effective supervisors, and criteria for evaluating supervisors. Chapter V suggests a theological grounding for the practice of supervision as a ministering style, using the biblical concepts of covenant, relationship, incarnation, judgment, and grace. The book concludes with the presentation in Chapter VI of a model of theological reflection utilizing this understanding of supervision in relationship to insights drawn from narrative theology. A case study demonstrates the use of the model in a typical supervisory/ministering situation. Overall it is my purpose to show how supervision can be a transformative experience for both individuals and the church.

The book doesn't really end there. The bibliography which follows the final chapter brings together some (still only some) of the developing resources that are available to persons who want to pursue the trails suggested here to greater length. Put together, I know of no other listing of supervisory literature as extensive as this one.

Running through the book is a dominant concern, namely, the enablement of the church's ministry. The patterns of supervision that have shaped the ministering styles in the past have tended to use laity to assist the "minister's" work. The model of supervision presented in this book describes a way of helping the whole People of God to see, to own, and to do the church's ministry. I have focused primarily on the pastor's supervisory task, because I believe that it is the key role which either keeps people in servitude or releases them for servanthood. I have utilized as my primary context the supervision of seminary students, because I have found in my twenty-plus years as a theological field educator that this is a place where life-long patterns of ministry can be influenced. It is not limited to that, however; what I describe here translates immediately into the actions of pastors who supervise laity, clergy and lay persons who coordinate or work in multiple-person staffs, judicatory persons who superintend pastors, institutional administrators or department heads, and pastoral/staff relations committees that work with their enablers in ministry.

The book is written, therefore, for supervisors whose central task in a ministry of supervision is to equip the saints for ministry. For that reason I will emphasize the pastoral nature of the supervision that I propose.

ENDNOTES

1. Charles William Stewart, *Person and Profession* (Nashville, TN: Abingdon Press, 1974), 164.
2. Ibid., 166.
3. Thomas W. Klink, "Supervision from a Clinical/Pastoral Care Perspective," *Report of the Proceedings of the Tenth Biennial Consultation on Field Education*, Berkeley, CA, January 15-18, 1969, 17-25.
4. "Theological Education as Professional Education," ed. Jesse H. Ziegler, *Theological Education* 5 (Spring 1969): 135-36.
5. See the recent book edited by David A. Steere, *The Supervision of Pastoral Care* (Louisville: Westminster/John Knox Press, 1989).

CHAPTER I

A CRY FROM THE WILDERNESS:
OPPORTUNITY AND NEGLECT

A number of years ago I went through what I now recognize as a crisis in my personal and professional life. I was in the tenth year of ministry after graduation from seminary. From all outward appearances, according to the way people and institutions measure such things, I was a successful pastor. I worked in an exciting parish, was challenged by growing recognition in community and denominational circles, and knew the liberating feeling of having options of ministry available to me. Colleagues and parishioners alike affirmed my work, and the future looked bright.

In spite of all that, deep inside of me some conflicting questions were tumbling around, like: Why am I really in this? Where is it all leading? In some respects it all seemed so unimportant, and I wondered whether the personal price I was paying in physical and emotional energy was worth it. I felt like the well had run dry. At the same time, I was highly committed to pastoral ministry and not about to abandon it.

In that time of need and in the providence of God's grace an unexpected invitation arrived in the mail to participate in an ecumenical pilot program in pastoral studies designed for persons between five and ten years out of theological school.[1] I accepted, and I shall always be glad I did, though I was not fully prepared for what happened. It proved to be a time of concentrated reflection on who I was, what I was doing, and how poorly or well I was doing it. It was an opportunity to bring myself and my ministry under the evaluative scrutiny of a pastoral supervisor/educator and eleven peers who, like me, were in a pilgrimage of faith.

I remember well how it unfolded as I got in touch with a style of education that was new for me: how the "leader," after calling us together for the first session of introductions, left the room and threw us upon our resources to decide what we wanted to do for the next ten days; how one participant nearly left and went home because, he said, he certainly hadn't paid his money to sit around pooling ignorance; how we struggled with our individual reasons for being there.

We spent ten intensive days exposing the isolated pieces of our several ministries to one another's critical but supportive assessment within the skillful enablement of a more experienced colleague (the "leader" who had temporarily left the group). I went home when it was over refreshed, cleansed, a better person, and a more sensitive pastor. I did not know then, but I know now that what I had experienced was my first peer group in pastoral supervision.

7

TWO INSIGHTS

I share this slice of my own life because of two important insights growing out of that experience which have helped shape my ministry. The first is that **the receiving of pastoral supervision is not limited to the laity**; pastors are in need of supervision also. Consequently, I began to gather small groups of my colleagues who shared my conviction for mutual encouragement and reflection upon our ministries. None of us thought of it as pastoral supervision; no such term was in vogue then. However, that is precisely what we were doing. It was the beginning of a continuing interest that I have carried to this moment.

Donald Houts reports two studies which corroborate this need. One study grows out of his work with one United Methodist Annual Conference over a twelve-year period. It identifies five primary areas of personal concern expressed by pastors: (1) loneliness; (2) conflicts regarding expectations placed upon spouses; (3) feelings of inadequacy; (4) intellectual and spiritual malaise; and (5) a lost sense of meaning regarding their work. The other study, gleaned from a report by Alfred Hazer and Thomas Klink to two other United Methodist Annual Conferences, identifies five personal problems for which pastors most often sought consultation at the Menninger Foundation: (1) over-extension (of energy and time); (2) imprecise competence; (3) inadequate resources; (4) an uncertain faith; and (5) lack of accomplishment.[2]

Houts's conclusion is that there is a fundamental need to develop a strategy for ministry to pastors. Accordingly, he organized a program among those for whom he held pastoral responsibility which provided for crisis intervention services, professional consultation, continuing education, clergy support groups, career assessment, marriage enrichment, and assistance in contracting with local church pastoral relations committees. He refers to it as pastoral care for pastors; it is on the edge of what I believe is effective pastoral supervision.

Lest we be tempted to conclude that this indicates a crisis peculiar to pastors, of equal significance is Houts's description of a number of similar issues confronting those who pursue other professional careers. He confirms my experience in working with supervisory persons in both community-based agencies and in parishes: namely, that professional life is subject to so many conflicts in technology, social practice, theological view, and management theory that "no professional is free from occasional strain and tension, though basically happy and competent in his/her work." And he adds that they, like pastors, are therefore in need of "continuing support."[3]

Houts's emphasis suggests that the receiving of pastoral supervision includes but is not limited to the laity. He lifts up a fact we tend to forget, namely, the extent to which our colleagues around us, regardless of profession, need our pastoral attention. But the inclusion in his program of assistance for pastors in contracting with their pastoral relations committees suggests the second germinal insight growing out of the slice of my own experience described above. It is that **the giving of pastoral supervision is not limited to the clergy**; laity can engage in pastoral supervision also.

So, early in my ministry we began to form small caring groups throughout our parish in which our members could gather regularly for mutual support and accountability. These fulfilled a number of purposes, among which was that of maintaining a network of caring persons throughout the congregation. One such group was an early morning breakfast group of which I was a member, composed of persons with a wide variety of education, skills, and occupations, but all lay persons except myself. It was one of the most remarkable gathering of Christians in which I have ever participated. It was in every sense of the word a group in pastoral supervision as we brought segments of our lives and jobs for personal, professional, and theological reflection and for decision-making.

The value of small sharing/caring groups in parish life is, of course, well known. What is not so well known is the potential of such groups for extending the supervisory ministry of both clergy and laity. One of the great problems for clergy persons (and other professionals) is the reluctance to accept ministry from others. It is with a kind of "messiah complex" that we appropriate the words of Jesus: "I came not to be served, but to serve . . ." (Mk. 10:45). It is not just our professional peers whose ministry we find it difficult to accept. Particularly, we have found it difficult to permit those who are supposed to be the recipients of our ministry to exercise their ministry to us.

The professionalization of the clergy assumes that the most expert among us should exercise the pastoral supervision. Tragically there have been pastors all too willing to assume the role of expert and lay people all too willing to let us do it. The result has been that when we have spoken of the ministry of the laity, we have tended to withhold a part of the ministry. Lay persons have business acumen and so assist in the administration of the church; they possess teaching skills, so they are relied upon for the operation of a church school; they can communicate, so the bravest (not always the most competent) among them read liturgy and on rare occasions preach from the pulpit. But they have resisted and we have failed to encourage their engagement in the supervisory ministry of the whole congregation.

Pastoring and supervising are ministries that belong to both laity and clergy. The potential and hazard of this claim can be seen in the way the church has dealt with it from its earliest days. I turn now to briefly trace that history.

THEOLOGICAL ROOTS

The biblical roots of supervision are planted in the covenant concept of the Hebrew/Christian tradition. God's covenant with Israel was one of promise and response; God offered life to a People with a condition of accountability: "I will make of you a great nation . . ." (Gen. 12:2), and "you shall keep my covenant . . ." (Gen. 17:9). Made first with one person (Abraham), the covenant had as its object the well-being and mission of an entire nation. Sealed originally with one act (circumcision), it came to be expressed in a complex discipline of observances. Yet, at its center was the simple relationship between God and a People expressed in the alternation of giving and receiving in worship and ethical action.

Through the centuries oversight of the covenant was committed to a series of persons (charismatic leaders, priests, judges, kings) in a history of response character-ized by both faithfulness and unfaithfulness. Life within the covenant became a pattern of brokenness and renewal to which Israel was periodically called to accountability—if not by rulers, then certainly by prophets: "The days are surely coming when I will make a new covenant . . . not . . . like the covenant which they broke . . . says the Lord" (Jer. 31:31-32). Thus the story of Israel is the story of a covenantal relationship between God and a covenant community in which the supervisory task was one of maintaining accountability to the covenant.

Like the Old Testament, the New Testament writings do not use the term "supervision," but they identify a growing set of functions for the oversight of the first Christian congregations as the new covenant community. The earliest reference to a division of responsibility in the church is in Acts where it is recorded that the twelve apostles, upon urging of the Hellenists, selected and appointed seven disciples to administer the distribution of food among the needy while they (the twelve) devoted themselves to the ministry of the word (Acts 6:1-6). There is a hint in this of a hierarchy of tasks suggested by the apostles: "It is not right that we should neglect the word of God in order to wait on tables" (Acts 6:2).

By late New Testament times there were three distinguishable offices in the church's developing life. One of the Pastoral Epistles uses three different words to describe the functions of these offices. **Bishops** were to "`care' for God's church" (1 Tim. 3:5); **deacons** were known as "those who serve" (1 Tim. 3:13); and **elders**, whom Paul had earlier called overseers whose duty it was "to shepherd the church of the Lord" (Acts 20:28), were to exercise rule over others (1 Tim. 5:17). In the case of the elders in particular, precautions were urged that they should "tend the flock of God" in an exemplary, non-domineering manner (1 Pet. 5:2). While it is not clear whether these originally constituted entirely separate offices, they all appear to bear supervisory functions performed by persons with diverse backgrounds and skills, nurtured by a pastor for the benefit of a pastoring ministry.

But to understand the New Testament roots of supervision it is necessary to press behind this development of function and/or office to the nature of the New Testament church. Paul uses the imagery of the human body to illustrate that all Christians are equally members of the body of Christ and that a variety of spiritual gifts have been given to them. He wrote that the purpose of the varied gifts is "that there may be no dissension within the body," but that "the members may have the same care for one another" (1 Cor. 12:25). Writing to the Galatians he instructed them to "bear one another's burdens," and so "fulfill the law of Christ" (Gal. 6:2). In the Epistle to the Ephesians, the author affirms that the purpose of God's gifts to the church is "to equip the saints for the work of ministry" in order that we may all be brought to Christian maturity (Eph. 4:12-13). In 1 Peter the church, meaning the entire membership of the church, is addressed as "a holy priesthood" in and through which the love and forgiveness of God is mediated to the world (1 Peter 2:5-9). And in the same Epistle, Christ himself is referred to as the "shepherd and guardian" of souls (1 Pet. 2:25).

Thus, "the ministry of pastoral supervision, as related to Christ's own oversight and shepherding, seems to have been taking place in the life of the church since near its beginning."[4] Believing the above to be saying that ministry in the church belongs to the entire community of faith, it follows that pastoring and supervising are inseparable tasks and that they are to be exercised by both clergy and laity. This holds true regardless of the context in which the ministry takes place; the "church gathered" offers a model of supervisory practice for the "church scattered." Therefore, the business manager, school department head, social worker, supervising pastor, or member of a lay pastoral relations committee in a congregation becomes a pastoral supervisor when she/he carries out these responsibilities within this tradition.

THE CHURCH EXPERIENCE

Across time the church has struggled with this matter. There have been seasons and situations when the church has been able to integrate these responsibilities and this identity into its understanding and practice. More often than not, however, it has pursued its supervisory task within a hierarchical arrangement that at least hinders, if not denies, the mutual accountability and caring responsibilities of the whole body of believers. There are several signs of this.

1. Pastors tend to avoid supervisory relationships. Partly, the argument (as indicated earlier) is that pastors are professionals and therefore work independently. More than that, the nature of ecclesiastical polity often isolates individual pastors into competing rivals. This is true within judicatory structures as well as between them. There is a general suspicion about supervision and a reluctance to engage in it lest it compromise one's authority and/or personhood. Many pastors simply prefer to "go it alone."

2. Pastoral relations committees are inclined to shun their supervisory task. Some, for reasons similar to the above, do not consider it appropriate for lay persons to supervise clergy persons. ("We don't have the right to do that.") Others do not see any need for it. ("Our pastor does everything so well that she/he doesn't need supervision.") More basic is the likelihood that most such committees do not understand and have never been prepared for their responsibility. And if any such committees are matched with pastors who guard against it, perfect conditions exist for nothing to happen. So while the church may provide for this supervisory relationship, there is no guarantee that supervision will get done.

3. Congregations differ in their supervisory relationship with the judicatory. Some tolerate the judicatory's intrusion into their life but keep it at arm's length. Others feel neglected through lack of attention and have given up any hope of recognition. Still others would welcome more contact but exercise little effort to initiate it. In all such cases their investment in the church-at-large is minimal.

4. Judicatory persons are occasionally frustrated in their attempts to fulfill their supervisory responsibilities with those committed to their charge. One or more of several possible reasons may prevail: multiple duties divide their time, the supervisory responsibility is unclear, pastors and/or congregations do not welcome their efforts, they have been thrust into a role for which they have limited preparation, or the level of trust on the part of those being supervised toward their supervisors negates any meaningful overtures of a supervisory nature.

It should be clear from this description of our condition that some of these factors are self-imposed; others are inherent in the situation. In either case they undermine the supervisory process which becomes blocked (that is, it doesn't happen at all), is done haphazardly (meaning sporadically and with little intentionality), or is crisis-oriented (in the sense of responding to brush fires every time an alarm rings).

A PARADIGM: THE UNITED METHODIST CHURCH

One church body that has addressed this concern is The United Methodist Church. As a member of that tradition, I can at least speak more accurately of its efforts to work at the issues involved. United Methodism's recent efforts in this regard evolve out of a study of the bishop and district superintendent offices in preparation for the 1976 General Conference. Further study and refinement has taken place in connection with the general conferences since then in 1980, 1984, and 1988. While this represents the experience of only one segment of the church universal, this denomination's struggle with supervisory issues can be instructive to others as well.

The *Discipline* of The United Methodist Church affirms that ministry in the church "is derived from the ministry of Christ" and that "all Christians are called to ministry" (§401).[5] Within that calling, some persons are "set apart by the church for the specialized ministry of Word, Sacrament, and Order" (§402.1). The latter are the ordained ministers who, in their ministry of Order, are charged with responsibility to "equip the laity for ministry" and to "exercise pastoral oversight" (§430.2).

Supervision, as the exercise of pastoral oversight, is clearly the responsibility of all ordained persons. **Bishops** "lead and oversee the spiritual and temporal affairs" of the church (§514.1) in the work of general superintendency. **District superintendents**, whose office is an extension of the general superintendency, are to "oversee the total ministry of the pastors and the churches" in their districts (§519); specifically, in regard to clergy, they are "to establish a clearly understood process of supervision for clergy of the district, including observation of all aspects of ministry, direct evaluation, and feedback to the clergy involved" (§520.2); in the case of churches, they are to meet and work with the Pastor/Staff Parish Relations Committees and Charge Conferences in the congregations on their district (§520.1). **Pastors** "oversee the total ministry of the local church" (§439), including "equipping and supervising" the persons in their charge (§439.2).

The *Discipline* is precise about the way bishops and district superintendents are to relate to their work assignments and peers. These two offices are linked together as "particular ministries" (§503) calling for "a collegial style of leadership" (§526). Thus, bishops are elected first to a Council of Bishops and then assigned to an episcopal area (§527.1). Likewise, district superintendents first become members of a Cabinet and then are appointed to a district (§529.1). This is The United Methodist Church's way of holding these persons accountable for their work and of providing a consultative and supportive system for both personal and professional growth. It is an appropriate peer supervisory system.

Consistently in theory, the *Discipline* provides for a similar arrangement for pastors; "all ordained ministers are first elected into membership of an Annual Conference and subsequently appointed to pastoral charges" (§527.1 and §529.1). In practice, however, the same quality of accountability, consultation, and support cannot and does not apply. Not only is the Annual Conference too large to provide this quality of peer relationship, but there is reluctance on the part of pastors to trust "the system" with the multiple facets of their lives and ministries. Also, most pastors are appointed to one-pastor charges where a degree of isolation from peers prevails. Even those appointed to some form of multiple staff may not experience the collegial supervisory process that the *Discipline* provides. Add to this the fact that lay pastors remain outside full Conference membership, and there emerges the prevailing pattern of a breakdown in the supervisory process.

To be sure, the *Discipline* says that among the duties of district superintendents are those of "building clusters for supervision" for probationary and local pastors "with the assistance of counseling or supervising elders" (§520.4); giving "pastoral support and care to the clergy and diaconal ministers and their families by traveling through the district . . . and maintaining the connectional order of the *Discipline*" (§522.1); providing "counsel with clergy concerning their pastoral responsibilities and diaconal ministers concerning their ministerial duties as well as other matters affecting their ministry and personal life" (§522.2); encouraging the building of "peer groups among the clergy and diaconal ministers for mutual support and discipline" and "systems of mutual support for clergy and diaconal families" (§522.3); consulting with the Pastor/Staff Parish Relations Committees to "update their profiles for appointment" (§521.3); and receiving "annually from each clergy person a report of his/her program of continuing education" and "to give counsel concerning future plans" (§520.5). When this occurs, we are fulfilling an historic and sacred function of ministry.

Thus there is in The United Methodist Church a long tradition and an ongoing serious attempt to provide an effective supervisory process for its clergy and its congregations. While that process is concentrated in clergy relationships, it has, for many years, taken seriously the role of the lay pastor/staff parish relations committee. It does not refer to the committee's role as "supervisory," but it is difficult not to think in supervisory terms when speaking of the committee's responsibilities to "confer," "counsel," "consult" with the pastor, and annually to "provide evaluation" for the pastor and staff (§269.2f). I contend that the committee's role in the church is supervisory so that in every United Methodist congregation there is a unique, specific, and mutual supervisory responsibility shared by clergy **and** laity. The point here is the mutual responsibility for supervising the church's total ministry.

There is one other significant piece of this supervisory pattern; that is the supervision of persons moving from lay to clergy roles. Candidates for ordained ministry move through a lengthy and structured supervisory process. That process begins with the recommendation by the laity of a local congregation of one of its members. It continues with assignment to a supervising pastor in order to search through one's motivation and suitability for ordained ministry (Candidacy); participation in a credentialing process, including theological education, under the guidance of a Board of Ordained Ministry; and, following graduation from theological school, two years of probationary ministry under the supervision of a district superintendent in order to establish eligibility for election to full ordination. This movement from Candidacy, through the Order of Deacon, to the Order of Elder requires a minimum of six years, all of which is under the supervision of those who, at the end of the process, will be one's "peers."[6]

I have referred to the United Methodist pattern as a serious attempt to provide an effective supervisory process for its clergy and its congregations. This has both positive and negative aspects. The positive side is that supervision is taken seriously at a policy level, and the Church has made giant strides in refining its process. The negative side has several dimensions:

1. There is little coordination of the several supervisory tracks that persons must take to move from candidacy to full ordination; the result is that some persons, particularly theological students, find themselves on more than one track simultaneously.[7]

2. Missing in the *Discipline* is any reference to supervised ministry as part of theological education, though all United Methodist seminaries require it; there are clear requirements for content courses in denominational history, theology, and polity, but none for supervision; nor does the church accept the schools' supervisory programs in lieu of its own.

3. The many responsibilities assigned to district superintendents makes it difficult for them to give supervision the time that it needs; the fact that they are physically removed from the pastors' settings adds a further complication.

4. While the supervisory role of the lay pastor-parish relations committee is acclaimed, there are few programs which adequately prepare those committees for their task.

A clue for approaching these concerns can be found in the precedent established by early Wesleyan practice. The Wesleyan tradition developed around the formation of lay-led local "societies" which were divided into smaller groups of "classes" and "bands." While these scattered groups were under the general oversight of itinerant preachers, the weekly meetings of laity were supervised by lay class leaders whose task it was to exhort and examine the members in a rigorous spiritual discipline. It was out of this system of mutual accountability that the clergy emerged, first as lay preachers, then, under the supervision of the traveling preachers, into the cadre of itinerant preachers and spiritual leaders who comprised the "connection of preachers." James Nelson insists that "this is the crucial point in the calling of ministers in the United Methodist traditions during the first century and a half of Methodism's development. The ministerial tasks of spiritual supervision of a class or leadership of a band was an intense spiritual exercise as well as a religious challenge."[8]

The preachers also had their own meetings (quarterly) where they went for spiritual nourishment, personal sharing, and supportive encouragement. Those were times, in addition to the annual conference sessions, when spiritual concerns were pursued even more vigorously than temporal matters. Thus the beginning of the current elaborate system of supervision began in a setting where mutual accountability was generously and vigorously exercised in the interests of the persons involved. However,

. . . by the end of the nineteenth century, the class itself had faded, and its vestiges in the meetings for public prayer and witness were fading. The meetings and conferences of the "connection of preachers" had largely been transformed into the images of their official minutes. The deep affection and intense involvement of the ministers for and with one another gave way to a spiritual isolation which the "lonely" circuit rider never knew. Members of the clergy, even in situations where they were assigned to the same station or church as members of a staff, often simply divided the labor and failed to submit themselves to each other's preaching, praying, and teaching. Even meetings designed to attain spiritual formation tended to become business-oriented or academic in character.[9]

I do not suggest an imitation of the Wesleyan system. That would be inappropriate for United Methodists as well as for churches of other traditions. I do plead, however, for a recovery of the tradition of supervision among clergy and laity that takes with utmost seriousness the mutual accountability for the ministry of the whole People of God. This can only happen if we can find it in ourselves to surrender our hierarchical systems of management and to become truly colleagues in ministry, willing to open ourselves to one another's lives and ministries in spiritual commitment and discipline.

THE PRIESTLY QUALITY OF SUPERVISION

Lesslie Newbigin tells that when he was Bishop of Madura in India, every person who was confirmed and received into the full membership of the church received a card on which was printed the text of 1 Peter 2:5 as a constant reminder of who they were: "You are a chosen race, a royal priesthood, a holy nation, God's own people, that you may declare the wonderful deeds of God who called you out of darkness into God's marvelous light." The priest is one who stands with God and with the people, to be the bearer of the people's worship to God and the bearer of God's acts of grace to people. This is Christ's ministry, and it is the ministry of the body of Christ. It takes place not just in liturgical celebration but whenever and wherever Christians hold one another before God in love and concern. However, as Newbigin claims:

> One of the tragic facts of Christian history has been the obscuring and distorting of the great scriptural doctrine of the royal priesthood of the whole Church, firstly by a clericalism which practically confined the priestly charac-ter to a professional ministry, and then by an understandable but lamentable counter-distortion which tried to assert the self-sufficient priesthood of every individual, apart from the organic unity of the priestly body of Christ.

> The truth is that it is only because the one priestly body has been given from the beginning a structure which includes a ministry based on and continuous with the ministry of the incarnate Lord Himself, that there is a priestly character in the ministry answering to the priestly character of the body. And the supreme function of the priestly ministry is so to minister that the whole body attains to and retains its true priestly character. What an unnecessary and pitiable thing it is to see these two things which belong together being placed against one another so that a clericalism which denies the true priestly character of the *laos*, the consecrated people of God, produces a laicism which neglects the true service of the ordained ministry.[10]

This suggests the priestly quality of supervision. The signs are for a returning interest in the equipping of laity for their priestly role. There is a revival of study, an increasing amount of preparation, and a growing involvement of lay persons in this ministry. I encourage that, and I see the equipping of laity for the pastoral

15

supervision of theological students as a participation in the current recovery of a practice that is virtually as old as the church.

A PERSONAL VIGNETTE

There is an even more personal reason why this approach to ministry receives attention here. As a graduate fresh out of seminary, I was assigned to organize and pastor a new congregation in a rapidly growing metropolitan area. Early in the life of the congregation a power struggle emerged which threatened not only to destroy that new outpost of God's kingdom but to drive a hopeful and enthusiastic young pastor right out of the ministry. In such a crucial time of need a district superintendent sat down with me and with the people of the parish to work through the conflicts. What he made available was an opportunity to ventilate the intense feelings, an arena for considering alternative solutions, a set of boundaries within which accountability could be exercised, a theological framework for decision making, and a continuing supportive relationship upon which everyone could depend. He was called a "superintendent"; he called himself a "pastor to pastors." For me and the congregation he was a pastoral supervisor who taught what that gift means when it is exercised responsibly; in particular it was his supervision that enabled me to hammer out my pastoral identity.

During an exciting seventeen-year pastorate in that congregation we worked to develop a supervisory model for our common ministry based upon that event, something for which theological education had not specifically prepared me. Later, as a college chaplain, I found myself expanding my supervisory role with college students, particularly in a volunteer program of ministry in cooperation with several social agencies and the public school system of an adjacent city. More recently my responsibility was to train and supervise the pastors and lay people who work with theological students in their own settings of ministry. In the meantime, I have benefitted from my own supervised clinical training. But my present concern is the development of a methodology that will make possible a shepherding and enabling ministry throughout the total church, as represented by the scattered congregations of Christians as well as the institutions in which they daily live and move and have their being. Pastoral supervision lies at the heart of this concern.

ENDNOTES

1. I refer to the Institute for Advanced Pastoral Studies, Bloomfield Hills, Michigan, whose founder and director at that time was the revered author, educator, and supervisor, Reuel Howe. I was a participant in the Institute's program during its first year.
2. Donald C. Houts, "Pastoral Care for Pastors: Toward a Church Strategy," *Pastoral Psychology* 25 (Spring 1977): 189, 190.
3. Ibid., 187, 189.
4. Editorial, "Pastoral Supervision--A Ministry of the Church," *Journal of Pastoral Care* 25 (September 1971): 145.
5. *The Book of Discipline of The United Methodist Church*. (Nashville, TN: The United Methodist Publishing House, 1988). All the parenthetical number references in this section refer to paragraph numbers in the *Discipline*.
6. There are exceptions provided for "Special Conditions." See §416 in the *Discipline*. At the other end of the process, there are also supervisory responsibilities attached to the movement of persons out of clergy and back into lay relationship.

7. There are efforts in process through The United Methodist Division of Ordained Ministry and theological school field educators to provide a more wholistic approach to the total supervisory process, but these must filter down into Annual Conference procedures before they will impact supervisory practice.

8. James D. Nelson, "United Methodist Heritage," *Spiritual Formation Resource Packet*, Section I, Paper C (Nashville, TN: Division of Ordained Ministry, Board of Higher Education and Ministry, The United Methodist Church, 1982), 3.

9. Ibid., 5.

10. Lesslie Newbigin, "Four Talks on 1 Peter," *We Were Brought Together, Report of the National Conference of Australian Churches*, ed. David M. Taylor (Sydney: Australian Council of the World Council of Churches, 1960), 97. The implications of this for pastoral supervision were discussed with Newbigin in a personal conversation, March 22, 1977, at Selly Oak, Birmingham, England.

CHAPTER II

PREPARING A WAY:
PRINCIPLES AND PRACTICE

It is surprising that, with such a clear biblical precedent and long practice of overseeing, pastoral supervision has received little attention in literature. This claim is made while recognizing that there are three academic disciplines in theological curricula which have dealt with some of the issues involved.

One discipline is church administration in which the management of the church's temporal life is addressed. A second is pastoral care which focuses on the care of persons in the exegencies of their daily lives, including the societal structures in which people live and work. The third discipline, newer to theological curricula, has focused attention on supervision as a distinctive way of doing ministry. I refer to field education (supervised ministry) carried out in the supervision of seminary students in their theological studies. All three disciplines have provided guidance in the supervision of ministry in both local parish and judicatory circles.

At the same time there is a wealth of information available from non-pastoral professions. Pastoral supervision at its best is an integrative art, drawing upon the wide range of resources available. There is a need to distill all this body of experience and theory into usable form for the exercise of ministry in its various settings. I propose to do that by means of a review of some of the literature in five professions. This will provide some interprofessional grounding and will permit the identification of some common principles and practices which can be useful in the church.

BUSINESS/INDUSTRY

Though some readers may question reference to business and industry as a profession, it is included here for two reasons. First, in 1969 Kenneth Andrews wrote that "it is the **management** of the activities and institutions of business that has become the newest profession."[1] This is consistent with James Glasse's thought when he identified professionals as persons who are educated, expert, institutional, responsible, and dedicated.[2] Persons in business and industry clearly possess these qualities as much as others. Second and more importantly, business and industrial practice has contributed much to our current images of supervision. There are also efforts to change the images, and those efforts are instructive to us.

HISTORY

The supervision of work in the production of goods and services goes far back in human history. As Edgar Schein points out: "The pharaoh building a pyramid faced problems fundamentally similar to those faced by the corporate executive of today. Both must figure out (1) how to organize work and allocate it to workers; (2) how to recruit, train, and effectively manage the people available to do the work; (3) how to create work conditions and reward and punishment systems which would enable the workers to maintain high effectiveness and sufficient morale to remain effective over long periods of time; (4) how to adjust their organization to changing environmental conditions and technological innovations; and (5) how to cope with competition or harassment from other organizations or groups within their own organization."[3]

Modern life has been dominated by bureaucracy as a social invention to structure and order organizational behavior. Bureaucracy is a system using a division of labor under a hierarchical authority structure to manage people for the achievement of organizational goals. Conceptualized by Max Weber in the early part of the twentieth century, a body of theory was developed based on a view of human unreliability and the need for control for the sake of efficiency and production. About the same time, under the influence of Frederick Taylor, there arose a similar view known as scientific management which promoted the professionalization of management. Its result was the same; in organizational theory, whether for economic or social purposes, human needs were made subservient to the organization.

Between 1935 and 1950 a new theory emerged known as the human relations approach. Whereas scientific management viewed people as existing for organizations, the human relations approach placed a premium on the well-being of workers—their personal feelings, sense of accomplishment, attitudes, beliefs, and opinions about their work. Under the influence of persons like Kurt Lewin and Carl Rogers, motivation, self-fulfillment, and worker participation in decision making were emphasized.

Two major studies contributed to this change. One, The Hawthorne Studies, involved an experiment at the Hawthorne plant of the Western Electric Company in Illinois in the late 1920s in which it was found that, by humanizing the working conditions through improved social relationships among workers and between workers and boss, morale, productivity, and the quality of work were increased. The other study known as The Tavistock Institute Coal-Mining Studies found that a change from small teams working in community to large groups under a single supervisor created a sense of isolation, conflict, and competition that became counter-productive.

Since 1950 there have been attempts to integrate the insights from these experiments and theories. In 1966 Warren Bennis observed about bureaucracy

that this form of organization is becoming less and less effective, that it is hopelessly out of joint with contemporary realities, and that new shapes, patterns, and models--currently recessive--are emerging which promise drastic changes in the conduct of the corporation and in managerial practices in general. So within the next twenty-five to fifty years, we should all be witness to, and participate in, the end of bureaucracy and the rise of new social systems better able to cope with twentieth-century demands.[4]

DEVELOPMENT

In 1960 Douglas McGregor, in his signal work *The Human Side of Enterprise*, described the contrasting assumptions operative in industrial management. The traditional view of direction and control he called Theory X, which holds that the average human being has an inherent dislike of work and must be coerced, controlled, directed, and threatened with punishment because of the desire to avoid responsibility. As a corrective, McGregor proposed a new set of assumptions called Theory Y in which he asserts that work is as natural as play or rest, that people will exercise self-direction and self-control when they are committed to objectives, that in the proper environment they seek and accept responsibility, and that the exercise of creativity in the solution of organizational problems is a widely distributed human trait.

Because of factors related to both productivity and human rights, business and industrial management was prompted to evaluate its practices. As a result, there were changes which reflect a more humanitarian approach. However, as McGregor points out, management made its initial changes "without changing its fundamental theory of management," so that, while there were exceptions, the assumptions of Theory X remained predominant.[5]

Growing out of McGregor's observations a third approach to management emerged called Theory Z. Based upon Abraham Maslow's hierarchy of human needs, Theory Z holds that human beings occupy different positions in the developmental hierarchy and therefore respond individually to responsibility and freedom. Therefore management must take the approach best suited to the situation, with the goal being to assist workers in their growth and self-actualization while still meeting the needs of the organization.[6]

Supervision in the business and industrial setting has been exercised essentially under the assumptions of Theory X. Supervisors have been viewed as individuals "having authority, in the interests of the employer, to hire, transfer, suspend, lay off, recall, promote, discharge, assign, reward or discipline other employees, or responsibility to direct them, or to adjust their grievances, or effectively to recommend such action. . . ."[7] While this does not prescribe any particular supervisory style, it does suggest a procedure of authority and control. Throughout the literature supervisors are referred to as "superior" and workers as "subordinate." The results of this approach are illustrated in some empirical studies reported by Gary Gimmell which support data that subordinates decide "not to disclose their feelings, opinions, and difficulties" to their supervisors because "they are afraid that their superior may punish them in some way for doing so."[8]

Attempts to correct such a dysfunctional managerial style prompted Paul Ecker and his colleagues to observe that "no well-run company will be found without a human relations program."[9] This move to stress human dignity became, on the one hand, indicative of a new climate in labor-management circles in which peoples' physical and emotional needs are taken seriously. On the other hand, a proposal by Alfred Lateiner for a conference method of creating a supervisory climate shows management's hand when describing the method as a "democratic way of giving orders and obtaining maximum performance." It gives supervisors the opportunity to delegate many routine tasks to their employees "with the knowledge that they will carry them out with a minimum of supervision." It will leave the supervisors free to "concentrate on more important things."[10]

This is a schizophrenic condition, because it places both supervisors and supervisees in a double bind, to which Ralph Reber and Gloria Terry allude when they refer to supervisors as "man-in-the-middle." Specifically: "Management usually expects the supervisor to put priority on higher production, lower costs, and exacting schedules. Subordinates, on the other hand, expect the supervisor to be understanding of their work problems, fair, helpful, and friendly and to represent them in their dealing with higher management."[11] The tension that arises when one seeks to speak for both interests characterizes the emotional climate in which business/industrial supervisors function. They have, in many instances, been selected on the basis of work experience but are expected by their supervisees to be experts in human relations.

In the midst of this ambiguity, there are those within the ranks who have pressed for a supervisory stance more consistent with Theory Y and Theory Z principles. Lateiner holds that supervisors should "blend a number of different qualities" such as knowing "company policies and philosophy," having "experience and knowledge of the work itself," and being able to "understand and handle people." They must not only be "informed in labor laws and union agreements" but also be able to "instruct workers . . . keep records," and "improve work methods."[12] This is supported by Ecker and others who write that the effective supervisor is "a master technician, a competent administrator, an expert in human relations, and, above all, a leader."[13]

Robert Katz identifies three primary managerial skills that are applicable to this task: (1) **technical skills**, meaning proficiency in the activity being supervised; (2) **human skills**, related to the ability to interact effectively with people; and (3) **conceptual skills**, making possible the ability to visualize the total organizational pattern.[14] Building upon that insight, Reber and Terry describe five qualities or attitudes required of good supervisors:

1. **Empathy** — projecting oneself imaginatively into the thoughts, feelings, and probable reactions of another person while maintaining an objective viewpoint;
2. **Self-awareness** — awareness of one's own behavior patterns and their impact on others;
3. **Acceptance of Individual Difference** — recognition, understanding, and acceptance of the variety of personality and behavior patterns among people;
4. **Perceptual Awareness** — understanding of and willingness to deal with the fact that people perceive events and situations differently;
5. **An Employee Orientation** — priority consideration of workers as human beings in terms of their development and needs.[15]

Two other supervisory functions deserve special comment. One is teaching. Supervision in business and industry is performed primarily in relation to experienced workers. New, inexperienced workers have traditionally been trained in the apprenticeship model, though technical schools have more recently taken over some of that role by providing training in specific job skills. Supervisors may be experienced and competent as workers, but they may not be good teachers. Thus, the organization's role in worker development remains an issue. The other function is evaluation. It is done, formally or informally, often with minimal concern for the worker as person. Here also there is no common view.

CURRENT STATUS

McGregor expressed the supervisory challenge for business and industry when he wrote:

> . . . Theory X places exclusive reliance upon external control of human behavior, while Theory Y relies heavily on self-control and self-direction. It is worth noting that this difference is the difference between treating people as children and treating them as mature adults. After generations of the former, we cannot expect to shift to the other overnight.[16]

It has been twenty-five years since Bennis predicted an end to bureaucracy and the advent of more appropriate social systems. Bureaucracy is still with us, but there has been some though not a total shift away from Theory X. Recent years have witnessed a strong interest in and numerous innovative implementations of Theory Z in major industries. William Hitt describes Theory Z as "a uniting of scientific management and human relations management."[17] During the last 25 years, he says, the most significant developments to arise from these two movements are management by objectives and participative management. He calls these the two key strategies of Theory Z.

Hitt provides a thorough analysis of four leadership styles: Theory X, the autocratic style with maximum concern for production; Theory Y, the benevolent style with maximum concern for people; Theory Z, a team approach with maximum concern for both production and people; and Theory L (laissez-faire), a hands-off style with minimum concern for both. He compares them in their approach to philosophy of management, planning, organizing, staffing and development, motivating, and controlling. He rates Theory Z as the most effective style across the broad spectrum of organizations and situations.

Included in Hitt's analysis is a continuum of leadership behavior ranging from boss-centered to subordinate-centered leadership. It is his claim that Theory Z provides the most flexible management system to benefit both the organization and the workers.

Finally, Hitt summarizes the values underlying Theory Z management as "a new concept of human beings . . . power . . . and organizational values which, spelled out, are:

1. People are usually good.
2. Treating persons as persons rather than as objects.
3. Viewing individuals as being in process.
4. Accepting and utilizing individual differences.
5. Viewing the individual as a whole person.
6. Prizing authentic behavior.
7. Fostering of trust.
8. Confronting others with differences.
9. Willingness to risk.
10. Viewing process work as essential to productivity.
11. Emphasis on cooperation."[18]

The implications for supervision in this development are of great significance. As

Hitt points out, each of the Theories carries its own set of advantages and handicaps into particular situations, and the one that is utilized will determine the way supervision is done. Supervisory practice in business and industry continues to be dominated by Theory X. Even so, the struggle to find the most effective approach continues with its impact upon workers' training, tenure of employment, involvement in decision-making, evaluation, and, ultimately, the success of the organization.

EDUCATION

The general field of education was selected for attention partly because it represents a specific concern of the writer as a pastoral educator, but partly also because of the serious efforts that have been made in this discipline to develop supervisory procedures. The particular focus in this review will be upon public education, because there is a recognizable tradition and sizeable body of literature upon which to draw. Several recent publications are especially helpful, because they indicate the current ferment in this profession surrounding the issue under discussion.

HISTORY

According to Ralph Mosher and David Purpel, supervision in the public schools began as school inspection for the purpose of "maintaining common standards of instruction" and "deciding on the retention or promotion of individual teachers."[19] It remained that until 1920, gathering about it a reputation as "snoopervision" because of its often authoritarian insistence on conformity. There was no clear designation of this responsibility; local school boards, local or district superintendents, state departments of education, educational institutions, and regional accrediting agencies variously, sometimes simultaneously, shared the task. As school systems became more complex toward the end of the nineteenth century, it was sometimes assigned as a more specialized duty to other staff persons but still always as a function of the school administration.

Between 1920 and 1950 two radically different theories of supervision emerged to impact the system. One, called **scientific supervision**, emphasized research in admin- istrative and teaching methods and viewed the supervisor as the one responsible for conducting the research and communicating the information for the sake of improved instruction. The other theory, referred to as **democratic supervision**, stressed the professional development of the teacher and saw the supervisory task to be that of protecting the integrity, releasing the talents, and supporting the personhood of the individual teacher. The result was the identification of three distinguishable foci of supervision. As Mosher and Purpel point out: "It is clear that democratic and scientific supervision represent deeply differing views on both the means and the ends of supervision. Historically, as one or the other tradition gained sway, varying degrees of emphasis have been placed on the role of supervision in evaluation and inspection, in curriculum development, and in teacher development.[20]

DEVELOPMENT

The democratic view with its emphasis on teacher development became the soil in which supervision found nurturance under the assumptions: "(1) that the individual teacher is the key agent of education; (2) that given proper support and strength, the teacher's talents can achieve full expression; and (3) that this talent is sufficient in the teacher and in the teaching profession to warrant extensive efforts to provide the resources of supervisory assistance."[21] This is not to discount curriculum development, but it is clear from the literature that, while teacher and curriculum development are the primary objectives of supervision (school inspection having been de-emphasized), the teacher came to be the central focus. Thus Mosher and Purpel's definition of the two tasks of supervision reflect the major body of literature, namely, "teaching teachers how to teach (which involves working with teachers as people) and professional leadership in reformulating public education--more specifically, its curriculum, its teaching and its forms."[22] It is clear, therefore, that while it remains an administrative responsibility, it has become, in concept at least, a teaching function. The supervisor has one foot in each camp!

Such a stance creates both hazards and opportunities. These grow out of the way in which the supervisory role is understood in a particular setting and the way in which the supervisor sees him/her self in the role. Adolph Unruh and Harold Turner claim that supervision involves three processes. The **social process** includes "stimulating, nurturing, and appraising the professional growth of teachers." The **psychological process** has to do with "problem mechanisms teachers and school personnel employ in their relations with others." The **educational process** provides for continuing education "utilizing workshops, institutes, consultants, independent studies, conventions, and school visits."[23] Exercised in this fashion, say these authors, supervision should be understood as educational leadership.

How this leadership is exercised, however, determines how it is received. If it takes seriously the autonomous development of the individual teacher, it is accepted, appreciated, and utilized constructively. If, on the other hand, it is perceived as the coercive ploy of the central administrative office, it is resisted and, on occasion, rejected. Unruh and Turner report several studies which identified factors contributing to teacher morale; supervisory behavior was one:

> Supervisors "caught in the middle" between the authoritarian administrator and genuine concern for the dignity of the individual teacher cannot shirk their responsibility to the person. They must, in conscience, respect the worth of each teacher and strive to work with him in a fair manner. Their concern for human relations can sometimes neutralize the negative aspects of authoritarianism.[24]

Heavy emphasis is placed in the literature on this democratic approach to supervision. Stanley Williams refers to it as "horizontal supervision" as contrasted to "vertical supervision," as a "helping" rather than a "telling" procedure. However, there is considerable discrepancy between what administration and faculty understand as being helpful. Whereas administrators tend to prefer directive methods as a means of maintaining quality control, the consensus among teachers is that they do not want the supervisor to deal with them autocratically; rather they want stimulation and coordination of their activities for the improvement of the curriculum. New teachers in particular recommend that a good supervisory program should include: "a thoroughly planned orientation program, workshops and group conferences, individual interviews or counseling sessions, classroom visitations, directed readings, and individual guidance from experienced teachers on the staff."[25] This compares with the types of help that experienced teachers desire as reported by Unruh and Turner: (1) individual personal problems, (2) materials of instruction, (3) methods of instruction, (4) professional problems, and (5) intellectual and cultural outlets.[26] This reflects the view of other writers.

One way that democratic supervision works out in practice is described as **clinical supervision**, described by Morris Cogan in his book by that title. Criticizing past reliance on technical assistance for improving education, he supports his call for a clinical approach with the claim that "American experience so far indicates that it is in the classroom, at the point of application, that new methods of teaching break down."[27] The beginnings are traced to the Master of Arts in Teaching Program at Harvard University in the 1950s where supervising teachers, student teachers, and university supervisors shared in the development. Building on the definition of clinical as the direct utilization of observable behavior, he distinguishes between **general supervision** which takes place outside the classroom in activities such as curriculum development, and **clinical supervision** which seeks the improvement of classroom instruction by focusing on what teachers and students do in the classroom.

Cogan outlines a cycle of supervision built around a supervisory conference in which the supervisor and teacher sit together as colleagues to discuss a teaching session that the supervisor has observed. The eight phases of the cycle provide for mutual planning of the teaching session, clarification of expectations for the observation, shared analysis of what took place, and renewed planning for another teaching session based upon insights gained in the conference. All this is done in a consultative way, the intention being that the supervisor and teacher be learning partners, sharing the decision making, with the teacher's needs being paramount. The central objective in the entire process is "the development of the professionally responsible teacher who is analytical of his own performance, open to help from others, and withal self-directing."[28] Cogan refers to the latter quality as self-supervision.

Cogan feels that in the context of clinical supervision it is possible for one to confront both dysfunctional teaching patterns and new effective methods without personal threat. By viewing their supervision as continuing education, teachers are enabled to make responsible decisions about their own development. The supervisory relationship also helps to alleviate the professional loneliness that many teachers feel. Once the teachers come to realize that the supervisory program is theirs, not the supervisors, their commitment to it is increased and the use of their own experience and resources improves. Critical incidents become teaching instruments for personal exploration and skill development according to the teacher's objectives. What was once viewed as remedial becomes growth-oriented.

Not everyone in public education is considered capable of performing the supervisory task. Those who do must be in possession of certain qualifications. Mosher and

Purpel refer to six supervisory skills: (1) sensitive to people and teaching problems; (2) able to analyze what is observed; (3) able to communicate ideas and perceptions; (4) expert in the teaching and curriculum field; (5) competent in interpersonal relationships; and (6) informed in social responsibility in terms of educational goals.[29] Williams identifies similar characteristics which affirm that the supervisor needs to be academically well-trained; emotionally stable; respected by students, colleagues, administration, and the community at large; and willing to experiment.[30] This assumes adequate self-understanding and specialized preparation, though it is recognized that supervisory competence comes primarily through the experience of supervising.

There is an implication in all of this of a close relationship between supervision and counseling. It is acknowledged that supervision utilizes counseling principles when it is responsive to the teacher as a person. The emphasis, however, is upon the teacher's professional identity. Some go so far as to suggest the special relevance of ego counseling to the supervision of teaching; others write in more cautious terms. All agree that the specific purpose is to help teachers become self-aware in terms of their teaching patterns so as to bring about improvement in their instructional abilities. Dysfunctional patterns need to be identified when they interfere with performance, but deep penetration of the personality is to be avoided. Change in behavioral patterns is left to the individual teacher's determination, as is any decision to seek therapeutic help for personality adjustment.

While the norm in the clinical approach is a one-to-one supervisor-teacher relationship, some emphasis is placed upon the use of group settings for supervision, thus increasing the availability of the supervisor as well as providing collegial relationships for the teachers. The place of evaluation is more controversial. While all agree that teacher evaluation is integral to the supervisory process, there is some disagreement over how it is to be done. There is consensus that the best evaluation is the teacher's self-evaluation. The tension between supervising and evaluating is crucial, and some writers in the field insist that the same person cannot do both. They feel, however, that when the supervisor reveals him/her self as open to evaluation and has established a sound clinical relationship with the teachers, resistance is lowered and it becomes a productive experience.[31]

CURRENT STATUS

Since its introduction, clinical supervision has received both support and criticism. Debate over its usefulness continues. On the one hand, critics argue that it is too time consuming, is incongruent with some school contexts, and that it is resisted by teachers who often prefer help from their peers rather than from their superiors.[32] Even one of its proponents, Lee Goldsberry, acknowledges that "personal experience supports the . . . research that supervision depicted in the literature bears little resemblance to the supervision actually occurring in schools."[33] On the other hand, Goldsberry maintains that clinical supervision, with its emphasis on colleagueship, collaborative goal setting, teaching values, and student learning is consistent with effective leadership. He appeals to supervisors to model the method, and he offers suggestions for implementing it.

The debate over the values of clinical supervision appears to have given birth to creative alternative methods of supervision in public education circles. These include variations on clinical supervision, peer supervision, team supervision, and the appropriate mix of technical, human relations, and managerial skills. Studies indicate that principals' styles, teachers' experience and readiness, and the methods used to introduce the supervisory program are all critically important factors in any supervisory approach. To that end numerous writers, too numerous to review fully here, have proposed options based upon the understanding that no one method is able to fit every situation but that a repertoire of methods and styles are needed. What is clear is that teachers respond most positively to supervision that treats them as colleagues and react most negatively to supervision that puts them in a subordinate position. Given that mix, Thomas Sergiovanni says that "supervisory work is among the highest callings available to educated men and women."[34]

Supervision as practiced in the public schools has no uniform definition or pattern. In 1972 Mosher and Purpel observed that: (1) With the notable exception of many urban school systems, professional educators have purposely de-emphasized the assessment or inspection function of supervision; (2) professional educators generally subscribe to the validity and necessity of a "supervision program;" (3) school systems have generally put limited resources into their supervisory programs; (4) by and large, teachers massively resist supervision, are suspicious of it and are reluctant to consider its positive dimensions.[35]

This assessment of the situation remains mostly true. However, an old issue has recently been revived. The current emphasis on the status of student achievement suggests that the assessment of teachers and of schools is of renewed importance. What effect this will have on staff development as a major supervisory task is an open question.

PSYCHOTHERAPY

The field of psychotherapy is a large one and embraces several professions. In spite of those who suggest that perhaps we have come to a point in time when psychotherapy should be recognized as a profession in its own right, it seems more accurate for our purpose to see it as a professional art which is practiced by specially trained persons in medicine, social work, ministry and other professional fields. Richard Chessick, a psychiatrist, appropriately points out that "not all psychiatrists ought to, can, or want to do psychotherapy," and "it is not necessary to have an M.D. degree to become a psychotherapist, although it is desirable."[36] The general discipline of psychotherapy has been selected for review here for three reasons: (1) it represents one branch of the medical arts; (2) it is a discipline upon which pastoral counseling and pastoral supervision have drawn widely for identity and methodology; and (3) there is a sizeable body of literature available.

HISTORY

Most of the literature on the teaching of psychotherapy through supervision of psychotherapists-in-training has been written since 1955. This does not mean that supervision was non-existent before that; rather, only recently has the process been conceptualized and analyzed. The experiential dimension of medical education has historically followed an apprenticeship model, but Sigmund Freud's experience led to the recognition that more was needed in the training of psychoanalysts. Therefore as early as 1902 he gathered about him a group of young doctors for conversation about their experiences and observations. This led in 1910 to his suggestion that a personal analysis should be part of the training of every psychoanalyst, and two years later he began stressing the procedure.

Known as the training analysis, this did not become a regular practice until the early 1920s when, under the influence of Max Eitingon in Berlin, the International Psycho-analytic Congress made it a requirement. This was followed in 1925 by the institution of three components in psychoanalytic training: the training (personal) analysis, the theoretical curriculum, and the supervised analysis. Supervision has been a part of the training since that time, with considerably more developmental thought being given to the subject in Europe through the 1930s. By the 1940s and 1950s in America it was common practice for clinicians to bring written accounts of their therapy sessions with clients to supervisors for discussion and analysis. It was not until the mid-1950s that educational philosophy was addressed in the United States, resulting in the adoption in 1956 (one writer says 1957) of the "Minimal Standards for the Training of Physicians in Psychoanalysis." These standards called for 150 hours of supervision with two supervising analysts in addition to the training analyst in order to:

1. Instruct the student in the use of the psychoanalytic method;
2. Aid . . . in the acquisition of therapeutic skills based upon an understanding of the analytic material;
3. Observe . . . work and determine how fully . . . personal analysis was achieving its aims; and
4. Determine . . . maturity and stability over an extended period of time.[37]

The earliest teaching materials for the education of supervisors and consultants was Florence Kaslow's *Issues in Human Services: A Sourcebook for Supervision and Staff Development* published in 1972. This was followed in 1977 by *Supervision, Consultation and Staff Training in the Helping Professions* by the same author, aimed at improving supervisory practice in cross-disciplinary settings. Both books identify supervision as a critical element in the education and work of psychotherapists.

DEVELOPMENT

Growing out of this brief historical sketch are two important facts about supervision in psychotherapy. One is that it depends heavily upon the psychoanalytic tradition for its identity. The other is that from the beginning supervisors have struggled with a still-unresolved question about the focus of their work. It may be stated this way: Is the aim of supervision to do therapy through students, instruct students in how to do therapy, or provide therapy for students? Or is it all three of these? The literature gives major attention to this question and can best be summarized by reference to the principle proponents of the several schools of thought.

The opinions cluster around two poles: **supervision as teaching** in which the students' learning of therapeutic theory and skill is central, and **supervision as therapy** in which the students' self-understanding and personhood is primary. Back of them, however, is a third concern about the clients for whom ultimately the supervision is carried out. The earliest expressions of supervision concentrated on the clients. It is generally agreed that they should be the final beneficiaries, but the supervisory question asks how to accomplish that. Should the supervisors, who are therapists, control the situation by using the supervisory conference to analyze the clients and tell the student-therapists working with the clients how to handle the cases? In such a move, the supervisors manage the cases, and the students serve as agents to carry out the supervisors' therapeutic program. William Mueller and Bill Kell refer to this as a "controlling supervisory model." They report that:

> Trainees emerging from such a supervisory experience seem usually to feel that they have learned something. However, they also are more ambivalent about the experiences, about themselves, and about the supervisor. In addition, they are usually less clear about their own identities as persons and as therapists. Commonly, therapists coming out of such training often say they are grateful for what they have learned but that they hope to do supervision somewhat differently themselves.

Their comments are often to the effect that they believe some kind of faith, belief, or trust in people is desirable but they are unclear how this can occur. What seems to be missing is the experience of a reciprocally trusting relationship although a wish or hope is still retained. It seems clear to us that the controlling supervisory model is somewhat successful in teaching. That it engenders a sense of trustworthiness, a strong sense of personal and professional identity, and unambivalent feelings about learning and development is much more questionable.[38]

In contrast, these authors think that conflict, including its resultant anxiety, is the central dynamic of all human relationships and that both therapy and the supervision of therapy must provide the opportunity for exploring and resolving it. In supervision the special sources of conflict are the clients' life experiences, the therapist-client interactions, and the supervisory relationship. Student therapists need to learn not only what is therapeutic but also how to use themselves therapeutically. The authors' "supervisory paradigm" calls for the creation of a warm, open, trusting relationship in which trainees, by working out their own emotional conflicts, are enabled to assist clients to do the same.

An important supervisory task, therefore, is to help therapists accept their own feelings and to use them in understanding what feelings their clients may activate in other people. Questions that supervisors should continually raise within themselves and with their trainees are: "What triggered that reaction and those feelings in you in your relationship to your client? What does that tell you about your client?"[39]

Nowhere is the struggle over this issue more clearly illustrated than in the book *Clinical Supervision of the Psychiatric Resident* where, based upon a lengthy review of literature in the field, Daniel Schuster and his colleagues conclude that there is no single accepted supervisory method. Consequently the authors propose the refinement of a model of supervision that moves trainees through a sequence of supervisory relationships designed to increase individual competence. While they follow primarily a one-to-one, apprentice-master arrangement, they recognize that psychiatrists, even more than other medical personnel, function out-of-sight of their colleagues. Therefore the development of a supervisory attitude is crucial, meaning that they encourage voluntary supervision as a continuing educational experience throughout their professional careers.

Schuster and others conclude that supervision is the most influential component of their training program.[40] However, the struggle identified earlier is evident in verbatim accounts of their supervisory staff consultations. They differ sharply in their understanding of what needs primary attention.

The author most frequently mentioned as representative of the supervision-as-teaching view is Sidney Tarachow who says: "The basic rule is that the teaching of the resident should be instruction in terms of the problems and needs of the patient, as expressed in the specific clinical phenomena of the patient. The supervisor is an instructor and not a psychotherapist."[41] While he insists on the correctness of this view, he admits that supervision approaches psychotherapy dangerously close.

On the other side of the issue, the authors considered to be most representative of the supervision-as-therapy approach are Rudolph Ekstein and Robert Wallerstein who base their understanding of supervision on the complex dynamics operative in the multiple relationships native to psychotherapy. They describe this in terms of a diagram called the clinical rhombus which identifies four primary participants: the **patient** who seeks therapeutic help; the **therapist** who provides the therapy as a student and thus receives supervision; the **supervisor** who is responsible for training the therapist and thus also has a responsibility to make sure both that the patient receives adequate care and that the standards of the clinical setting are upheld; and the **administrator** of the clinical setting who is obligated to see that the best interests of all participants are protected.

Although the supervisor and student are the immediate participants in a one-to-one supervisory relationship, the self-interests, integrity, and emotional needs of all become a part of the supervisory situation, often in conflicting ways. The supervisory task is (1) to help the students understand this, particularly the way in which their own participation affects the several relationships, and (2) to provide the intellectual and emotional conditions in which such total awareness can contribute to the students' growth as therapists.

From the outset the authors insist that this is a learning process, not a disguised form of psychotherapy. Ideally utilized, the supervisory process will constitute for students "a form of self-discovery, a constantly critical evaluation" of what they are doing and of what they are being taught. It will help them toward those "inner commitments" they need in order to learn the use of psychotherapeutic techniques.[42]

The inner commitment of which the authors speak is the students' professional identity. The acquisition of skills is not enough; students need also to become clear about who they are. This is true also of supervisors who, because of their own inner needs, may be tempted to simply create extensions of themselves rather than assist their students to grow into mature, autonomous, competent professional persons. Good supervision promotes self-determination. Psychotherapeutic help, in addition to supervision, may become necessary in particular cases to resolve emotional barriers; but identification as psychotherapists with the corresponding inner discipline, along with the improvement of therapeutic skills, is a prime objective of supervision.

31

Ekstein and Wallerstein therefore suggest that supervision in psychotherapy has two purposes. One is to maintain quality professional service; the other is to help students become qualified professionals. In light of this, one way of doing supervision would be to make a distinction between the professional self and the personal self of the students. Supervision would then direct its attention to change in the professional self, and change in the personal self would be referred to psychotherapy.

While this is one supervisory model, these authors feel that the two "selves" cannot be so neatly divided. They speak of the supervisory process being directed toward two kinds of related concerns--**learning problems** and **problems about learning**. Learning problems consist of the predisposition of students to act in patterned ways toward their patients. Problems about learning refer to the characteristic ways in which students relate to their supervisors. Both have their source not only in what students bring to the experience but what patients and supervisors also bring by way of personal experience and psychological make-up. Supervision addresses both sets of problems with the understanding that students learn "through becoming aware of and working toward the resolution of the problems . . . (their) learning poses."[43] These are problems not only of theory and skill but also of emotion.

The term that Ekstein and Wallerstein use to describe this is **the parallel process** by which they mean that the way students function in the therapeutic relationship with patients is frequently reflected in the way they respond to the supervisory relationship. Thus, the way they give help and the way they seek help are functionally related. The same can be said about supervisors. Effective supervision depends upon the identification and understanding of these patterns in order that effective therapy can occur. Only as students are "helped in the resolution of such difficulties" in themselves will they be able to "see objectively enlarging aspects of the patient's problems. It is as though we work with a constant `metaphor' in which the patient's problem in psychotherapy may be used to express the therapist's problem in supervision--and vice versa."[44]

It is this emphasis that puts Ekstein and Wallerstein on the side of supervision-as-therapy, but they seek to disclaim that. What they do claim is that they wish to enrich the original two methods of training psychotherapists--personal analysis and didactic instruction through the use of the parallel process. While they think it desirable for trainees to have a personal analysis, experience indicates that it is not necessary for all persons. "Modern training has at different times placed different emphases on the importance and significance of the personal therapeutic experience for the future practitioner on the one hand, and the supervision of his work on the other hand. The tendency today seems to be to emphasize the desirability of both forms of experience as a part of clinical training."[45]

Joan Fleming and Theresa Benedek represent a middle view between teaching and therapy as the primary foci of supervision. They see the supervisory responsibility as one of selecting the method and emphasis most appropriate with each particular trainee. This demands that attention be given to theoretical understandings, technical skills, and personal identity. Supervision therefore moves through a series of tasks which have both learning and therapeutic goals, but always stopping short of the psychoanalysis of the trainee. The end-goal is to bring the student, like the patient, to "a point of independence and new insights."[46] Or as Florence Kaslow suggests, the behavior of the supervisor in the supervisory session will itself provide "a much more compelling model of how a session should be conducted than does his/her verbalizations about the structure of a therapy hour."[47]

CURRENT STATUS

Regardless of which theory one prefers, training in psychotherapy has moved from a condition in which the pioneers in the field had little formal training to one in which today's students go through several years of preparation, a significant part of which is supervised practice. The primary method is a one-to-one conference in which trainees bring case material to their supervisors for analysis, though group supervision is not uncommon. Evaluation is a painful but necessary part of the supervisory task, and procedures vary.

The struggle between controlling and egalitarian methods continues. There is one view that sees some trend toward the latter. Describing what she observes as "two forces in America, one operating from above down and one operating from down upward," Margaret Rioch offers the opinion that "the `you are up; I am down' situation is not likely to obtain for very long. The balance is untenable."[48] Actually, she takes a dim view of the value of supervision at all:

> The question may well be raised as to how, when all these forces are operative, any effective work is done at all in supervision. The answer is that it often is not. In fact, more often, nothing is accomplished, work is not done, and supervisees sit through interminable hours because there are certain requirements in the program which gives them certificates that they need in order to make a living. The less we have of "sitting through," the better. But just as in learning to play the piano, the most important thing is to practice, and to have the stimulation of a teacher to whom we can go once a week or so and show what one has done. In learning to practice and to present one's work to a teacher, one also learns to listen to oneself. This is probably the most important aspect of teaching the piano and of supervising psychotherapy that there is. One learns to listen to oneself.[49]

The over-arching goal of supervision is to make it possible for persons to function independently as competent therapists, and there is considerable pressure to create the opportunities and the motivation necessary for ongoing supervision through voluntary professional consultation. Kaslow's early suggestion that there are three major teaching processes--supervision, consultation, and staff training--remains true. Her lengthy treatment of models and paradigms for the supervision of therapy continue to be useful. In this connection Richard Hogan describes four levels of development for student therapists with a corresponding model of supervision appropriate to each level. They move from dependency to limited autonomy to budding peership to mutual consultation.[50]

In 1963 Daryl DeBell wrote that supervision should provide students with the opportunity to observe and reflect on their conduct of an analysis and thereby readjust and refine their observing instrument. They should "be constantly occupied with the translation of the clinical material into theoretical forms, and with the reverse. This process is virtually limited to supervision and its analogues, the case conferences, and its exercise is vital if the student is to become more than a rule of thumb technician."[51] More recently Irving Weiner and Robert Kaplan have described the task as help for beginning therapists in "(a) learning to integrate treatment techniques with personal authenticity, (b) learning to recognize the boundaries of psychotherapy and of themselves as effective agents of behavior change, and (c) learning to achieve an appropriate sense of professional identity and responsibility."[52]

Allen Hess acknowledges that "as supervision develops, more attention must be given to the definition, training, and possibly credentialing of supervisors. While it is likely that supervisors will continue to be defined by the training institute, academic department, or clinic, professional standards will be developed for supervisor education. These developments make the need for definition and research on the supervisory process even more urgent."[53]

SOCIAL WORK

There is a long and close relationship between social work and pastoral work, both being referred to frequently as helping professions. Their institutions are mutually supportive and often parallel each other in concern and work. It is not uncommon for persons in these fields to change professions from one to the other. Of particular relevance to our purpose here, however, is the fact that it is one of the professions that has given attention to conceptualizing the supervisory process. Clinical Pastoral Education has drawn upon it for its supervisory theory and practice, taking its original cue from social work. It is important, therefore, to review its literature.

HISTORY

The first references to supervision were usually in connection with the controlling functions of licensing authorities or funding boards to which social work agencies were accountable. However, in 1878 the Charity Organization Society movement began as a way of overseeing alms-giving practices. Volunteer workers (friendly visitors) were assigned to visit families to investigate their needs, offer personal support, and provide some behavioral influence. As the procedure grew, paid agents representing the Society were made responsible for recruiting, training, coordinating, and encouraging the volunteers. Each agent, in cooperation with a district committee, would oversee a group of lay volunteers who, in turn, provided the direct service to clients. The extensive social needs, difficulty of the work, and rapid turnover of volunteers forced the agents to spend a large part of their time consulting with visitors. This was done sometimes in groups but more commonly in individual conferences, using the visitors' case material as the major source for learning. By the turn of the century all the components of social work supervision as it is known today were in practice, though the term did not appear in the literature with this usage until the mid-1920s.

Mary Burns points out: "Supervision has been the traditional method of transmitting knowledge of social work and skill in practice from the trained to the untrained, from the experienced practitioner to the inexperienced student or worker."[54] Though the first supervisors had no formal training for their responsibility, their practice led to the gradual development of a body of wisdom used in specialized training programs until, early in the twentieth century, the first schools of social work were established. This resulted in some shift of responsibility and methodology, but social work continued to rely on supervision in the agency setting as a major method for educating and sustaining its professional workers. It was by no means a static process; a great deal of ferment arose in the field, particularly concerning its use with experienced workers, but it remains integral to the profession.

DEVELOPMENT

Supervision in social work has been variously defined, but most writers agree that it includes at least two elements, **administration** and **teaching**. A third element, mentioned under different titles and with different descriptions in several sources, is identified by Alfred Kadushin as **support**. These principal supervisory functions, he maintains, are complimentary, and:

All are necessary if the ultimate objective of supervision is to be achieved— a purpose above and beyond the more limited purpose of each of the three. The **ultimate objective** of supervision is to offer the agency's service to the client in the most efficient and effective manner possible. It is toward that goal that the supervisor administratively integrates and coordinates the supervisees' work with others in the agency, educates the workers to a more skillful performance in their tasks, and supports and sustains the workers in motivated performance of these tasks.[55]

Kadushin describes the administrative, educative, and supportive functions of supervision in clear detail but acknowledges that there is some difference of opinion over their applicability. The principle controversy grows out of a feeling among experienced social workers that educational supervision is inappropriate once they have achieved professional status. There is full agreement that for students, inexperienced workers, and para-professionals, supervision meets a necessary educational need. Speaking also as an educator, Betty Jones calls field instruction "the practice activity that tests out and acts to integrate the whole of professional education and from which emerges the beginning professional practitioner."[56] Many experienced workers, however, believe that intermi-nable educational supervision "suggests that the worker does not know enough, is not fully competent, is incapable of autonomous practice."[57]

Betty Mandell complains that continued supervision has tended to increase dependency, leading to the accusation that social work is only a semi-profession "partly because of its lack of full autonomy."[58] On the other hand, Evelyn Stiles, while acknowledging that staff supervision is not analogous to student supervision, counters the criticism with the strong suggestion that it is not supervision itself but the quality of it that makes the difference.

In discussing the possible deleterious effects of supervision, it is essential to distinguish between good supervision and poor supervision. Is it the ineffectiveness of supervision or the ineffectual use of supervision with which the professional needs to be concerned? The belief that supervision in itself fosters dependency seems contrary to social work concepts about dependency. The elements of dependency that exist in any significant relationship do not necessarily impair a person's functioning. When dependence is met appropriately, the result can be an increase in a person's independence. Thus a good supervisor can help a worker increase . . . knowledge, productivity, and creativity.[59]

Social workers are also vocal, though less so, in their criticism of supportive supervision. The issue here is not its legitimacy but the form it takes. As has already been pointed out, the first supervisors, the paid agents, spent considerable time encouraging and inspiring the lay volunteers. With the emergence of dynamic psychiatry in the 1920s attention in social work supervision began to be focused on the workers' attitudes as they affected their relationships with clients. The modification of attitudes through the resolution of personality conflicts became a supervisory aim. Burns feels that while this "was essentially incompatible with the administrative and teaching components of supervision" which required workers to be held accountable for their own activities and progress in professional development, "the therapeutic function has left vestiges in the supervisory process."[60] The current objection by workers is not emotional support but attempts at therapy. They welcome the former but resist the latter.

Kadushin defines supportive supervision "as those interventions that reinforce ego defenses and strengthen the capacity of the ego to deal with job stresses and tensions."[61] Leonard Bloom and Cherie Herman compare the supervisor's function to "an emotional Geiger counter which clicks" when one senses the workers are "concealing a significant level of emotional tension and over-involvement" in their jobs. They warn that supervisors must also avoid becoming over-involved in the workers' problems lest workers feel that their personal lives are "being unwarrantably invaded."[62]

Common practice sees supervisors giving attention to workers' personal problems only as they interfere with their professional work. The general procedure is to assist workers in identifying such patterns and encourage them to get therapeutic help in another relationship if necessary.

Administrative supervision, on the other hand, is accepted as a "given" in social work. Kadushin claims that "even if all workers were well trained, were objectively self-critical, and had developed a level of self-awareness that eliminated the need for educational supervision, even if all workers were so highly motivated, so self-assured, so rich in inner resources that they felt no need for supervisory support, administrative supervision would continue to be necessary as long as the workers were employees of an agency."[63] As several writers maintain, it is hard to separate them; all are necessary.

Kadushin calls for a democratic approach to supervision which includes the worker as a full and equal participant in the process. In research that he conducted among 750 supervisors and an equal number of supervisees, he found an increased emphasis being given to training at the Master's level, though only 47% of those supervisors had completed a formal course in supervision. While the individual case conference was identified as the norm in methodology, improved techniques and more egalitarian relationships were being utilized. There was mutual agreement that service to clients and the professional development of supervisees were the primary objectives, while personal development of the supervisees was rated among the three least important objectives.

At the same time, when asked to name their satisfactions in supervision, the supervisees identified shared responsibility for cases, support in difficult cases, help with problems, and personal growth. Their dissatisfactions were that the supervisors too often failed to plead their cases before administration, were not critical enough of their work, and did not give enough specific help with cases.[64] Clearly there is considerable ambivalence in the social work field about supervision.

Attention has been given to some alternatives as a way of meeting some of the criticisms about supervisory practice. One is the use of consultation as a sequel to supervision for the experienced professional. Lydia Rapaport defines consultation as "a problem-solving process wherein a more knowledgeable professional, the consultant, or expert, gives information and help to a less knowledgeable professional, the consultee."[65] The purpose is to strengthen consultees in their designated professional role by: increasing their knowledge and skills, modifying their attitudes and behavior so that their specific problem may be solved, or generally enhancing their work performance for the ultimate benefit of the clientele they serve. She sees this as the growing area of social work practice and puts it into the stream of development of other professions.

Rapaport claims that in some case-work agencies consultation is a substitute for supervision with the following advantages: (1) it is geared to solving specific work problems; (2) it provides freedom to select particular consultants on the basis of expertise; (3) it is voluntary, being initiated by the consultee who also maintains responsibility to decide how to utilize the input; (4) it focuses on the consultee's precise need; (5) it is contractual. As a process it is "a time-limited, goal-oriented, and segment-focused transaction."[66] Consultation is more acceptable to experienced social workers, especially as a substitute for educative and supportive supervision.

Kadushin has developed these ideas by showing how consultation is both distinctive from and similar to supervision, sometimes fulfilling the same purposes. He suggests that what ultimately distinguishes the consultant from the supervisor is "the possession of some special knowledge and skill different from, or beyond that, possessed by the supervisor." With this understanding, "consultation might be regarded as an adjunctive function to supervision or a supplementation of supervision."[67] The use of consultation is understood appropriately as an interprofessional activity.

According to Kenneth Watson private agencies developed the supervisory method that became the model for the profession, essentially a tutorial model borrowed from psychiatry with an emphasis on creating self-awareness in the supervisee. Dissatisfied with this, a number of other models have been tried. No one model is adequate, but "what is needed is differential supervision with a range of options."[68] Concentrating on the administrative and educative functions, he describes six differential models of supervision as possibilities:

1. **Tutorial** - Supervisor and worker meet in a one-to-one relationship. This is most useful with inexperienced workers but may be used by more experienced persons on request. Conferences are regular and frequent. The teaching-learning component is important. The worker is directly accountable to the supervisor who shares responsibility for the worker's cases, evaluation, and linkage to the agency.

2. **Case Consultation** - Usually a one-to-one relationship on request of the

worker who sets the agenda and is responsible for decisions. This is usually utilized with more experienced workers. It is case focused and time limited. The consultant carries a heavy teaching role but has no responsibility for the worker's cases, evaluation, or linkage to the agency. The worker may use different consultants for different needs.

3. **Supervisory Group** - A group arrangement of one supervisor and several workers which functions much like the tutorial model except in a group setting. It is most effective where workers are fairly homogeneous in training and experience. Meetings are held regularly with agenda determined by the supervisor. Decisions, however, are left to the workers with accountability to the supervisor. Teaching is a strong component. Evaluation is done by the supervisor on a one-to-one basis. Linkage to the agency is through the supervisor.

4. **Peer-Group Supervision** - Has no designated supervisor; rather all members are equal. This model requires mature workers who share common areas of competence. Chairship is designated by the group or rotated. Meetings are on a regular basis with agenda mutually determined. Workers are responsible for their own decisions. There is no formal teaching; learning is individual and a by-product. Case accountability and evaluation are provided outside the group, but linkage to the agency is through the group leader.

5. **Tandem Supervision** - Similar to the peer-group model but includes only two workers functioning in peer relationship without a designated leader. It is informal, case-centered, and held on request. Teaching is incidental. There is no case accountability, evaluation, or linkage provided.

6. **The Team** - A group with heterogeneous membership. Meetings are regular with agenda determined by the group with room left for crisis situations. Decisions are made by the team through group process, but individual workers are responsible for carrying them out. There is a designated leader who carries no supervisory status. Learning is the responsibility of individual workers. Evaluation is done cooperatively by the worker, team leader, and administrator assigned to oversee the team but is not a group member. Linkage to the agency is through the team leader.

"Social work supervision," says Watson, "has vacillated between perpetuating a tutorial model that needlessly restricts and infantilizes competent workers and abandoning this model for some type of group method that it hoped would do the supervisory job more efficiently."[69] It should be pointed out that the tutorial model is commonly used in work with social work students, and in actual practice there are numerous adaptations of all the models being used with social workers.

These issues come to a head in a study done by a social work educator, Carlton Munson. He agrees that there is considerable uncertainty within the social work profession in regard to supervision, growing out of a rejection by many social workers of traditional supervisory methods and the more recent trends toward consultative models of staff relationship. While the long-standing definition of supervision as embracing three principal elements—administration, education, and helping—continues to be a valid description of supervisory functions, the way these are interpreted and utilized needs clarification.

Munson proposed that supervision in social work be clearly distinguished from the consultative function, that it be limited to administrative concerns (working conditions, case distribution, personnel policies, etc.), and that the authority for policies and decisions be lodged in the supervisor. Consultation, he feels, is a separate function and should be performed by a different person for purposes of assisting social workers in the handling of their case load; consultation should be voluntary and advisory, with the authority for decisions lodged in the worker. In this arrangement, the educational and helping functions, traditionally assigned to supervisors, should be left to the self-determination of workers as mature, autonomous professionals. Should a situation arise in which personal problems interfere with the ability to function effectively, workers may be confronted, but both the supervisor and consultant should coordinate their observations and efforts in this regard. Therapy, if needed, could be contracted separately with the consultant but, more preferably, with a third person.

Munson feels that this model clarifies the supervisory and consultative functions, lodges authority appropriately, and solves the problem of workers feeling "de-professionalized." He concedes, however, that in the case of social work students, the traditional three supervisory functions (administration, education, helping) are probably best assigned to one person. In this regard, he distinguishes between "field instruction" for the student and "supervision" for the social worker. "Field instruction," he feels, more appropriately describes the traditional three supervisory roles.[70]

CURRENT STATUS

The open, honest struggle over the purpose and role of supervision in social work continues. On the one hand Charles Levy boldly states that: "Social work personnel are in a bind, and this calls for a special set of ethics to guide the supervisor's conduct."[71] He suggests that supervisors should act to safeguard the workers' rights regardless of whether it is the immediately best or most practical procedure, assign workers with maximum opportunity to succeed and then evaluate fairly, give primary consideration to the workers' growth whether or not it benefits the agency and its clientele, help workers come to an accurate appraisal of their professional aspirations and opportunities, and provide workers with an accurate understanding of the expectations upon which their work will be carried out and evaluated.

On the other hand Munson, who has become a prominent spokesperson and writer in this development, maintains that: the conflict over the educational component of supervision remains unresolved, particularly in the disagreement between schools of social work and social work agencies over how to handle field instruction; group supervision which, along with consultation, was viewed as an alternative to promote worker autonomy has not been widely implemented, though autonomy remains an issue; the balance between advice and support for both experienced and inexperienced practitioners is continuing agenda; and, while the structure of supervision remains essentially the same, its content is changing from supervision of the person to supervision of the position, meaning that there is some erosion in the supportive function.

At the same time, old issues have taken on new faces. According to Munson's research, workers experiencing burnout identified good, supportive supervision as their main source of help; unfortunately little attention is given to stress management in supervisor training. Supervisors are urged to give attention to the revised Code of Ethics adopted by the National Association for Social Work in 1980, though there is no separate code for them. Certification of supervisors is a concern. Evaluation is a necessary part of the supervisory process though not necessarily a troublesome part, Munson says, if his proposed supervisory process is utilized; he maintains, however, that a distinction must be made between administrative evaluation and evaluation of practice. The latter is a supervisory function; the former may involve other persons.[72]

Finally, Munson calls for flexible supervisory approaches to meet different situations and unique settings. "Given the diversity in agency resources, agency size, worker education, worker experiences, personalities, and worker supervisory preferences, it seems unrealistic to seek one best model of supervision. It is realistic to select a model that is best suited to a given situation. When the supervisor and supervisee are willing to work at it, such a flexible system is attainable.[73]

CLINICAL PASTORAL EDUCATION

In this fifth and final profession selected for review the literature on pastoral supervision consists of two groups. One is a body of materials that deals with policies and guidelines for clinical pastoral education; included in this group are some published articles by supervisory persons which serve to build a fund of knowledge consistent with the official organizational documents. The second group is a collection of published and unpublished articles directed to the adaptation of the guidelines to other settings and programs, particularly in terms of extending the clinical method to broader uses by theological schools; many of these are written by clinical pastoral education supervisors, but some are by seminary field education persons with clinical backgrounds who are responsible for the clinical experiences of their students. This following review includes the first group of writings; the second group will be considered later.

HISTORY

The early twentieth century saw theological schools steeped in a curricular style which emphasized almost exclusively a theoretical approach to learning. Signs of change appeared in 1913 when William Todd, a minister, proposed clinical-type training for clergy, and in 1918 the idea received official attention at the first Conference of Theological Seminaries and Colleges in the United States and Canada. In the summer of 1923 some concrete action was taken by Bexley Hall, an Episcopalian Seminary in Ohio, by assigning several students to some social agencies in Cincinnati. The students worked in the agencies during the week and on weekends met with a Dr. William S. Keller in his home to reflect on their experience. This grew into a year-around arrangement which lasted until the seminary moved away to merge with an eastern school in 1944.

During the same period a physician, Richard Cabot, conceived the idea that clergy should receive a year of clinical training under supervision as a means of learning pastoral practice. With his encouragement Anton Boisen, a mental hospital chaplain, brought two seminary students into Worcester State Hospital in Massachusetts in 1925 to work with mentally ill patients. That event marks the beginning of Clinical Pastoral Education (CPE).[74]

CPE, with over six decades of history, has attempted to correct a rigidly academic theological education by engaging students in experiential learning under supervision. The change, said Boisen, "is the attempt to begin with the study of living human documents rather than with books and to focus attention upon those who are grappling with the issues of spiritual life and death."[75] The word "clinical" means "bedside" and describes accurately the usual location for clinical pastoral education. While the hospital is not the only place where human needs abound, it is the setting in which the program has flourished. The critical factor, however, is not the location but what takes place in whatever location is utilized. As Carroll Wise says:

> Some of the most fundamental lessons that the theological student must learn cannot be taught within the four walls of any classroom. They may be learned only as the student comes into firsthand relationship with human beings suffering from the maladies that afflict mankind. Such teachings can take place in the wards of mental or general hospitals, or in prisons, provided adequate theological and scientific supervision and instruction are present.[76]

It seems clear that Boisen intended to introduce a more dynamic way of doing theological inquiry, but the theological schools rejected the method as academically insufficient. This led to the formalizing of the CPE movement under several coordinating associations. In 1967 these associations combined to form the Association for Clinical Pastoral Education (ACPE), "the standard-setting, accrediting, certifying, resource agency in the field of clinical pastoral education. It accredits institutions, agencies and parishes as clinical pastoral education centers to offer programs of CPE and certifies supervisors to conduct these programs."[77]

Through the years a progressive arrangement of programs have been offered in a variety of settings. A basic unit of CPE requires a minimum of 400 hours over ten or more weeks, but advanced programs are available for persons with specialized interests. Beyond that, a few persons continue in education to become certified supervisors of the programs. It is the education for and practice of supervision that particularly interests us in this paper.

DEVELOPMENT

CPE is unique among the professions because it requires that its supervisors meet particular levels of training and competence for that function. Those accepted as supervision candidates must possess the qualifications of demonstrated pastoral, professional, and clinical competence, to which are to be added other competencies under specific objectives.

The goal of Supervisory CPE is to learn the art of supervision through: continuing education in the theories related to supervision using conceptual models from theology, the behavioral sciences, and education; an opportunity to practice supervision under the supervision of a CPE Supervisor; and the opportunity to integrate the theory and practice of supervision in one's pastoral and personal identity and begin to focus his or her identity as an educator. Specific objectives of Supervisory CPE are:

1. Conceptual Competence
   a. To achieve competence in using conceptual models from theory and practice to understand and articulate pastoral supervisory methodology.
   b. To develop a philosophy of CPE, including an appropriate educational model, which integrates theory and practice and to be able to articulate and demonstrate this philosophy.
   c. To gain a thorough understanding of organization and program development with emphasis on organization and development of a CPE program.
   d. To become knowledgeable of and critically conversant with the literature relating to the field of clinical supervision.

2. Supervisory Competence
   a. Competence in CPE Program Management
      (1) To develop ways of using a wide variety of program resources such as patients or parishioners, treatment or rehabilitation programs, interdisciplinary staff and CPE supervisory staff, theological consultants, library, administrative structures, and community resources for the CPE student's learning.
      (2) To develop the ability to use appropriate clinical education methods such as verbatims, taped pastoral conversations, interviews, team interviews, administrative meetings, clinical seminars, didactic seminars, and supervisor-student sessions.
      (3) To develop the ability to conduct a CPE program, making use of the theological perspective inherent in the CPE program's ministry.
      (4) To develop the ability to assist students in taking responsibility to formulate a plan of learning and to evaluate the results of the learning experience.
   b. Competence in CPE Group Supervision
      (1) To acquire the ability to facilitate the development of group interpersonal interaction as a pastoral concern.
      (2) To develop the ability to lead a small group of student peers, enabling the students to use their response to the program as a learning experience.
   c. Competence in CPE Individual Supervision
      (1) To develop the ability to understand the individual student through: awareness of the student's religious history; sensitivity to the student's psychological patterns; and respect for the student's individual learning patterns.
      (2) To develop the ability to supervise the student's pastoral work, giving attention to unique patterns of personal and professional development; and the ability to facilitate the student's moving toward pastoral identity.
      (3) To develop the ability to use one's personality and personal history as a teaching tool and as a resource in shaping one's personal supervisory style.

(4) To develop competence in the process of defining and evaluating the student's pastoral and personal resources and in the ability to use supervisory methods.

3. Pastoral Education Competence
   a. To develop professional identity as a clinical pastoral educator.
   b. To integrate educational theory, knowledge of behavioral science, theology and pastoral identity into one's own supervisory function.

Certification of supervisors takes place through rigorous examination by appropriate committees of peers, and it is maintained only by continuing practice. Failure to function in actual supervision of CPE students for more than three years may result in the loss of supervisory status unless one's competency to continue is reaffirmed by one's peers. All centers in which supervision takes place must meet certain accreditation standards, but those in which supervisory training is done must meet additional standards which include (1) multiple staff resources in teaching supervision, (2) a peer group of those learning supervision, (3) didactic instruction in supervision, and (4) one-to-one supervision of the candidates' supervision.[78]

Engagement in supervision applies equally to all who seek the CPE experience—seminarians, ordained clergy, and lay persons. All become students in the context of the program. Unlike the other professions described in this paper, there is no struggle over whether it is more appropriate for experienced or inexperienced practitioners.

While each center is free to develop its own program format, the usual pattern is: the involvement of several students in pastoral acts; the writing of case material (verbatim records of conversation, anecdotal notes of pastoral contacts, et cetera) for presentation to a supervisor-led peer group for analysis; interpersonal relations group sessions in which personal growth concerns are discussed; and individual one-to-one sessions with the supervisor, usually built around the students' case material. The students determine the agenda in the case seminars, interpersonal relations sessions, and supervisory sessions; and they are held accountable for their work and growth. Other elements such as the use of didactic material, worship opportunities, and inter-professional dialogue vary but are integral to the program. All of them fall within the responsibility of the supervisor to whom the students are accountable.

While at the beginning CPE supervisory process was developed and passed along more through practice and tradition than written materials, in recent years supervisors have been active in sharing their ideas and experience through publication. One such writer is Thomas Klink who, in the absence of any official definition, has on several occasions sought to conceptualize it. Acknowledging that "the process of supervision itself is probably even less clearly understood than the identity of the supervisor who carries it out," he has suggested several versions of a definition, one of which he claims represents common elements selected from a number of professions, mainly CPE:

(1) Supervision is a unique and identifiable educational procedure; (2) it requires as supervisor one who is both engaged in the practice of his profession and duly qualified to supervise; (3) it assumes as student a candidate seeking fuller qualification in the practice of his (intended) profession; (4) it requires for its setting an institution within whose activities there are functional roles in which student and supervisor can negotiate a "contract for learning"; (5) the

roles of both supervisor and student must be appropriate to their particular professional identity (in this case the Christian ministry); (6) lastly, supervision requires for its environment a wider community of professional peers associated in a common task.[79]

Supervision takes place, Klink says, under the impact of anxiety for both students and supervisors. For this reason a structure of time, place, and responsibilities is provided to lend stability and motivation for informing practice with knowledge. Critical to the process is the "cross-grained experience" which is "a situation in which one is confronted with demands calling for responses contrary to one's presently ingrained character."[80] Such situations arise in any or all of the experiential components of CPE, including the supervisory relationship in which they may be reflected upon and hopefully resolved. Supervision, therefore, must be seen as a process which causes students to be confronted with themselves and the way they function. It is "working with a student who is working with patients, not working with patients through a student."[81] This distinction is basic.

Armen Jorjorian identifies eight major foci in CPE supervision: (1) didactic instruction; (2) response to administrative expectations of the training program and institutional staff; (3) clinical observation and understanding of the patients' pastoral needs; (4) pastoral relationships with patients; (5) relationship with a peer group; (6) relationship with the supervisor; (7) relationship with God and the Church; and (8) each students' relationship with him/her self. The supervisory act is tentative and qualified, he says, and "requires a decision as to whether focusing on the student-patient relationship or . . . on the student-supervisor relationship is going to be the most fruitful course."[82] In a unit of CPE, all of the foci would normally receive attention, but only when and as appropriate with each individual student.

Ronald Sunderland points out that the clinical rhombus of Ekstein and Wallerstein can be expanded in the CPE setting in a multi-dimensional way to include not only the patient, student, supervisor and administration but also the patient's family, the center's professional staff, faculty persons, the students' peers, and the church.[83] Supervision may focus on any or all of them over the course of the students' involvement. As in other professions, however, it stops short of therapy which should be pursued, if necessary, with another professional.

John Patton and John Warkentin speak to this latter concern when they declare that "there should be no attempt to change the character structure" of students but that it is essential to focus upon "the `being' as well as the `doing' of the minister." Good supervision "must come within a hair's breadth of psychotherapy." It is:

> . . . holding up a looking-glass to the supervisee and challenging him, like Alice, to go through the looking-glass to a deeper level of professional practice and understanding. I want him to move toward what he sees in the mirror, which appears different from the assumptions about himself that he brought into the supervisory hour. A good supervisory situation is sort of like a house of mirrors that you go through with someone who encourages you to learn from all that you see there.[84]

As early as 1971, Charles Gerkin felt that CPE had come to a point in its history when it needed to rethink its structure and program of using primarily institutional centers to train persons already committed to the church. He proposed this as a means of: meeting the demand of seminary students not yet committed to the ministry but using seminary as a time to work through life goals; meeting ferment in the ministry by helping pastors remain in the parish as opposed to seeking an alternative ministry; capitalizing on the pluralism in CPE while maintaining some consensus and tradition; supporting the search for new bases for doing the work of theology; responding to preventive and group models of care in addition to the curative model; and recognizing ministry to structures as well as to individuals as a necessary and legitimate arena for action.[85] How this would change the supervisory process was not made clear, but it does suggest possible innovations.

One of the innovations that has received some attention is consultation, not as a substitute but as a corollary of supervision which for the pastoral profession has been limited to the CPE model and setting. Using the medical model as their example, Patton and Warkentin suggest that a student should be free to contract for consultation which is voluntary, more free, and less demanding on the consultant. In particular, they think that consultation is a neglected but useful procedure for clergy outside of CPE; denominational officials in their superintending tasks and pastors in their parish duties could benefit from a consultative approach which has most of the earmarks of the supervisory process. They believe that fear of conflict and the question of confidentiality are barriers to its acceptance, but "using the consultation opportunities which are already built into church structure can be a big move toward better church health."[86]

Another suggested innovation is the extension of the supervisory process to the ministry to structures. Defining supervision as "the process of being responsible for the methodical creation of conditions in which the student can develop his own unique styles of ministry under systematic guidance and evaluation," Robert St. Clair proposes a theory of supervision based upon Lewin's social field theory.[87] He believes that in the arena of social problems supervision has been abandoned in favor of consultation and theological reflection has been replaced by action. He seeks to build a bridge and proposes:

> The full range of personal/social tasks initiated by perception of an event are called for by a field theory view of supervision. The fuller significance of the event is shot through the mind and lived again in dialogue with self, the supervisor, and others. Dimensions are enlarged, corners are illumined, and lines drawn from the event to other bodies of knowledge, like the behavioral sciences. Finally, the intern faces the ontological quest, searching for the core meaning, the fundamental matrix of interpretations about the world we live in. This theologizing grows out of the nuclei of life and illumines again ancient words of scripture and tradition.[88]

St. Clair suggests that in such a setting: supervisors must have first-hand knowledge of and be participants in a ministry to structures; supervision should include other staff persons periodically, including lay persons or committees; and more than one student should be assigned to the setting, though this is not necessary. It is clear that St. Clair has the urban context in mind, and he further suggests four foci for the supervision: (1) ministering skills, (2) empathy, (3) task commitment, and (4) self-awareness.

CURRENT STATUS

Clinical Pastoral Education has continued to be institution-centered. What began as a way of supplementing the church's pastoral education has existed for more than a half century outside the formal structures of theological education and the church. In the meantime, increasing numbers of seminarians, ordained clergy, and lay people are turning to it either as a way of improving their present work or finding an alternative ministry. Participants have benefitted from the opportunity to receive personal and professional evaluation. Research done in the mid-fifties showed that most participants grow in the ability to function professionally in ministry, especially in their self-understanding and professional identity.[89] Supervision is seen as the key component.

Building upon other studies, Lawrence Beech reports research on the effects of CPE in counseling practice, showing that "clinically educated pastors exercise a style of authority which tends to be more open, free, and accepting.[90] A later study reported by Gerald Grant raises questions about the permanence of such growth, suggesting that a little learning may make participants more assertive without necessarily reducing their defensiveness. However, tests did indicate positive movement in self-confidence, motivation, trust, and interpersonal relationships.[91]

It can be detected from this review that we cannot speak of supervision in CPE without also speaking of theology. Boisen's original intention to create a more experiential way of studying theology runs as a thread through the CPE story. While it is somewhat more visible in actual practice than in the literature, this component has often become lost in the more personal interests of self-understanding and professional skill development. Though these are also legitimate foci for pastoral education, it is important to recognize, as Seward Hiltner did on the fiftieth anniversary of CPE's beginning, that, "the basic theological concern from which Boisen began has continued to occupy, at best, only a secondary position in most training centers."[92]

An important contributing factor to this condition has been the ambiguity in identity among CPE supervisors. In research published in 1980, Anthony Seaton-Johnson and Craig Everett affirm the centrality of professional education and clinical supervision in CPE but point out the tendency among theologically trained clergy-supervisors "to enhance their present roles with embellished psychological degrees and/or identities."[93] This represents, they feel, the struggle of CPE "to clarify its own identity along side an increasingly competitive range of other clinical disciplines."[94]

This state of ambiguity is receiving increasing attention in CPE circles. A decade ago ACPE, in cooperation with the Association of Theological Schools (ATS), conducted a year-long study of what ACPE persons expect of ministry. Its results are compared to an earlier ATS study done in the 1970s with theological schools, called the "Readiness for Ministry" project. Persons within ACPE both hail and criticize the results. Its critics point out its low view of the ministry of lay persons, its limited reflection of women's issues, and its seeming neglect of theological reflection on its own results. At the same time, it appears to represent an ongoing attempt to address the issue raised by both Boisen and Hiltner. Clyde Getman maintains that in it "supervisors placed themselves firmly among theologians in the Church."[95]

There is strong evidence that Getman's observation is accurate. The theological nature of supervision is receiving attention. The parish as a context for the supervision of ministry, suggested early in CPE's history, has been legitimized. Ethical concerns raised in supervision are being addressed, including gender issues and the shortage of ethnic supervisors.[96] As of 1988 there were over 800 active and inactive supervisors certified by ACPE within a total membership of 4600 persons and organizations. The supervision of persons in ministry and the teaching of supervision remain dominant ingredients of the program.

SUMMARY

It is apparent from this review that supervision is a dynamic process and that it is in a dynamic stage of its development. Being central to all five professional fields reviewed here, it is under a great deal of study. Business and Industry is not yet fully in touch with the potential in the human side of enterprise; the pressure to put production rather than people at the center of its concern is intense. Public education has taken a long leap in moving from school inspection to clinical supervision, but its efforts to institute its new insights with students and especially full-time teachers are still in developing stages. Psychotherapy seeks to escape a multi-relational dependence upon other professions, each of which has its own supervisory styles; at the heart of that engagement is the attempt to find ways not only to train competent psychotherapists but to continue the professional development of its members. Social work, with its long history of supervision, reveals a high commitment to the idea but much ambivalence about its applicability; though not alone in the struggle, this profession like others raises the question about consultation as an alternative with its experienced workers as an ongoing professional discipline. CPE alone has a systematized concept and structure of supervision, but it appears still to be going through an identity crisis in its relationship to the church; the indications are that it is increasingly inclined to address its theological task, though it remains officially outside church structures.

One other body of literature remains to be consulted. That is material, some growing out of CPE practice, which addresses the efforts of theological education to adapt the clinical method to its curricula. That will be addressed in the next chapter.

END NOTES

1. Kenneth R. Andrews, "The Progress of Professional Education for Business," *Theological Education* 5 (Spring, 1969): 145.
2. James D. Glasse, *Profession: Minister* (Nashville, TN: Abingdon Press, 1968), 38.
3. Edgar H. Schein, *Organizational Psychology* (Englewood Cliffs, NJ: Prentice-Hall, 1967), 2.
4. Warren G. Bennis, *Changing Organizations* (New York: McGraw-Hill, 1966), 4.
5. Douglas McGregor, *The Human Side of Enterprise* (New York: McGraw-Hill, 1960), 46. For a more detailed description of Theories X and Y, see 33-48.
6. See Abraham Maslow, *Eupsychian Management: A Journal* (Homewood, IL: Richard D. Irwin, 1965). For the impact of Japanese industry on American Management, see also William G. Ouchi, *Theory Z* (New York: Avon, 1982).
7. J. J. Famularo, *Supervisors in Action* (New York: McGraw-Hill, 1961), 25. Taken from the National Labor Relations Act, Section 2, §11.

8. Gary Gimmell, "Managing Upward Communication," *Personnel Journal,* February 1970, 107-10. Reported in Ralph W. Reber and Gloria E. Terry, *Behavioral Insights for Supervision* (Englewood Cliffs, NJ: Prentice-Hall, 1975), 157.

9. Paul Ecker, John Macrae, Vernon Quellette, and Charles Telford, *Handbook for Supervisors* (Englewood Cliffs, NJ: Prentice-Hall, 1959), 3.

10. Alfred R. Lateiner, *The Techniques of Supervision* (New London, CT: National Foreman's Institute, 1954), 21.

11. Reber and Terry, *Behavioral*, 7.

12. Lateiner, *Techniques*, xiv-xv.

13. Ecker, *Handbook*, 15.

14. Robert L. Katz, "Skills of an Effective Administrator," *Harvard Business Review* 33 (January-February 1955): 33-42.

15. Reber and Terry, *Behavioral*, 9-13.

16. Douglas M. McGregor, "The Human Side of Enterprise," in Reber and Terry, *Behavioral*, 59. Reprint of an article carrying the same name as McGregor's book, in *Management Review*, November 1957.

17. William D. Hitt, *Management in Action* (Columbus, OH: Battelle Press, 1985), 20.

18. Ibid., 15-18.

19. Ralph L. Mosher and David E. Purpel, *Supervision: The Reluctant Profession* (Boston: Houghton Mifflin, 1972), 18.

20. Ibid., 17.

21. Ibid., 19-20.

22. Ibid., 63.

23. Adolph Unruh and Harold E. Turner, *Supervision for Change and Innovation* (Boston: Houghton Mifflin, 1970), 17-20.

24. Ibid., 82.

25. Stanley W. Williams, *New Dimensions in Supervision* (Scranton, PA: Intext Educational Publishers, 1972), 120.

26. Unruh and Turner, *Supervision*, 165-66.

27. Morris L. Cogan, *Clinical Supervision* (Boston: Houghton Mifflin, 1973), 4.

28. Ibid., 12.

29. Mosher and Purpel, *Reluctant*, 72-74.

30. Williams, *Dimensions*, 127-28.

31. For a discussion of the relation of supervision to counseling, see: Mosher and Purpel, *Reluctant*, Chap. 6, 113f.; Cogan, *Clinical*, Chap. 5, 58f.; Unruh and Turner, *Supervision*, Chap. 7, 149f. The reader is referred to Unruh and Turner, Chap. 9, 204f. for a discussion of supervision through the use of group techniques.

32. See Shirley A. McFaul and James M. Cooper, "Peer Clinical Supervision: Theory vs. Reality," *Educational Leadership* 41 (April 1984): 5-9 for the report of an experiment and a review of literature around this issue. See also two critical responses to the McFaul/Cooper article in the same issue: Lee F. Goldsberry, "Reality-Really?" and Robert J. Krajewski, "No Wonder It Didn't Work!", 10-11.

33. Lee F. Goldsberry, "The Realities of Clinical Supervision," *Educational Leadership* 41 (April 1984): 12. Cf. Cheryl Granade Sullivan, "Supervisory Expectations and Work Realities: The Great Gulf," *Educational Leadership* 39 (March 1982): 448-51. Goldsberry's article also has an excellent bibliography.

34. Thomas J. Sergiovanni, ed., *Supervision of Teaching* (Alexandria, VA: Association for Supervision and Curriculum Development, 1982), 189. See also: Allen A. Glatthorn, *Differentiated Supervision* (1984) and Carl D. Glickman, *Developmental Supervision* (1981) both also published by the Association for Supervision and Curriculum Development; and the following, all in *Educational Leadership* 41 (April 1984): Robert J. Afonso, Gerald Firth, and Michael Neville, "The Supervisory Skill Mix," 16-18; William E. Bickel and Nancy J. Artz, "Improving Instruction Through Focused Team Supervision," 22-24; and Jim Sweeney and Dick Manatt, "A Team Approach to Supervising the Marginal Teacher," 25-27.

35. Mosher and Purpel, *Reluctant*, 21.

36. Richard G. Chessick, *Why Psychotherapists Fail* (New York: Science House, 1971), 40.

37. Bertram D. Lewin and Helen Ross, *Psychoanalytic Education in the United States* (New York: W. W. Norton, 1960), 257.

38. William J. Mueller and Bill L. Kell, *Coping with Conflict: Supervising Counselors and Psychotherapists* (Englewood Cliffs, NJ: Prentice-Hall, 1972), 193.
39. Ibid. See 122-29 for the author's discussion.
40. Daniel B. Schuster, John J. Sandt, and Otto F. Thaler, *Clinical Supervision of the Psychiatric Resident* (New York: Brunner/Mazel, 1972), 96.
41. Sidney Tarachow, *An Introduction to Psychotherapy* (New York: International Universities Press, 1963), 303.
42. Rudolph Ekstein and Robert S. Wallerstein, *The Teaching and Learning of Psychotherapy* (New York: International Universities Press, 1972), 58.
43. Ibid., 141.
44. Ibid., 180.
45. Ibid., 246.
46. Joan Fleming and Theresa F. Benedek, *Psychoanalytic Supervision* (New York: Greene and Stratton, 1966), 237.
47. Florence W. Kaslow, ed., *Supervision and Training: Models, Dilemmas, and Challenges* (New York: Haworth Press, 1986), 3.
48. Allen K. Hess, ed., *Psychotherapy Supervision* (New York: John Wiley and Sons, 1980), 70. See Chap. 6, "The Dilemmas of Supervision in Dynamic Psychotherapy," by Margaret J. Rioch.
49. Ibid., 76.
50. Richard A. Hogan, "Issues and Approaches in Supervision," *Psychotherapy: Theory, Research, and Practice* 1 (August 1963): 139-41.
51. Daryl E. DeBell, "A Critical Digest of the Literature on Psychoanalytic Supervision," *Journal of the American Psychoanalytic Association* 11 (July 1963): 548-49.
52. Hess, *Psychotherapy*, 41. (See Chap. 4, "From Classroom to Clinic: Supervising the First Psychotherapy Client," by Irving B. Weiner and Robert G. Kaplan.)
53. Ibid., 529.
54. Mary E. Burns, "Supervision in Social Work," *Encyclopedia of Social Work* (1965), 15:785.
55. Alfred Kadushin, *Supervision in Social Work* (New York: Columbia University Press, 1976), 20-21.
56. Betty Lacy Jones, ed., *Current Patterns in Field Instruction* (New York: Council on Social Work, 1969), xi.
57. Kadushin, *Supervision*, 436.
58. Betty Mandell, "The Equality Revolution and Supervision," *Journal of Education for Social Work* 9 (Winter 1973): 47.
59. Evelyn Stiles, "Supervision in Perspective," *Social Casework* 44 (January 1963): 24.
60. Burns, "Supervision", 786.
61. Kadushin, *Supervision*, 201.
62. Leonard Bloom and Cherie Herman, "A Problem of Relationships in Supervision," *Social Casework* 37 (July 1958): 404-08.
63. Kadushin, *Supervision*, 436.
64. See Alfred Kadushin, "Supervisor-Supervisee: A Survey," *Social Work* 19 (May 1974): 288-97.
65. Lydia Rapaport, "Consultation," *Encyclopedia of Social Work* (1965), 15:214.
66. Ibid., 217.
67. Alfred Kadushin, *Consultation in Social Work* (New York: Columbia University Press, 1977), 45.
68. Kenneth W. Watson, "Differential Supervision," *Social Work* 18 (November 1973): 80.
69. Ibid., 87.
70. This summary is based upon an interview that I had with Carleton E. Munson on October 7, 1976, at the University of Houston, Houston, Texas, where Dr. Munson teaches in the Graduate School of Social Work. The written source is "The Uses of Structural, Authority, and Teaching Models in Social Work Supervision," (Ann Arbor, MI: University Microfilms International, 1975) (ASW dissertation, University of Maryland, 1975).
71. Charles S. Levy, "The Ethics of Supervision," *Social Work* 18 (March 1973): 15.
72. The reader is referred to Charles E. Munson, *An Introduction to Clinical Social Work Supervision*, (New York: Haworth Press, 1983).
73. Ibid., 124.
74. For a thorough treatment of this development, see Edward E. Thornton, *Professional Education for Ministry* (Nashville, TN: Abingdon Press, 1970).

75. Anton T. Boisen, "The Period of Beginnings," *Journal of Pastoral Care* 5 (Spring 1951): 15.
76. Carroll A. Wise, *Religion in Illness and Health* (New York: Harper and Brothers, 1942), 264.
77. *The Standards of the Association for Clinical Pastoral Education* (Decatur, GA: Association for Clinical Pastoral Education, 1991), 1. The following descriptions of procedures, standards, and objectives are taken from this document.
78. Ibid., 10-12.
79. Thomas W. Klink, "Supervision," in Charles Feilding, *Education for Ministry* (Dayton, OH: American Association of Theological Schools, 1966), 176-77.
80. Ibid., 192.
81. Ibid., 194.
82. Armen D. Jorjorian, "The Meaning and Character of Supervisory Acts," *Journal of Pastoral Care* 25 (September, 1971): 156.
83. Ronald H. Sunderland, "A Concept of Ministry Which Employs the Supervisory Process Derived from Clinical Pastoral Education," (Unpublished S.T.M. Thesis, Perkins School of Theology, Southern Methodist University, 1968), 53.
84. John H. Patton and John Warkentin, "A Dialogue on Supervision and Consultation," *Journal of Pastoral Care* 25 (September 1971): 166-68.
85. Charles V. Gerkin, "Clinical Pastoral Education and Social Change," *Journal of Pastoral Care* 25 (September 1971): 175-81.
86. Patton and Warkentin, "Dialogue," 173.
87. Robert J. St. Clair, "Toward a Social Field Theory of Supervision," *Journal of Pastoral Care* 23 (September 1969): 143.
88. Ibid., 146.
89. Ernest E. Bruder and Marian Barb, "A Survey of Ten Years of Clinical Pastoral Training at Saint Elizabeth's Hospital," *Journal of Pastoral Care* 10 (Summer 1956): 86-94; Ernest E. Bruder, "Training and the Mental Hospital Chaplain," *Journal of Pastoral Care* 11 (Fall 1957): 136-45; and John R. Thomas, "Evaluations of Clinical Pastoral Training and 'Part Time' Training in a General Hospital," *Journal of Pastoral Care* 12 (Spring 1958): 28-38.
90. Lawrence A. Beech, "Supervision in Pastoral Care and Counseling: A Prerequisite for Effective Ministry," *Journal of Pastoral Care* 24 (December 1970): 236.
91. Gerald Grant, "An Objective Evaluation of an Eleven-Week Supervised Pastoral Education Program," *Journal of Pastoral Care* 29 (December 1975): 254-61.
92. Seward Hiltner, "Fifty Years of CPE," *Journal of Pastoral Care* 29 (June 1975): 92.
93. Anthony Wayland Seaton-Johnson and Craig A. Everett, "An Analysis of Clinical Pastoral Education Supervisors: Their Identities, Roles and Resources," *Journal of Pastoral Care* 34 (September 1980): 149.
94. Ibid., 158.
95. Clyde J. Getman, "CPE Supervisors: Psychologists or Theologians?" *Journal of Pastoral Care* 36 (September 1982): 175. The results of the ACPE study referred to is published under David S. Schuller and Merton P. Strommen, *Expectations of Ministry: The View of Clinical Pastoral Educators* (Dayton, OH: ATS and ACPE, 1981). A summary of the study can be found in G. Wade Rowatt, "What Does ACPE Expect of Ministry?" *Journal of Pastoral Care* 36 (September 1982): 147-59. A series of symposium articles critiquing the study follow in the same issue.
96. For examples, see Tjaard G. Hommes, "Supervision as Theological Method," *Journal of Pastoral Care* 31 (September 1977): 150-57; Herbert E. Anderson, Homer W. Ashby, Jr., and David L. Lindberg, eds., "Supervision of Ministry in a Parish Context," Symposium in *Journal of Supervision and Training in Ministry* 10 (1988): 106-231; and Marie McCarthy and David B. McCurdy, eds., "Supervision and Training as an Ethical Endeavor," Symposium in *Journal of Supervision and Training in Ministry* 12 (1990): 106-229.

CHAPTER III

MAKING A HIGHWAY IN THE DESERT: CHARACTERISTICS AND IMPLICATIONS

The foregoing review of supervision literature serves two purposes. First, it makes it possible to identify some basic characteristics of supervision found to be operative in five major and related professions. Second, it provides a body of information from which we can draw implications for pastoral supervision in the church. It is the purpose of this chapter to expand on these observations.

THE BASIC CHARACTERISTICS OF SUPERVISION

DIVERSITY

The first characteristic of supervision is its diversity. There is no single definition or set of components which can be described as representative of supervision as a whole. In most cases the same can be said for any one profession. There are numerous definitions, each one specific to the particular administrative philosophy, learning theory, or therapeutic orientation of the practitioner. Likewise, there are numerous components which tend to be specific to the setting in which it takes place. CPE has conceptualized its process and described its practitioners more precisely than the other professions, and this makes for considerable uniformity in CPE programs, but there is both uniformity and diversity within each of the professions as well as among them.

Diversity can also be seen in the different objectives to which supervisory activity is committed: a product or service, teaching, client help, and ministry. Specialized objectives require the use of dissimilar methods, at least in part. Thus there is some hazard in trying to identify common characteristics which can be said to be basic to supervision as a whole. Yet, it is possible to find some common threads, which suggests that somewhere in the commonality and the diversity there may be properties which can be extended to the church. If diversity can be understood to mean adaptability to and flexibility in the range of unique settings and needs, then diversity is one of supervision's characteristic strengths.

QUALIFYING EXPERIENCE

The second characteristic is that supervision is the qualifying experience by which entrance into a profession is achieved. The methods vary: apprenticeship, a period of supervised experience by persons already fully certified, or a certifying process of peer review. Although not clearly conceptualized or uniformly practiced in business and industry, entrance into the rights, privileges, and responsibilities of the profession in all five professions is through supervision where candidates are declared worthy by their colleagues.

Through much of its history there have been some educational, peer review, and/or ordination or consecration processes operative in the church. Through the years there has been change in the way these elements have been emphasized, but there is no comparable supervisory requirement by which persons are assessed as ready to practice ministry, nor is there any formal preparation for those who do the supervision. Within the past three decades increasing attention has been given in theological education to such requirements; this development will be reviewed shortly.

Current procedures vary for persons entering ministry, but they consist generally of some kind of examination before a committee of persons with only partial knowledge of the candidate and with differing standards by which evaluation is made. In the case of superintending persons, the right comes by appointment or election. The question to the church from other professions is clear: is supervision a more appropriate qualifying experience than these current procedures? I propose that it is. This suggests that there be a careful selection and educational program for clergy and laity to supervise those who are in the credentialing process.

DUAL PURPOSE

The third characteristic of supervision is its dual purpose. While there are many outcomes toward which it points, there are two common purposes underlying the several professional approaches. One is the **utilization of professional skills**; supervision is responsible for delivering something: the "something" may be a product, knowledge, human service, or ministry. In any case, supervisors enable supervisees to work with some set of skills. Furthermore, the product or service or ministry is intended to be useful, helpful, and important to the public or the special group toward whom it is directed.

The other purpose is the **development of professional identity**; supervision is responsible for helping supervisees come to a definition of their professional role. This involves helping supervisees think of themselves as craftspersons, teachers, psychotherapists, social workers, or ministers. Professional identity represents the maturity to have a clear, consistent understanding of who one is.

There is a difference between simply the skill to do a job and identification with that job in a way that brings the individual's total being to bear upon the use of the skill. The question can be put this way: Do we perform professional acts or do we participate in a profession? This is sometimes referred to as professional socialization; the term professional identity is preferred because it is a matter of identifying ourselves in a particular way, not simply participating in a professional function.

Supervision is uniquely suited to help fulfill these dual purposes precisely because it works with persons at the point of their immersion in the professional role. It necessarily addresses both the application and meaning of what supervisees do at the point of involvement. This makes it particularly useful for the pastoral profession where there is no other single function charged with this simultaneous dual responsibility. One of the criticisms of CPE in the church is that it sets up the risk of luring clergy out of pastoral ministry through the development of specialized skills and a new identity. The criticism itself points to one value of supervision, because such a career change indicates professional uncertainty in the first place. Moreover, what appears in such instances to be a change in career may be a change only in function, since the identity that CPE supervision seeks is, in fact, pastoral.

There are today a variety of alternative ministries to which committed Christians are attracted. At this point in time at least, the church has a dual responsibility: one is to create a supervisory program that will make it possible for all Christians to clarify and carry out their own unique role in the general vocation of ministry; the other is to provide particular supervisory experience by which pastoral identity as a professional role can be achieved and constantly clarified. While CPE now makes such experience available to a limited number of persons, the challenge to the church is to take responsibility for its own supervisory task rather than delegating it to other professions or a specialized ministry outside its own structure.

CLINICAL NATURE OF THE CONTEXT

The fourth characteristic is the clinical nature of the context in which supervision takes place. While the word "clinical" has a medical origin, it has grown in common usage to be a more inclusive term. Webster's *Third New International Dictionary* (1981) includes in its definition an understanding of clinical as applying "objective or standardized methods to the discussion, evaluation, and modification of human behavior." This broadens the term to include other fields besides medicine where direct involvement in or observation of human activity makes possible the critical reflection upon case material.

In harmony with this, the word clinical has come to be applied to a variety of contexts in addition to hospitals: penal institutions, mental health centers, social agencies, parishes, private offices, classrooms, and business/industrial establishments, in all of which people may be engaged in pursuits upon which our cultural survival depends. The critical element that makes a setting clinical is not that people are in crisis but that they are in need, whether that need may be described as economic, educational, emotional, social, or spiritual.

This distinction between crisis and need is of prime importance to pastoral supervision where the clinic may be an urban congregation at worship or a rural ministry to migrants. As William Spafford said years ago, given adequate supervision people "should be able to relate to and learn from the county welfare worker, as well as the ward nurse; the county agent, as well as the occupational therapist; the head of the county health unit, as well as the staff psychiatrist."[1] It follows that the church in its varied mission is an arena in which supervision is not only appropriate but also demanded.

INTENTIONALITY

Need must, however, be supported by intentionality, the fifth basic characteristic. All of the professions reviewed here give conscious, thoughtful attention to the manner in which supervision is carried out. It is not something that just happens; there are processes and expectations that guide the activity. These are more evident and more highly developed in some professions than in others. With the exception of CPE, there is some lack of clarity about both process and expectation, but in each profession, supervision is done intentionally.

This is not always the case in pastoral settings. In some traditions churches have permitted students to engage in pastoral work in which there has been little or no system or design to their oversight. Even when there have been efforts to bridge some of that gap, intentionality is not assured. Some students may dependently rely for direction on the pastors to whom they are assigned, who may be all too willing to manage the students' every move; other students who prefer to be left alone may be assigned to pastors who are all too willing not to be bothered. Both situations may be deliberate and are certainly ineffective. Both also call for supervision, but neither is fully intentional in the sense of having a mutually designed process and set of expectations to guide the activity. The same can be said about the pastors' work with lay people, other colleagues on the staff, and relationship to judicatory officials charged with the pastors' oversight. Pastoral supervision, if it occurs at all, is often haphazard or crisis-oriented.

Several of the professions address this by insisting that supervision takes place only within a contractual arrangement between supervisors and supervisees. CPE calls this a "contract for learning." It might more accurately be described as a learning/serving contract, because supervision takes place within objectives that include both education and work. In any case it is a mutual agreement on process and expectation within a larger framework of objectives specific to the context. It is not only something that binds them to accountability but is something upon which they can depend for relationship. Most of the professions reviewed have some form of supervisory contract, though it is not always obvious and clear. Good pastoral supervision depends upon such intentionality.

ESSENTIAL FUNCTIONS

This suggests a sixth characteristic of supervision. In one way or another all of the professions stress three essential functions--**administrative**, **educational**, and **therapeutic**, though they do not all identify them under these terms. Unanimously they see the **administrative function** as maintaining the boundaries within which the total supervisory task takes place: work assignment, accountability, coordination of resources, communication, interpretation of policies, and general oversight. This necessitates a responsible use of authority and power, which in itself adds to the burden upon the other two functions depending upon the way supervisees respond to their use. There is also considerable ambiguity with which supervisors must live, because it places them in the competitive arena of a number of "publics." Most literature describes supervisors as being in the middle between management and workers, but it is even more complicated than that. The question for supervisors is: For whom is supervision provided? Is it for the management of the clinical center, the recipients of whatever work or service is done, the community at large, the profession represented by the supervisees and/or the center, the supervisees, or the supervisors? Supervisors move among all of these concerns, each of which has some investment and expects some recognition, and they must therefore administer these multiple and sometimes conflicting interests.

It is a common view also that the **educational function** depends upon some form of observation, experience, and correction although, as supervisors in business and industry point out, teaching has received too little attention so that too often supervisees are primarily self-taught through trial and error. Public education is increasingly stressing a procedure of mutual planning, observation, evaluation, and continued planning, with supervisors providing both material and personal resources for their supervisees. In psychotherapy, social work, and CPE where supervisees do their work largely out of sight of supervisors, case material and the case conference are utilized as a way of analyzing what happened. The latter three frequently use didactic material which may include reading and/or formal instruction. Always supervisors are expected to model the desired level of expertise by being competent professionals in practice. Whatever form the teaching takes, supervision is intended to perform a teaching function as a way of helping supervisees achieve a higher level of professional competence.

The **therapeutic function** is less uniformly understood but is present by the very fact of focusing attention on supervisees as persons. This focus is more verbalized than practiced in business and industry, and in public education it is more a goal than a realization; yet in both there is increasing realization of an attention to the total life situation that supervisees bring to their work. In both of these professions there is an appeal for supervisors to be better equipped with counseling skills in order to be more sensitive and helpful in the supervisees' normal problems of daily life; it follows that they would then also be more effective in assisting persons in crisis to get adequate help. Psychotherapy, social work, and CPE take more responsibility than that, though this varies among supervisors. All agree that supervision, by its very nature, tends to force dysfunctional life patterns into the open but that any attempts at personality change should be left to another qualified professional in whatever way supervisees may chose to seek help. However, among psychotherapy and CPE supervisors in particular, there is a deliberate attempt to utilize the supervisees' total experience, including the emotional components, as supervisory agenda.

All three supervisory functions—administrative, educational and therapeutic—are legitimate and necessary foci for pastoral supervision. Specifically, pastoral supervision takes place in administrative structures with all the boundaries and ambiguities native to such structures. It has an educational purpose, whether that be the theological training of seminarians, the continuing education and professional growth of ordained clergy, or the equipping of lay persons for effective ministry in the church. And it certainly has as its major objective the growth into wholeness of the persons with whom it is utilized.

From its beginning the church has given attention to these three essential functions, although one or another has been emphasized more than the others (sometimes at the expense of the others) at particular periods in its history. Indeed, three essential functions do not adequately represent the church's attempt to fulfill its mission. The supervisory question for the church is how to ensure that the essential functions, however many, are faithfully expressed. The fact is that the church, like business and industry, sometimes becomes distracted by institutional demands of program production, worker deployment, organizational policy, and economic survival at the expense of persons and mission. Can an excellent supervisory process help the church remain focused on the essentials? I believe that it can.

DYNAMIC PROCESS

Seventh, supervision is characterized by its dynamic process. This is best summarized by saying that supervision, as it has emerged in the professions reviewed here, belongs equally to the supervisees and to the supervisors. This means that both have a voice in what happens and that in whatever occurs the freedom of supervisees to engage in self-actualization as well as work management is central. This is usually done in the context of a one-to-one or small group relationship to which supervisees bring needs or questions, growing out of experience, for supervisory help. While supervisors may suggest items for discussion based upon their observations, the agenda "belongs" to the supervisees in the sense that they must "own" it; otherwise nothing constructive will happen. The process depends upon the supervisees' ability and willingness to identify problems in professional performance and to submit them to supervisors who can help in analyzing them. If there is a lack of ability or willingness to do this, psychotherapy in addition to or instead of supervision may be needed.

It is important that the autonomy and individuality of supervisees are not only protected but encouraged. While there is still a temptation in some professions, particularly Theory X circles, to manage the supervisees' lives, the supervisory process being described here promotes self-determination. Thus, the solution to particular work situations, how one relates to people, or what is done about a revealed need for counseling are left to the supervisees for decision as much as possible. Obviously, wrong decisions may sabotage the supervisees' careers, but that is a necessary risk in supervision. Both the clinical centers and the supervisors must live with the supervisees' right to fail, as painful as that is. Supervision, therefore, is not management in the sense of control; rather it is relationship in the sense of creating an atmosphere in which responsible decisions can be made.

This suggests a collegial style of supervisory relationship. The participants are committed to wrestle together with the problems that confront the supervisees, recognizing each other as responsible persons who bring unique resources to the encounter. Supervisors usually have more education, experience, and status than their supervisees. However these are not "advantages;" good supervision does not occur because of any personal superiority but rather because of a superior process. As Patton and Warkentin point out, young psychotherapists can supervise older colleagues because both the felt need and the available process make it possible for them to bring their combined competence to their meeting.[2]

This dynamic process cuts directly across the hierarchical methods which have sometimes characterized the churches' superintending practice, as it does in the professions reviewed here. The desire to be treated as responsible adults, to adapt McGregor's thought, is present in the ministry as much as in business and industry. New styles of education, as well as personal investment in more authentic life styles, are prompting seminarians, ordained clergy, and laity alike to demand more participation in determining their own futures and the future of the church. Pastoral supervision, utilizing the process described later, provides a necessary alternative.

SPECIALIZED EDUCATION

If the pastoral supervision alternative is to gain acceptance, however, an eighth characteristic of supervision must prevail, namely specialized education. This is expressed in the literature as both hope and fact. All the professions reviewed recognize the need for it; some require it; others make provision for it. There is much truth in the observation that supervisory skills are best learned in the act of performing them, but that simply points to a necessary part of the educational process rather than a substitute for it. It suggests that supervisors must learn their art through their own supervised practice of it.

The quality of the supervision being described here suggests a unique and identifiable responsibility which is too important to be left to anyone who happens to be in the right place at the right time. Professional status alone is not sufficient reason to make people supervisors. Not all the persons who are competent in their particular fields are capable of, should be, or want to be supervisors. Nor is everyone who wants to supervise automatically thereby capable of doing so. Too long have supervisors been selected by such inadequate criteria. The skills of supervision are precise, specific, and demonstrable; supervision deserves their expert use. This is as true for the church as for any other organization.

SELF-SUPERVISION

The ninth characteristic is included because it is the objective toward which all the others point. It is that the ultimate goal of supervision is self-supervision. Since one mark of professionals is that they be able to function competently alone, they must be fully in command of the necessary skills; and they must have sufficient self-understanding that they can do what needs to be done with full awareness of what and why it is done. Professionals must make appropriate decisions before acting and be able to analyze and describe afterward what happened. This is not meant to imply that professionals are never under some other person's supervision; rather it recognizes the reality of professional life. To be able to have both one's skills and emotions in command is utterly essential. To be aware of one's strengths and weaknesses, to be able to evaluate one's own performance, to have both the ability and motivation to make necessary changes, is to possess the characteristic described as self-supervision.

It is this characteristic for which many professionals appeal when they suggest that good supervision should move toward consultation. Such a request normally takes "profession" seriously, though there is the danger that it could grow out of a desire to escape the demands of self-supervision. The argument is that fully qualified professionals are able to supervise themselves, which includes being able to make responsible judgments about when they need to seek consultation. There is some indication that some who press this argument view supervision not as the dynamic process described here but in a more authoritarian way. On the other hand, the concept of self-supervision is not meant to rule out consultation; rather it suggests that even competent professionals need to structure consultative relationships into their practice in full recognition that the demands of their work will often force them to function alone.

This is as applicable to pastoral supervision as any other field. The same professional demands apply. Some ecclesiastical structures, however, make on-going supervision an ubiquitous reality in ministry. This should encourage both clergy and lay people to demand excellent supervision within these structures **and** to develop the skills of self-supervision.

EVALUATION

One final basic characteristic of supervision seen in the five professions considered here is that of **evaluation**. While it is viewed as a necessary part of the supervisory task, it is an element with which there is considerable discontent. There are some suggestions that supervisors should not evaluate, though it is recognized that evaluation is inevitable; it is communicated to supervisees in non-verbal as well as verbal responses, in the failure to give evaluative feedback as much as in formal assessment. Behind the uneasiness are supervisors' concerns about personal status, use of authority, the supervisory relationship, and the possible harmful effects of negative judgments. After all, the supervisees' professional future may ride on the supervisors' reports! Supervisees are threatened by the same concerns, growing at least partly out of past one-sided, arbitrary procedures of which they have been victims.

There are differences, however, in the manner in which evaluation is conceptualized and handled. Even within particular professions the format, content, process, and even purpose vary. In business and industry the word evaluation is not common; some writers do not use it at all in describing supervisory functions. What they do refer to is judgment or rating of performance; some employees are helped to work out programs of self-development based on strengths and weaknesses, the objective being efficiency and increased production. While promotion or salary increase may be the reward for the supervisees, it is the company's interests that are primarily served.

Public education confesses more vulnerability in this aspect of supervision than any other. While some in the field insist that teaching, not teachers, constitutes the focus of evaluation, others claim that in actual practice teachers themselves receive primary attention usually in terms of the effectiveness of the total instructional program. In psychotherapy this dual responsibility to both person and institution is also present, the goal being to select candidates for or screen them out of the profession. Here the process is used with students exclusively; there is no description of evaluation in terms of established practitioners.

Social work has stressed evaluation with both students and experienced workers more than any other profession, partly because of its special public accountability. The right of agencies to do this is not questioned, but resistance by experienced workers is widespread because they have not always found the evaluations to be helpful. Here again, while the workers' personal growth is a concern, the enforcement of professional standards is of primary concern.

CPE, though emphasizing evaluation as a supervisory responsibility, has not fully articulated its rationale or method in its literature. In practice, however, more than any of the other professions, it has given primary attention to the personal and professional growth of the student rather than achieved competence. This may be because CPE works with persons preparing for a variety of functions in the profession of ministry; within its own ranks, in evaluating candidates for supervisory certification, considerable stress is placed upon professional standards as well as personal and pastoral identity.

There are important similarities that stand out in the literature. With some exception for business and industry, all recognize the establishment of clear and specific criteria, accepted from the beginning by supervisors and supervisees, as a basis for evaluation. There is unanimity in seeing it as an ongoing process, with each supervisory conference providing opportunity for feedback in relationship to particular professional performance, and a formal evaluation conference at the end as an over-all assessment of strengths and weaknesses. Mutual planning and consultation between supervisors and supervisees is increasingly accepted as the normal procedure, with a positive supervisory relationship being essential as a foundational prerequisite. Self-evaluation is utilized as a corollary to the supervisors' assessments, with a growing emphasis being placed on helping supervisees take responsibility for the process and result. It is also generally agreed that evaluation of supervisees invites feedback to and about the whole system, including the supervisors. Seen in such dynamic terms, at least some of the threat to supervisees is removed as they come to understand that they are full participants in a system-wide process.

In the midst of these similarities, however, there is one other important difference. In all of the professions studied with some exception in CPE, the purpose of evaluation is to approve trainees as practitioners; and, except in psychotherapy, it is used also to determine their right to remain within the profession. CPE, however, evaluates on two levels: seminarians and clergy who function in the general life of the church are evaluated in terms of personal and pastoral identity, the certifying power belonging to other groups or institutions; only in the case of persons seeking supervisory status does CPE evaluation become a certifying process.

The significance of this for pastoral supervision is that many clergy persons have no access to a supervisory evaluation process which either determines their readiness for or their progress within professional practice. Most judicatory bodies have their own particular methods of assessing the candidates who seek ordination or consecration. There is little consistency or coordination among these processes, however. As for post-ordination assessment, many persons in ordained ministry are denied the benefit of regular professional evaluation. The result frequently is either frustration and eventual attrition from the ministry or the perpetuation of ineffective pastoral performance. A few solve the problem by consulting a career counseling center. The clear indication is that the church could strengthen its hand considerably by developing more adequate evaluation programs in its supervision of ministers.

The assessment of ministry is at the heart of the church's life and certainly of the supervisory process. Evaluation is threatening both for persons and congregations. Part of the problem is that evaluation has traditionally been seen as exterior to the ministry being performed, that is, done by some authority from "outside." But the key to evaluation is self-evaluation. The discovery of methods is involved, but motivation is an even more basic problem. Experience indicates that evaluation instruments are not as important as openness and the desire to look critically at what one is doing. What happens to evaluation is also important; if it is used to rate, compare, determine success or failure, possibly reward or punish, it has a slim chance of being effective. Supervision must enable evaluation that is thorough and is utilized responsibly in the growth of the minister as well as the ministry.

LINGERING ISSUES

There are some additional matters which are more appropriately referred to as lingering issues than as basic characteristics of supervision. They are critical concerns as we make a highway in this desert.

One of these lingering issues is **authority**. Everybody agrees that supervision involves the use of authority, but they disagree on their understanding of how it is to be used. Even when it is recognized as an inherent component of the supervisory task, there has been reluctance to deal with its implications. In spite of the frequency with which it is named as an issue, it may be the most neglected element while, at the same time, impacting all participants in deeply significant ways. Studies in the relationship between authority and power, the opportunities and limits of authority, the role of both organizational structure and personality patterns, and the implications of authority patterns for supervisory style are all on-going concerns. What seems clear is that this issue must be dealt with in the preparation of supervisors for their work; the written word is not adequate. This suggests a major agenda in supervisory education.

A second lingering issue is **confidentiality**. Suanna Wilson writes: "Social workers, psychiatrists, psychologists, physicians and others have long argued that absolute trust is essential between client and helping professional if the treatment process is to be effective. Trust cannot be fully achieved unless all personal information shared during the counseling process is kept `confidential.'"[3] If this were to be stated to include the supervisory process, most supervisors would agree; it is acknowledged in all the professions studied except business and industry. There is a problem, however, in what one means by confidentiality. As Wilson points out, "absolute confidentiality" often promised to clients may be impossible. The use of case analysis in supervisory sessions suggests that "relative confidentiality" is a more reasonable expectation.[4] Supervisors and supervisees alike are caught in the middle ground between these two understandings. It certainly is a concern in pastoral supervision and is a deterrent if not an excuse for many pastors in their reluctance to participate in peer-group supervision. "After all," pastors say, "the person sitting next to me may become my next district superintendent."

Wilson raises a related and more basic issue, however, when she speaks of **trust**. Supervision involves a relationship, but as much or more than many other relationships it relies on trust. Relationships between supervisor(s) and supervisee(s) are two-sided. On the one hand we may know each other as colleagues, as Christians, or as part of the same organizations; we may get along in a reasonably cooperative way. On the other hand, privately (or not so privately) we tend to be suspicious, mistrustful, and envious.

It is difficult for us to relate on deep levels or submit our work/ministry for one another's scrutiny. We resist revealing too much about ourselves to each other lest rejection take place. We are reluctant to "spill our guts" to somebody who may evaluate us or become our supervisor. Congregations are not always sure that the theological school or judicatory needs to know everything that is going on. My work in training pastoral supervisors tells me that there is a crisis of trust in the church that impedes the supervisory process.

A fourth issue is **ownership**. The necessity of supervisees "owning" the supervisory agenda has been identified as part of the dynamic process in supervision. What is being suggested here is that ownership of supervision in our ministry is crucial. Ownership is created by helping all those involved be participants in the shaping, doing, and evaluating of it. That which is remote, handed down, exterior, needs to become immediate, personal, interior. Then it belongs to "us." A crucial issue for supervision, therefore, is creating ownership so that whatever it is that is "out there" (the job, the client/parishioner, the problem) can no longer be ignored or relegated to the irrelevant because "it" has become integral to the personal or corporate self. This includes the supervisor's ownership of the supervisory task.

A fifth lingering issue is **identity**. Creation of professional identity in supervisees as one of the dual purposes of supervision is discussed above. I am alluding here to the supervisor's professional identity. CPE speaks of pastoral identity—the identification of oneself as a pastor. Just as this is necessary to doing pastoral work, having a supervisory identity is important to being a supervisor. Good pastoring is also good supervising, because the care and affirmation of persons is basic to the enablement of effective ministry. But the issue is that effective supervision requires an identity. In my training of supervisors I find that frequently neither clergy nor lay persons identify themselves as pastoral supervisors prior to training, with the consequence that supervision rarely occurs in any creative way until that identification comes. At the center of this is an understanding and appropriation of authority—one's own and that of others.

Sixth, an issue that waits for more adequate attention is **inclusiveness**. Perhaps one reason for its neglect is its complexity, but it appears that there is a more basic resistance. By inclusiveness is meant openness of the supervisory ranks to persons of multi-ethnic backgrounds and to both male and female genders, full acceptance of women in the authority role, non-discriminatory use of language, and the practice of equality both among supervisory colleagues and between supervisors and supervisees. Not only do the professions differ radically in the way they have treated these matters historically, but there is wide variance in the way they are currently responding to them. There is not even universal agreement that inclusiveness is an issue. CPE has made a conscious effort to educate its supervisors in gender issues and to refine its practice. In the other professions there is genuine interest but less official attention given to it.

Seventh and finally is the issue of **certification**. All of the professions studied are concerned about the quality of supervision, and they have some criteria for selecting the persons for doing it, although the criteria are not always spelled out. All except business and industry have made attempts to regularize the selection of supervisors. Public education and social work have criteria that may or may not be consistently applied. Only CPE has formalized this into a process which certifies supervisors and rigidly monitors the process of certification. The church has both formal and informal policies for the supervision of ministry, and in recent years there has been an emerging interest in the certification of persons for this responsibility. The foregoing review indicates that we may be on the edge of development in this issue.

Running through all of these issues is an underlying concern for supervisory **style**. The patterns range from hierarchical to collegial. Attention has already been called to Hitt's continuum of leadership behavior. Carl Glickman, writing out of the public education arena, suggests a helpful continuum of supervisory behaviors based upon supervisor strengths, supervisee needs, and situational demands.[5] It has particular applicability to pastoral supervision. Together the principles and practice in the five professions just reviewed have paved the way for a sixth profession which, as much or more than all the others, has wrestled with these issues. We turn to that development now.

SUPERVISORY METHOD IN THEOLOGICAL EDUCATION

The foregoing observations about the nature of supervision provide an important part of the foundation upon which pastoral supervision can be constructed as a unique way of doing ministry. It is important now to consider the way supervision has emerged as a significant component in the curricula of theological education.

In 1969, I engaged in a research project designed to identify the essential elements of the clinical method in theological education. On the basis of that study it was possible to identify five basic elements in the clinical method: (1) first-hand experience with people in their native environment; (2) supervision by a qualified professional person; (3) opportunity for inter-disciplinary work with professional persons; (4) contact with people of differing religious persuasions or none; and (5) peer-group learning through participation with persons engaged in the same or similar experiences.[6] Of these five elements, supervision was clearly ranked as the critical element. With that as a foundation, a program for using the clinical method in theological education was then proposed.

The above represents one attempt to establish a method for engaging theological students in experience-based education, and supervision lies at the heart of it. Other persons in other schools have made similar efforts. These have grown out of studies by the American Association of Theological Schools (now Association of Theological Schools or ATS) in the late 1960's projecting curriculum revisions appropriate for theological education. Called the "Theological Curriculum for the 1970's," it included major emphasis on supervision as a means of reflecting on contemporary human problems and specific areas of ministry.[7]

Also in 1969 the Association of Field Education Directors (now Association for Theological Field Education or ATFE) held its Tenth Biennial Consultation around the theme of supervision. Representatives from several professional disciplines were asked to present their views on supervision as a means of identifying grounds for the supervision of seminarians. No conclusions were reached which could be said to represent a definition or model for use by the schools represented by the Association. What it accomplished was to awaken an interest in supervision to the degree that since that time it has been one of the dominant concerns among field education directors and a highly visible item on theological faculty agenda.

Among the observations made by Klink in his address to the Tenth Consultation, two were that (1) supervision has certain "common generic qualities" growing out of its use in many occupational fields and that (2) its procedures are thus sufficiently "different in meaning, practices, intentions, and settings as to merit attention to its varied characters."[8] Speaking of the "exciting possibilities" in supervision, he said:

It is a field of action; it is a style of work; it is a mode of change; it is a device for growth and progress which has many possibilities. And the recognition of the variety of possibilities of place, of organization, of goal, of style, the recognition of these and the making of advised decisions within them consti- tutes, I think, the intellignet [sic] promise of the utilization of the field of supervision in theological education.[9]

Supervision has received attention at each of the biennial consultations of ATFE since 1969. The way these consultations have addressed the issue has been to look at the total role of field education as the integrating component in seminary curricula. Supervision has figured prominently in the discussion.

In 1975 Jesse Ziegler, the Executive Secretary of AATS, raised the key supervisory issue for theological education: "How can the study of Scripture, theology, church history, sociology, psychology, and other disciplines bearing some relation to religious faith and institutions prepare one for practice of ministry? How can abstract ideas be translated into the concrete realities of ministering to persons in their joys and in their troubles?"[10] Theological field educators have led the way in pursuing these questions in the intervening years.[11] They have been joined by a number of clinical pastoral educators who have been involved in the supervision of seminary students and are increasingly seeking to relate clinical methods to the broader interests of theological education. Three specific questions related to supervision occupy the minds of all such persons.

THE QUESTION OF MODELS

One question is: What model of supervision is most appropriate in practice-based education? To address this question it is necessary to distinguish models of supervision from models of field education. George Baldwin and Paul Maves speak for most field educators when they say: "We have come to view models of field education as having meaning when they are seen as being seminary-specific. The only model that really makes sense is the one that grows out of the opportunities and limits that the particular seminary situation represents."[12] There are many models for engaging students in practice-based programs, and each one arranges its supervisory component to fit the model being used. Many of these have benefitted from the involvement of CPE supervisors in helping to provide both the initial design and continuing consultation, so that a number of schools follow clinical methods.

Wayne Oates, in an article directed toward a model of supervision for Doctor of Ministry students, uses the CPE model as a starting point. He speaks of a collegial approach to supervision and describes its goals, content, and style in CPE terms. Yet, he says: "This need not imply that one model of supervision be used. . . . It does mean that an even **quality** of supervision be developed in all differing models. . . .[13]

Working out of the same background and with quality as his concern, Arthur Travis proposes two models of practice-based education for understanding supervision. One is a "work model" in which the primary task is "to produce a product or deliver a service." The other is an "'education-through-work' model" in which the supervisory task is "to complete the supervisee's integration of professional development and identity." Both operate with "the notion that supervision functions in a 'work' milieu." Based on the assumption that supervision takes place in an institution which functions as a clinical setting, he believes that "optimally all levels of the institution should promote the dual tasks of providing service and education." In such a setting the supervisory responsibility is:

1. To be competent in the process of supervision;
2. To keep the institution structures clean and the boundaries clear so that distortions, resistance, and evasion can be addressed as they occur in the supervisees' work;
3. To keep an equal focus on the supervisees' work, learning, and professional selfhood development;
4. To create an ambiance of freedom, creativity, and challenge so that maximum growth can occur inside the supervisees;
5. To provide supervisees with critical feedback appropriately timed so that it can be internalized.[14]

John Gessell, in a position paper relating CPE to the theological curriculum, outlines the values that clinical training offers to students but acknowledges: "There is nothing to prevent the seminaries, however, from establishing their own criteria for including into their educational environments any clinical opportunities they choose, and for providing their students with the necessary supervision. This will place the educational responsibility where it belongs, in the seminary."[15]

In harmony with this, theological schools utilize both parish and non-parish agencies as clinical centers for their students. "The educational problem . . . is to construct an educational environment in which the changing forms of contemporary consciousness can be included. And so to the traditional purposes of clinical pastoral training is now to be added that of widening the environment of theological education to include the values and the realities of a pluralistic culture composed of organized and disorganized sets of related variables."[16] The characteristics of supervision practiced in the various disciplines used as clinical settings are therefore useful in constructing whatever model(s) of supervision is/are appropriate to theological education.

Donald Beisswenger, moving beyond the CPE model, has developed a grid showing seven modes of supervision (work, instructor, apprentice, training, resource, consultation, and spiritual guide) as "dominant educational mechanisms" in terms of five factors (primary goal, supervisor's task, focus of attention, dynamics, and locus of dominant control). A particular mode, utilizing the five factors appropriate to that mode, constitutes a model of supervision. He points out that schools tend to use one or a combination of modes, with one usually being dominant.[17]

Jacob Elias, writing as a Mennonite, suggests that a theology of church and of ministry requires a model of supervision more consistent with its ecclesiology. He criticizes other models for their preoccupation with the individual and their failure to include the Covenant Community (the congregation). He proposes a "wholistic congruent model of supervision" which is defined as "the individual and communitarian process of exercising oversight over a ministering person in the context of the Christian community and as a representative of that community in mission to the world. This includes the discerning of gifts for ministry, the enabling of the exercise of these ministering gifts, and the equipping of this ministering person for his or her specific ministries."[18]

Working out of a Lutheran tradition, Russell Seabright has proposed a model of supervision designed to integrate the social awareness and ministry functioning of students. Seabright believes that "each student should have the experience of reflecting upon the `tyrannies,' the insurmountables, having his/her consciousness about it reach new dimensions, and engage in activity designed to transform it." Contrasting his model to that of Andrew White who emphasizes the formal and functional power of supervisors, Seabright acknowledges that his may not be a model for all supervisors and all settings. Even so, he maintains: "I would be willing to hypothesize that its use would be more adequate to the demands of mission of church in world than are most of those models from which we now function, whether it be the CPE model or the more classical, functional definition of supervision. . . ."[19]

The ferment in the development of supervisory models is obvious and challenging. There is great variation even while the persons involved search for some minimal continuity. What is striking about this development is the increasing concern to give to whatever models emerge a sound theological grounding and purpose rather than a simple utilitarian rationale and use.

THE QUESTION OF EDUCATION

The second question occupying the minds of ATFE members is: How can supervisors be educated for their responsibilities? One of the first persons to address this question was David Steere who carried out an experiment in training pastor supervisors for the field education program of which he was director. Using a supervisory model adapted from CPE, his program was centered in the concept that supervision is learned by supervised practice; thus the primary function of the training staff was to "supervise supervisors in their supervision."[20] Seminars served as working sessions in group supervision. Position papers were distributed prior to the training and used as the basis for discussion. Electrical recordings of supervisory sessions with students were used as case material.

Conceptual approaches included the learning problems and problems about learning of Ekstein and Wallerstein and the analysis of supervisory games after the Berne Transactional Analysis model. This occurred over two weeks of intensive sessions during consecutive school years.

At the end a Supervisory Assessment Questionnaire was used to test the effectiveness of the training. This revealed that there was a significant difference in the quality of supervision given by those who were trained as compared to a control group who were not trained. The trainees produced measurement comparable to that of a second control group of CPE supervisors. The conclusion was that "field education supervisors may be trained in such a program to alter patterns of supervision significantly in the direction of the quality of supervision offered in clinical training."[21]

Charles Stewart reports a similar project which convinced him that "supervisors can be trained for the parish setting, taking account of the insights of clinical pastoral training but also being aware of the unique locale of the parish to build in elements which will make it more useful for the field education student."[22] His training consisted of three hours a day for two weeks. The components were: sensitivity training; multiple staff training; and supervisory training using the CPE model. Training was followed by monthly supervisory conferences with small groups of supervisors. Three styles (models) of supervision were presented: (1) father-son in which the supervisor dominates; (2) elder brother in which the supervisor guides the student in developing his/her own roles; and (3) peer-peer in which the supervisor treats the student as equal. The conclusion was that students and pastors should be matched according to their personalities and according to the styles of supervision which are employed.

These early experiments have given birth to a number of educational programs or courses in supervision across the United States and Canada. Some are confined to particular school settings while others represent the combined efforts of theological educators to work ecumenically. Most of them are designed specifically to prepare persons to supervise students while others are attempting to provide, in addition, resources for the larger church.[23]

For several years I, with others, have taught a basic supervisory course for pastors and other professional persons.[24] The course is offered in two different schedules: the intensive schedule, covering five days; or the extended schedule, meeting one half-day per week for ten weeks. In either schedule participants meet in supervisory work sessions for a minimum of thirty hours. The format is to engage the participants in the experience of bringing concrete acts of their own ministry for supervision by their peers as a way of helping them experience both the supervisor and supervisee roles. In addition they share case material from their supervisory work and group leadership in the course for analysis and evaluation. Didactic material is provided for reading and discussion in connection with issues which emerge in the group process. Peer feedback and evaluation along with that of the leader(s) is provided to assist participants in refining their self-evaluation as supervisors. While no tests have been administered, we have seen a high degree of growth in the attitudes, qualities, and skills used as a basis for evaluation. The stated goals of the course are:

1. To provide an action-reflection educational experience in supervising, being supervised, and reflecting on that experience as primary data for learning;
2. To create a group setting in which support and trust can be experienced as a paradigm for other supervisory relationships;
3. To investigate theories and models of supervision as a way of building flexibility and intentionality into practice of supervision;
4. To help develop self-awareness through clarification of the dynamics and issues within the participants which impact their supervision of others;
5. To engage in a supervisory method of theological reflection, based upon the

relatedness of belief and action, which can be translated into the participants' own supervisory situation; and,

6. To help participants own and appropriate their role as supervisors.

Paul Morentz, a psychiatrist, addressing the 1969 ATFE Consultation, said that "in general terms one can say that the supervision of supervisors is accomplished by giving them good supervision," but that "there are few places where a supervisor can learn these specific skills," so "part of the task of the supervisor of supervisors is to provide instruction in some of the more basic skills of supervision." This task, summarized, is: (1) to assist in the change of identity of supervisors, (2) to help supervisors handle their fears as they may be uncovered in the task of supervision, (3) to teach them certain specific skills, and (4) to explore with them certain intangible factors which are essential to effective practice of a profession.[25]

Morentz's suggestion of change in the supervisors' identity raises a critical issue. Should the education of supervisors be designed to make all supervisors look and function alike, or are there varieties of valid supervisory styles which need to be refined for use in different situations? Certainly, particular settings and circumstances demand particular behaviors. My experience is that supervisory identity does not mean the "cloning" of persons but rather the willingness and ability to function appropriately in the immediate supervisory moment. This calls for knowledge and competence in a range of supervisory models along with awareness of how one's being impacts these. The important thing is that supervisors know when and how to use the model most fitting to the occasion. While I am suspicious of attempts to validate one model as superior to others, I do believe that collegiality must be stressed in light of the traditional tendencies toward hierarchical patterns. Supervisors' education, therefore, must address itself to some basic essentials. Participants should be helped to:

1. Identify the supervisory models and theories from which they already function;
2. Clarify the meaning of their supervisory knowledge and acts;
3. Recognize how their supervisory style(s) affect their supervisees;
4. Become skilled in a range of supervisory methods;
5. Create relationships appropriate to the model of supervision being used;
6. Reflect theologically on the implications of the supervisory model being used;
7. Learn how to engage their supervisees in supervisory conversation, including theological reflection; and,
8. Come to an identity as pastoral supervisor.

THE QUESTION OF THEOLOGY

The third ATFE question related to supervision is: What is the role of supervision in practice-based education as a means of fostering theological inquiry? The first half of the decade of the 70's witnessed the emergence of practice-based education as an increasingly important component in the curricula of theological schools. Both research and experience indicate that the supervision of such practice is central in fostering educational value. The approach to supervision has been greatly influenced by CPE. However, since the theologizing function in clinical supervision has received less attention than other functions, theological curricula using the clinical method have tended to perpetuate this neglect in their programs of practice-based education.

Pastoral educators are being challenged to approach their task more theologically. They have struggled with the realization that the theologizing element in the action-reflection process has often suffered. This is partly due to the fact that field supervisors have not always been adequately trained to facilitate **theological** reflection. However, back of the training failure there may be, again, inadequate models of field education. An article by James and Evelyn Whitehead points out that "one's model of field education will profoundly influence how one goes about doing this theological reflection" and that this will "have consequences for supervision."[26]

The Whitehead article discusses three models of field education in terms of four components, two components—supervision and theological reflection—being of interest to us here. One model is the "**Application of Theology in the Practice of Ministry**." Supervision in this model is concerned with how well students are able to relate theology to experience, how correct the connections are between theological categories (e.g. sin, redemption, grace) and ministerial practice. The role of supervisors is to help students learn how to determine the appropriate theological answers to the questions arising in practical ministerial experience. Theological reflection in this model "focuses on how the individual pastoral experience is to be interpreted in the light of the tradition," is "most often one-directional," and produces a situation in which students await the "reflection of `professional theologians'" and then attempt "to apply this reflection" to their own pastoral experiences.[27]

A second model is described as the "**Acquisition and Development of Ministerial Skills**." In this model the role of supervision is to ensure that students acquire particular skills, and since supervisors usually identify themselves as practitioners and trainers of such **specific** skills, they will not be expected to assist students in the theological implications of these skills. As a result, "very little theological reflection is likely to occur. . . . The student's time is consumed in learning the skill of another discipline—an important practical skill, but one whose theological implications are rarely explored."[28]

A third model of field education is known as the "**Locus of Pastoral Theology**." Theological reflection, they say, is two-directional: students learn how to allow their experience to question their theological tradition as well as how to allow their tradition to confront their experience. "Hopefully the student here learns a **habit** of critical reflection, a specific method for approaching the theological question that will arise in his ministry, a method that will yield pastoral decisions at once **theological** and **his own**."[29] It is unfortunate that the authors omit any overt reference to the supervisory task in this model.

The Whitehead article highlights the ATFE question about the role of supervision in practice-based education as a means of fostering theological inquiry. Richard Bollinger speaks to the same concern when, in response to the question, "What is Pastoral Supervision?" he says:

> Broadly speaking, supervision is part of theological education and should be seen as one of the processes that leads to the formation of ministers. Supervision provides a key function in this process, namely at the point of applying theory to practice. The practice of ministry requires that the beliefs

and values of Christian faith be made operational in real life situations with real persons. The supervisor is a boundary keeper in this operation, or to use other terminology, a socializing "agent." He assists the student -minister to confront his own beliefs and traditions as they come into play in the actual work of ministry. In this sense, the supervisor "does theology" at the boundary between intellectual and beliefful appropriation of the tradition and the experiences of involvement in the lives of people in the service of that tradition.[30]

C. Roy Woodruff suggests three ways of "doing theology": dogmatic theology (what I say I believe), systematic theology (what I believe I believe), and experiential theology (what I show I believe). He says that all of these, along with biblical theology, are useful, but that "the theological method most relevant for the supervisory process is . . . experiential theology." By experiential theology he means theological reflection on and in the midst of the existential human situation. To be useful it must engage dogmatic and systematic theology in dialogue. Its value lies in its involvement of emotion as well as mind: "to do theology adequately means to use the whole self."[31]

This understanding of theological method is not totally new in seminary circles but it is only beginning to seriously impact the way supervision is done in theological curricula and the church at large. Bernard Cooke presses the supervisory concern when he says:

Related closely to such queries is a shift in theological method that has been gradually gaining ground in recent decades. This shift involves a move away from the assumption that theology can use as its starting point the formulations of belief that are traditional within a given community. Neither solemn conciliar dogmas nor the biblical texts can lay claim to self-sufficiency as "word of God": there is a sense in which the human experience of faith in those verbalizations and the human experience of faith that today is able to identify with that earlier faith-experience stand as a prior "word" and therefore as a prior source for theology, and to some extent as a prior norm.[32]

Writing as a systematic theologian, Lucien Richard confirms the struggle to find adequate ways of studying theology. He feels that the difficulties in theologizing field experience represents a fault not with field education but with the structure of theological education. "With our positivistic understanding of revelation, we have made tourists out of our theological students. They are trained to become map-readers, and in the process they lose their inner drive for discovery. . . ." The meaning of this is that we need "an empirical theology" that can free us of "a church-centered and Scripture-centered theology. An empirical theology is one that is open to God's Word in all life."[33]

The way this concern takes shape in the creation of models of theological reflection will be addressed in Chapter VI. In the meantime, ATFE continues to search for models of supervision, supervisory education, and theological reflection which are adaptable to the variety of situations in which they must be implemented. The characteristics of supervision identified earlier assist in the search precisely because they are basic to supervision but diverse in applicability.

PASTORAL SUPERVISION IN THE CHURCH

Theological education takes place in the context of the church, but the gap between church and seminary is a tragic and real fact. There is a great amount of suspicion, mistrust, and competition on both sides. Each feels threatened by the other, with the church accusing the school of being isolated from its life and the school charging the church of hiding its collective head in the sand.

It is significant that supervision of the practice of ministry is proving to be at least one means of building a bridge across the chasm. By being invited into an adjunct faculty role as supervisors, pastors get the message that their professional expertise is being recognized and that they have something important to contribute to the training of the persons who are to be their colleagues. By being designated a teaching congregation or clinical parish, lay people come to believe that they are being taken seriously, that they really are a necessary arm of the seminary, that they can have a share in preparing their future pastors for their careers. By being included in the placement and overseeing function, judicatory personnel become interested in what happens to their pastors, local parishes, and the students who work with them; they gain an investment in the program. Supervised seminary field experience, whatever its particular form, has made church laity, pastors, judicatory personnel, and the seminary available to each other so communication and collaboration can take place. This is a crucial step forward in church-seminary relations.

Pastoral Supervision in the church is still in a developmental stage, but there are some promising efforts that are taking place to foster growth. These are occurring on three fronts. One front is the **training of judicatory superintendents** who are charged with oversight of denominational persons and structures. The United Methodist Church has, on occasion, included introductory supervisory workshops into its annual training event for district superintendents. In the same denomination some bishops' Cabinets have sought consultation around supervisory issues. A few such persons have taken the initiative to engage in supervisory education on their own.[34] All such attempts provide encouraging signs that growth in supervisory theory and practice is being taken seriously, but they are far too infrequent.

A second front is the **emerging use of supervision with pastors of churches**. CPE centers have included parish pastors in their basic units of clinical education, sometimes within their parish, making it possible for the pastors to receive supervision for their pastoral work and to continue afterward with more sensitivity to supervisory processes. Occasionally some pastors contract with supervisors in CPE, pastoral counseling, or other interprofessional centers for on-going supervision. Or, as already indicated, some pastors are "turned on" to the idea through their training and participation as supervisors in seminary field education programs.

In recent years it has become acceptable among pastors to seek supervision for their counseling ministry. Unfortunately the practice of seeking supervision for other pastoral acts has not caught on as strongly among most pastors. There have been scattered attempts to design peer supervisory groups to meet the latter need, and participants are pleased with the results.[35] All of them seek effective methods for utilizing one's own pastoral events and/or situations (cases) around which to engage in conversation with peers.[36]   Robert Leslie and Emily Mudd applaud all such efforts when they write: "Ministers should be among those who first embrace this style of lifelong learning with enthusiasm. Through a pattern of continuing education, with a strong emphasis on supervision, they can stay equipped to nurture the continuing growth of their people, by continuing to grow themselves."[37]

Henry Adams, writing out of his experience with the Academy of Parish Clergy, proposes consultation as an alternative to supervision.[38] Building on this idea, Donald Houts reports an experiment with consultation teams among pastors. He based his experiment on the conclusion that the supervision **of** peers **by** peers is unrealistic and actually represents a misunderstanding of supervision. His thesis is that peer consultation may, under certain conditions, be a preferable and more effective supervisory investment for some clergy. He worked with peer consultation teams who were willing to contract for five days of training and eleven weeks of one-on-one consultative relationship with another person. Throughout his paper, however, he uses supervisory terminology and methods, and in the "typical response" that he quotes to reflect participant evaluation of the experience, the experiment is referred to as "the peer supervision project."[39]

These attempts to find alternatives to supervision bring to attention a supervisory problem referred to in Chapter I: pastors tend to avoid supervision. Consultation at least puts the burden of responsibility upon the individual pastor to seek help. It is significant, however, that the methods used are drawn from supervision. It is my contention that we must find ways to define and do supervision which will engage even reluctant pastors in a process that they can experience as useful and helpful.

The third front on which efforts are being made to develop **pastoral supervision is with lay people**. Some experiments have been done in equipping lay people in the work of pastoral care within the supervision of their pastor. One of the earliest of these was designed by Ronald Sunderland who taught lay persons and their pastors in the principles of pastoral visitation and of reflecting together on those experiences. The lay persons worked as volunteer lay pastors, wrote verbatims of their visits, and met with their pastor for supervision.[40] Howard Clinebell reports a similar experiment with different results. His conclusion was that the missing element in his program was supervision which, he concludes, is a critical factor in any such effort.[41]

Doors are also opening for laity as they are trained to serve on special committees to aid in the supervision of seminarians assigned to their parish for field education. Invariably such persons claim that they gain new awareness of themselves, broadened understanding of ministry, deepened commitment to the church, and increased appreciation for the educational task of the church. Many of them become quite skillful in the supervisory process. A growing number of selected lay persons are being brought into supervised field education, thus expanding the role of lay persons in the supervision of ministry.

In 1977 Patricia Drake began an extended study focusing on the involvement of laity in the theological education of seminarians. Building upon the experiments of numerous theological educators in their field education programs, she developed a comprehensive rationale and program that has been widely used in theological schools. It reflects the combined experience of educators, students, and lay persons and provides assistance in recruiting, training, implementing, and evaluating lay committees in field education. The processes used emphasize small group building, feedback, covenant making, spiritual formation, theological reflection, and assistance in writing case studies. The materials are available for seminary use.[42]

Simultaneously but separate from Drake's work Julianne Hallman designed a creative program for preparing and supervising "Teaching Parish Committees" that has been implemented and expanded through use. It represents one of the most thorough programs of lay participation in supervision that exists in theological education.[43]

SUMMARY

The review of literature from several professions in Chapter II has done three things. One, it has made possible the identification of ten basic characteristics of supervision which can be used to formulate a model of pastoral supervision that has inter-professional grounding. Second, it has identified several issues which need attention in any pastoral supervision model. Third, it has prompted a review of developments around this issue in the church, both in theological education and in the broader church among pastors and lay people. The implications are that these are both historical precedents and current pressures which demand that programs of pastoral supervision be instituted on a significant scale.

Three words have emerged out of this study to lend substance to such efforts: reflection, empowerment, and transformation. These are not new concepts for the church; rather they have been adopted from the church. What is new is that they have become essential language for the world to describe its need for more responsiveness to human values in the workplace. Oppressive, manipulative, insensitive, and haphazard approaches to supervision will no longer be tolerated. The challenge to the church and to other institutions is to translate this new language into principles and practices that take equally seriously the persons who work and the work that they do. It is to meet this challenge that the following model of supervision is proposed.

ENDNOTES

1. William B. Spafford, "The Question of Extensive Training," *Journal of Pastoral Care* 7 (Spring 1953): 34.
2. John H. Patton and John Warkentin, "A Dialogue on Supervision and Consultation," *Journal of Pastoral Care* 25 (September 1971): 170.
3. Suanna J. Wilson, *Confidentiality in Social Works* (New York: Free Press, 1978), 1.
4. Ibid., 2-4.
5. See Carl D. Glickman, *Developmental Supervision* (Alexandria, VA: Association for Supervision and Curriculum Development, 1981), 10.
6. Kenneth H. Pohly, "The Clinical Method in Theological Education" (Ann Arbor, MI: University Microfilms, 1969), 53. (Unpublished Doctor of Ministry Dissertation for Vanderbilt University.)
7. See Charles Feilding, *Education for Ministry* (Dayton, OH: American Association of Theological Schools, 1966); also *Theological Education* 4 (Spring 1968), 683-86.

8. Thomas W. Klink, "Supervision from a Clinical/Pastoral Care Perspective," *Report of the Proceedings of the Tenth Biennial Consultation on Field Education*, Berkeley, CA, January 15-18, 1969, 17.

9. Ibid., 25.

10. Jesse H. Ziegler, "Editorial Introduction," *Theological Education* 11 (Summer 1975): 262-63.

11. See Doran C. McCarty, *The Supervision of Ministry Students* (Atlanta, GA: Home Mission Board, Southern Baptist Convention, 1978); George I. Hunter, *Supervision and Education-Formation for Ministry* (Cambridge, MA: Episcopal Divinity School, 1982); *Theological Field Education: A Collection of Key Resources*, Vols. 1-5 (N.p.: Association for Theological Field Education, 1977-1986); and the *Report of Proceedings of the Biennial Consultations of the Association for Theological Field Education.*, 1969-89.

12. George W. Baldwin and Paul B. Maves, "Creating a Model for Field Education," *Theological Education* 11 (Summer 1975): 265.

13. Wayne E. Oates, "Pastoral Supervision Today," *Pastoral Psychology* 24 (Fall 1975): 22.

14. Arthur E. Travis, Jr., "Supervision: Some Assumptions." (Paper presented to the St. Mary's Seminary Department of Field Education, Houston, Texas, April 1974), 1-2.

15. John M. Gessell, "Clinical Pastoral Training and the Curriculum for Theological Education: A Position Paper," *Journal of Pastoral Care* 22 (September 1968): 165.

16. Ibid., 170.

17. Donald F. Beisswenger, "Differentiating Modes of Supervision in Theological Field Education," *Theological Education* 11 (Autumn 1974): 51-58. Persons going through my own supervision education program have benefitted from their use of Beisswenger's models and have expanded on them.

18. Jacob W. Elias, "Supervised Ministries in the Free Church Tradition," *Report of the 17th Biennial Meeting of The Association of Professional Education for Ministry*, Duquesne University, Pittsburgh, Pennsylvania, June 19-21, 1982, ed. LeRoy H. Aden, 65. Cf. McCarty, *Supervision*; Hunter, *Supervision*; Kenneth H. Pohly, *Pastoral Supervision* (Houston: Institute of Religion, 1977), and others.

19. Russell F. Seabright, "A Model of Supervision for the Integration of Social Awareness and Ministry Functioning During a Year of Internship in Lutheran Theological Education." Un-published Doctor of Ministry Project for United Theological Seminary, Dayton, Ohio, 1984, 146-65. Cf. Andrew J. White, "Supervision: An Invitation to Dialogue." (Unpublished paper written for Lutheran Theological Seminary at Philadelphia, 1983).

20. David A. Steere, "An Experiment in Supervisory Training," *Journal of Pastoral Care* 23 (December 1969): 207.

21. Ibid., 216.

22. Charles W. Stewart, "Training Pastoral Supervisors for Seminary Field Education," *Journal of Pastoral Care* 25 (March 1971): 24.

23. The earliest ecumenical program was the biennial Institute on Supervised Ministries, sponsored by the schools in the Boston Theological Institute, Boston, MA. Other examples of which I am aware are: the on-going supervisory courses at Andover Newton Theological School, Newton Centre, MA; the annual workshops in Pastoral Supervision, co-sponsored by Iliff School of Theology and St. Thomas Seminary, Denver, Colorado; the Program on the Ministry of Supervision, sponsored by St. Stephen's College, Edmonton, Alberta; and the Ohio consortium training co-sponsored by several seminaries in Ohio and Kentucky.

24. I refer to our program at the Center for Supervisory Studies (CSS) at United Theological Seminary, Dayton, Ohio. This facet of the Center's program serves the Supervised Ministry (Field Education) and Doctor of Ministry Programs at the seminary, as well as the church and community at large. For persons who wish to engage in it as part of an academic program, this constitutes a course under the title "Principles and Practice of Supervision" in the curriculum of United Theological Seminary. It is the prerequisite course for other supervisory courses also provided by CSS.

25. Paul E. Morentz, "The Supervision of Supervisors." (A paper presented to the Tenth Biennial Consultation on Field Education, Berkeley, California, January 15-18, 1969), 51.

26. James D. Whitehead and Evelyn E. Whitehead, "Educational Models in Field Education," *Theological Education* 11 (Summer 1975): 273.

27. Ibid., 272-74.

28. Ibid., 274-76.

29. Ibid., 276-77.

30. Richard A. Bollinger, "What is Pastoral Supervision?" *Theological Field Education: A Collection of*

Key Resources (N.p.: Association for Theological Field Education, 1977), 1: 53. (Paper originally prepared for the Division of Religion and Psychiatry, The Menninger Foundation, February 20, 1973.)

31. C. Roy Woodruff, "Theological Reflection in the Supervisory Process," *Journal of Pastoral Care* 34 (September, 1980): 199.

32. Bernard Cooke, "The Current State of Theological Reflection," *Theological Field Education: A Collection of Key Resources* (N.p.: Association for Theological Field Education, 1981), 3: 73. (Reprinted from *Bulletin of the Council on the Study of Religion* 10, no. 2.)

33. Lucien Richard, "The Existing Malaise in the Theologizing of Field Experience," *Theological Education* 9 (Autumn 1972): 69.

34. Two recent examples are the Doctor of Ministry programs carried out at United Theological Seminary by District Superintendents Julian M. Aldridge, Jr., of the Western North Carolina Conference and Paul C. Bailey of the Virginia Conference of the United Methodist Church.

35. An example is an early morning breakfast group, composed of pastors in a particular denomin-ational group, that meets weekly. There are similar interdenominational groups.

36. James D. Glasse, *Putting It Together in the Parish* (Nashville, TN: Abingdon Press, 1972), 84-105.

37. Robert C. Leslie and Emily Hartshorne Mudd, *Professional Growth for Clergymen* (Nashville, TN: Abingdon Press, 1970), 192.

38. Henry B. Adams, "Consultation: An Alternative to Supervision." *Journal of Pastoral Care* 25 (September 1971): 157-64.

39. Donald C. Houts, "Consultation Teams: A Supervisory Alternative," *Journal of Supervision and Training in Ministry* 3 (1980): 17.

40. Ronald H. Sunderland, "A Concept of Ministry Which Employs the Supervisory Process Derived from Clinical Pastoral Education," (Unpublished S.T.M. Thesis, Perkins School of Theology, Southern Methodist University, 1968), 103.

41. Clinebell, Howard J. "Experiments in Training Laity for Ministry," *Pastoral Psychology* 22 (June 1971): 35-43.

42. Patricia G. Drake, ed., *Building Stronger Lay Committees* (Washington, DC: The Alban Institute, 1983). An annotated list of resources available from the Institute is included.

43. Julieanne Hallman, "The Development of and Implications for the Teaching Parish Committee as an Integral and Vital Partner in Field Education." (Ann Arbor, MI: University Microfilms, 1980). (Unpublished Doctor of Ministry Project for Andover Newton Theological School, Newton Centre, MA.)

CHAPTER IV

LOWERING MOUNTAINS AND BRIDGING VALLEYS: MODEL AND METHOD

It now becomes possible to conceptualize a model for pastoral supervision. It should be kept in mind that what is suggested here is designed to be used in a range of settings in which pastoral supervision might be carried out. Not all elements would fit every situation. For example, the complete model is most appropriate for use with students in an educational setting; adaptation to a local church for use with a group of lay persons might necessitate some adjustments. That is its strength, I believe. Thus every supervisor is both free and challenged to build his or her own model to fit a particular context.

The description has been kept as brief and concise as possible so that it can be easily utilized. It is intended as an educational instrument, not as an instant outline that anyone can apply indiscriminately. Therefore, education in work with the model in supervised practice is assumed.

A DEFINITION OF SUPERVISION

Defining supervision is a difficult task, as the review of literature shows, partly because it is a dynamic discipline under growth and change and partly because it is used in such diverse settings. In spite of the hazards, however, I venture to do so. My experience with supervision on both sides—as supervisee and as supervisor—leads me to define it as a pastoral event.

Pastoral supervision is a method of doing and reflecting on ministry in which a supervisor (teacher) and one or more supervisees (learners) covenant together to reflect critically on their ministry as a way of growing in self-awareness, ministering competence, theological understanding, and Christian commitment. Such a definition assumes implementation of the basic characteristics of supervision described earlier. Some expansion of this definition follows.

Supervision is pastoral. It is something that Christians do as part of their work whether they are judicatory officers, pastors, teachers, heads of departments, or church lay leaders. But it is pastoral in function as well as office in the sense of its shepherding nature, that is, its care-giving. This includes everyone involved—supervisees as well as supervisors. The giving and receiving of care is something in which all supervisory participants engage.

Supervision is a way of doing ministry. To the degree that it is integral to the church's life, we have tended to see it as a way of getting ministry done, suggesting that it takes place somewhere outside of ministry like an external control. I suggest that supervision is a way of doing ministry—a methodology, a style, for ministry. It provides a way for persons to engage in the same ministry as colleagues, as co-participants. Thus it is both integral to and formative for ministry.

Supervision is convenantal. It occurs within an agreement in which persons say to each other: this is what we will do together and for which we will hold one another accountable. This is a dynamic process which allows for the covenant to be reshaped as needs change and persons grow. Its purpose is to set priorities, establish structure, provide boundaries, and identify procedures around which ministry can occur and be evaluated. It is something mutually negotiated and binding.

Supervision is reflective. Supervision occurs within a supervisory conversation in which the participants reflect critically on their ministry. While there are identifiable stages through which such a conversation normally flows, the objective is to help people tell and confront their own life story in ministry as a way of making appropriate faith (action) responses. It is reflective in that the supervisors assist the supervisees in seeing themselves and their ministry more accurately, clearly, and creatively.

Supervision is intentional. Although what happens in the supervisory conversation cannot and should not be programmed, it has intentionality. There are at least four growth-oriented purposes: to help people understand themselves more clearly; to assist in the development and refinement of ministering competencies; to sharpen and clarify theological understanding; and to deepen Christian commitment, whatever direction that may take. It is not haphazard or accidental; it has goals and occurs with regularity.

THE COMPLEX NATURE OF THE SUPERVISORY RELATIONSHIP

There have been a number of attempts to diagram the relationships inherent in supervision. Each such attempt is rooted in the context in which supervision takes place. I have been influenced by the clinical rhombus of Ekstein and Wallerstein which grew out of the practice of supervision in psychotherapy and Sunderland's adaptation of it for use with lay pastors.[1] Figure 1 shows the complexity of the supervisory relationship because of its multiple potential participants and components.

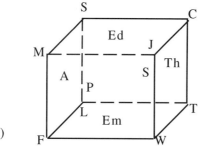

(Figure 1)

The potential **participants** in any supervisory relationship are represented here by the corners of the cube as follows:

M - Minister (student, clergy or lay)
S - Supervisor
C - Consultant
J - Jurisdictional superintendent
F - Family constellation of minister
L - Location in which ministry is performed
T - Theological school
W - World (immediate and remote)

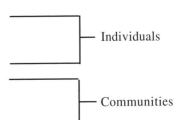

Individuals

Communities

Of these eight participants, some are individuals who, though they function as single persons in this instance, also bring certain community involvements with them to the relationship. Other participants are better described as communities which, while made up of individuals, influence the relationship as systems instead of (or at least more than) as individuals. All of the participants make some impact on the supervisory relationship, the force of the impact varying according to the issues introduced for supervision.

For example, a student minister may bring for reflection a confrontation with his or her church administrative council over what the council feels is a neglect of adequate home visitation. Their criticism might be expressed as a judgment of incompetence or laziness. The actual fact may be that the student's family is objecting to the required additional absence from home during the evenings when the visits have to be made in order to find the parishioners at home. Perhaps the council has failed to take this seriously or the student has failed to explain the reason in order to protect the family.

In any case, in terms of the diagram the student minister (M), the supervisor (S), the family (F), and the location (L, in this case the church council) are all immediately involved as participants. The theological school (T) will become involved if the issue becomes more complicated.[2] Thus, if one were to draw lines through the cube to represent the many possible combinations of involvement, the complex nature of the supervisory relationship would become obvious.

There are, in addition, six **components** of the relationship which constitute the tasks that belong to supervision. They are represented here by the sides of the cube as follows:

A   -   Administrative (providing accountability; giving feedback, evaluation)
Ed -   Educational (teaching knowledge, skills; providing resources)
Em -   Emotional (giving care, support; guiding to therapeutic help)
P   -   Professional (assisting in identity formation as persons, ministers)
S   -   Social (facilitating interpersonal, interprofessional relationships)
Th -   Theological (enabling reflection on meanings)

All of the components come in for attention in supervision, though it may take more than one supervisory session to address them adequately. All are integral to the relationship, however. In the example cited above, the administrative (A) component to which the church council gave immediate attention may need to be set aside temporarily in order to deal with the emotional (Em) and social (S) components. The professional (P) component looms as an inevitable concern, and the educational (Ed) component may be more important than appears on the surface. The theological (Th) component not only cannot be avoided but is foundational to all of the others and must set the tone for considering them.

To illustrate from the example, the supervisor will have to deal with the supervisee's feelings early in the supervisory session, not only the feelings growing out of the confrontation with the church council but those growing out of the supervisee's family relationships. Unless this is done, little can be accomplished. There may be ruptured relationships both at home and in the congregation that need healing. Reflecting theologically on the confrontation has the potential for moving the session beyond feelings to the discovery that either or both the supervisee and the Council may not understand the purpose of pastoral visitation, or that the supervisee doesn't know how to do it well and therefore avoids it; the family situation could be a "cover" for lack of understanding. Thus, the supervisor must exercise her/his role as teacher and pastoral theologian as well as boundary keeper. There are other possible scenarios that may include helping the supervisee and/or congregation refine their identity and understanding of ministry. In any case, the visitation task will not be enhanced aside from attention to all the components (tasks) in the supervisory relationship.

The relationship may be made even more complex by the manner in which the persons and systems beyond the immediate participants react. They, along with the supervisee, must eventually be helped to understand and address the total situation, not just the visitation task.

THE DYNAMIC NATURE OF THE SUPERVISORY PROCESS

Supervision has two foci: the persons in supervision and the ministry they perform. They are equal and simultaneous concerns for supervisors and are diagrammed in Figure 2:

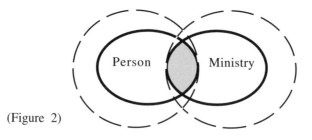

(Figure 2)

The material to be supervised consists of acts or situations of ministry upon which supervisors and supervisees reflect critically as a way of understanding what took place, why they developed as they did, and what can be learned from them. The "world" of the person and of the context in which ministry takes place are larger than the immediate focus of any particular supervisory hour. They include all the participants and components described above (Figure 1), represented here by the dotted extension of the circles in Figure 2. Supervision focuses on the immediate acts or situations of ministry brought for supervision, represented by the overlapping area (shaded portion).

This can best be described as an action-reflection flow, with supervision occurring (being "located") in that flow as shown in Figure 3 below:

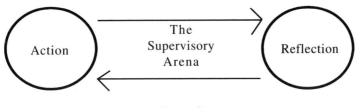

(Figure 3)

Thus, persons in ministry (supervisees) come for supervision (reflection upon ministry with supervisors), return to ministry with new insights and tools, to return later for more supervision. The process flows between action and reflection.

SUPERVISORY INSTRUMENTS

There are numerous forms in which the acts or situations of ministry can be brought for supervision. Experience indicates that written material is most useful, though circumstances sometimes dictate that it be described verbally. Klink has suggested eleven methods of reporting, described in more or less detail as to content and use.[3] They are included here with my own description and interpretation.

The observation report in which one describes, as fully and concretely as possible, an event to which one is a spectator. It is a phenomenological method, with emphasis on observing the setting and behavior rather than making decisions and judgments. It carries the lowest risk-taking of all the instruments.

The journal or diary of experience which provides reflective thought on one's ministering activity or situation. It tends to be discursive and inclusive rather than focused. At its best it provides access to the supervisee's feelings, motives, and values; at its worst it is a rehearsal of meaningless detail.

The common ministry event, meaning the mutual involvement of supervisors and supervisees, in acts of ministry such as a worship service or pastoral visit, followed immediately or at least soon with discussion of the event. Its advantage is that all the information is available to all of the participants, and it permits mutual supervision.

The verbatim account of a pastoral conversation consisting of a word-for-word account of a pastoral visit, street conversation, exchange in a committee meeting, or any other significant verbal encounter. It is done by recall after the event and may or may not accurately reflect what happened. It is one of the more difficult instruments to prepare; it is the one of primary use in CPE.

The electronic recording of a pastoral encounter using either or both audio and video equipment. It is the most objective reporting instrument; it eliminates the writing and reading tasks, and it provides the most complete system of reporting. On the other hand, it is the most time consuming of the instruments used in supervision and is not practical for use in limited time frames. It also requires permission (in writing and perhaps with witness) of the parishioner being recorded.

The critical incident report, a free-form way of reporting a recent event which is of critical or at least concerned importance to the supervisee (e.g. an official board meeting, a social gathering, a retreat experience, or a personal encounter). It provides maximum selectivity in what and how to report about both verbal and non-verbal encounters, but a useful guideline is to describe the event in terms of what made it critical for the supervisee.[4] This is one of the most widely used supervisory instruments.

The Plan of Ministry summary which can be used as follow-up to contact with a person or situation. This might involve a preaching schedule, youth meeting(s), Bible study, or a counseling relationship. It may be offered at the supervisee's initiative for feedback and evaluation, or it may be submitted as a requirement of the setting; in the latter case it is the most controlling of the supervisory instruments.

The process note, used most often in counseling situations. It reports a single encounter and consists of a summary of general impressions, details about the flow of the encounter (usually summaries of verbal exchanges rather than a verbatim), a review of the total encounter, and an appraisal of what took place in connection with goals and purposes.

The interim summary which includes a summary of an initial contact and plans with a person or group, a summary of subsequent events, an estimate of how things stand currently in the situation, and an identification of the on-going questions which emerge out of the contact. The emphasis is on goals and progress rather than methods and personal involvement. It is time consuming but particularly appropriate to consultation.

The case summary, a retrospective review of a ministering situation for the purpose of gaining the greatest possible learning from an event now completed. Being free from the concerns of pastoral decisions, this instrument allows more speculative consideration and tends to be used with that in mind, though its issues can be translated into current situations. Klink says that the only difference between the interim summary and the case summary is that the first involves work in progress while the latter involves work completed. There are also other models of case writing.[5]

The role-play (psychodrama) which involves "playing out" a situation by taking roles and "living out" the event in a new way. It is especially useful when the written reports or the pressure of an actual pastoral situation fail to provide sufficient basis for reflection. It provides an effective way to deal with feelings, to help supervisees become "unstuck" from a certain ministering style, or to call forth ministering responses that would not arise or be heard in simple conversation.

These do not exhaust the possibilities; imagination can invent others. The only requirement is that the instrument be accurate and useful. The purpose is to provide something that will identify the ministry to be supervised in a responsible manner. The written instrument need not and should not be long (one or two typewritten pages); but it must be precise. What appear to be negative experiences or failures are often the most useful material from which to learn, even though they are the most threatening to present. Even so, positive experiences which call for celebration are appropriate. However, case materials that always show one's strengths and hide one's weaknesses need to be challenged.

THE MINISTRY REFLECTION REPORT

For years my colleagues and I used the critical incident in our supervision of students, but we found both supervisors and supervisees objecting to its name. By trial and error we have developed our own version of the critical incident report which we call the "Ministry Reflection Report." While we continue to find supervisees exercising creative liberties with a variety of instruments, the ministry reflection report has become our instrument of choice in the supervision of our students' ministries and in our basic supervision course for the students' supervisors, Doctor of Ministry students, and other supervisors, both clergy and lay (e.g., pastors, religious, judicatory leaders, educators, social workers, spiritual directors, institutional and department heads).

The Ministry Reflection Report is a written description of an event or situation in ministry which is prepared to invite reflection upon our practice of ministry. It is the means by which we provide "live" case material for the supervision of our ministry. It is to be written in a format that follows the stages of a supervisory conversation so as to facilitate the conversation. It is to be one or two single-spaced, typewritten pages. The outline, agenda for content, and suggested procedures for writing are below.

1. Choosing the event or situation
   a. Think about the many events and situations which have had a significant impact on your ministry;
   b. From the many, select one that has current concern for you and in which you have a strong investment of emotional, mental, and/or spiritual energy;
   c. Both positive and negative experiences in ministry make appropriate cases.
2. Preparing to write
   a. Recall as much as you can of the details involved in the event or situation; "feel" your way into it as fully as possible;
   b. Make some notes or write a reasonably full account of the event or situation, which you can later reduce to a brief narrative, in order to make sure you have it accurately in mind.
   c. Analyze the event or situation, utilizing the outline for writing (see #3 below); make some notes for the five categories.
3. Writing the Ministry Reflection Report
   a. **Information.** Describe the event or situation in a way that a reader can get a mental picture of it. What happened? Who was involved? What was your role? How did you and others respond? What was the result?
   b. **Evaluation.** Relate the effects of the event or situation on you and other persons involved. What emotions did you experience? How did the other people react? How has it affected you personally? How has it affected you

professionally? What are the key issues for you?

c. **Analysis**. Sketch your interpretation of the event or situation as an occasion for ministry. What made it "ministry"? What made it positive or negative? What factor or forces were at work to influence it? What personal knowledge or experience does it challenge? What options are possible as a continuing ministering response?

d. **Theological Reflection**. State the theological meanings found in the event or situation and in your response to it. What personal beliefs and/or convictions are evidenced in or challenged by it. How did or could your religious experience shape your ministering response? What biblical, historical, and/or cultural insights relate to it? What "truth" informs you? What ultimate concerns do you have concerning it?

e. **Commitment**. Set forth the implications growing out of the event or situation for your future ministry. How is this like what you might experience in the future? What have you learned from it? How can its benefits be continued or its hazards be avoided? What ministering response do you intend to make?

THE SUPERVISORY CONVERSATION

Supervision is a conversation, meaning that the interaction involves all the persons present. It is not a time for a supervisor to interrogate a supervisee as a judge questions a prisoner. It is a dialogue. The supervisor (and other supervisees if there is a group) helps by listening, making observations, and raising questions as a way of enabling the supervisee to see the problem or event more clearly. Supervision provides a mirror for the supervisee to reflect on the situation and see it in all of its dimensions from a new perspective, not in a passive way but as a means to making responsible decisions about self and ministry.

The conversation begins with the supervisee describing the act or situation of ministry brought for supervision, using whatever instrument has been selected as most appropriate. It then moves to drawing out from that description the dominant feeling(s) and the central issue(s) needing attention. There follows a discussion of alternative ways of viewing and understanding the issue(s), drawing upon the supervisor's or group's experience but especially upon the resources of the supervisee (experience, insights, imagination, etc.). This leads to theologizing, which is an attempt to understand what this means for life and ministry in light of the sources of Christian faith. Finally, the conversation should result in the supervisee making a responsible decision in terms of a faith (action) response. The task of the supervisor is to help the supervisee tell his or her story and to reflect upon it. It is the supervisee's hour, and this includes working at the issues, not being given packaged answers.

Although questioning as interrogation should be avoided, the conversation can be facilitated if certain key questions guide it. They are not to be considered an "agenda" but are rather suggestive of the flow and progression appropriate to the process. However, the progression is not precise; it is frequently changed or the "parts" intermixed. The goal is to enable the supervisee to think in these terms so the conversation will unfold without the necessity of the questions being raised. They can be stated in terms of stages.[6]

1. **Informative Stage** — The focus is on getting an accurate picture of the event or situation:
   a. What took place? Or, what is the situation?
   b. What was your role? As a person? As a minister?
   c. How did you respond?
   d. Who were the other participants? How did you interact with them?
   e. How is this related to other events or situations?
   f. How typical is it? Is it part of a pattern?
   g. How does the situation stand now? Is there unfinished business?
2. **Evaluation Stage** — The focus is on the core issue(s) so as to sort out what the real problem is and/or what needs attention first:
   a. What emotions did you experience?
   b. What are your feelings about it now?
   c. How do you feel about the other people involved?
   d. How do you feel about your place of ministry? About what you are doing?
   e. In what way are or are not your expectations being fulfilled?
   f. How does this event or situation correspond with others in your life?
   g. What would you do differently if you could?
   h. How does all this affect your ability to minister?
   i. What are the key issues for you? What is most important?
3. **Analysis** — The focus is on removing the obstacles and finding among alternative possibilities the one that seems most viable for continued ministry in the situation:
   a. What do you want to have happen? In supervision? In the situation?
   b. What is your interpretation of the situation now?
   c. What would you change? What would that require?
   d. What do you see as alternatives?
   e. What would happen if . . . ?
   f. What is your role as a result of the experience?
   g. How can the continuing situation best be confronted or handled?
4. **Theologizing Stage** — The focus is on meanings so as to draw from this experience and prior or new knowledge those elements that now become "truth" in light of the gospel:
   a. What have you learned from this experience?
   b. What new insights do you have about self, human nature, church, world, God?
   c. At what points does your experience intersect with the Christian gospel? In what ways?
   d. What does this have to say to you about ministry?
   e. What are the implications for yourself as a minister? Weaknesses? Strengths?
   f. How do you feel about ministry? About yourself in ministry?
   g. What emerges as ultimate concern for you?

5. **Commitment Stage** — The focus is on decision in terms of choosing a ministering response:
   a. How is this situation like those you anticipate in the future?
   b. How do you anticipate responding to them?
   c. What are you going to do about the situation brought for supervision?
   d. What is your next step?
   e. What resources do you need?
   f. What faith response (action) must and will you make as a Christian as a result of this decision?

CONDITIONS FOR EFFECTIVE SUPERVISION

In the face of its diversity, there are some conditions that are essential to supervisory effectiveness. A great deal has been learned from the professions reviewed in Chapter II and from our experience in theological education. It is possible now to state this in language that applies to the church in its broader ministry in both the gathered and scattered congregation.[7]

CONTEXT FOR MINISTRY

Supervision occurs in a work milieu, and this milieu assumes some presence of need. More simply, supervision requires a context in which meaningful work takes place, some setting that calls forth a ministering response to human situations. It may be "religious" or "secular," but a ministry of supervision assumes a context that has transformational potential, that is, a context in which persons and institutions may be strengthened in ministry. This assumes that the remaining components described below are in place or can be created.

EXPERT SUPERVISOR

The presence and action of an excellent supervisor is **the** critical condition for effective supervision. People can work, learn, and grow even in deprived contexts if there is a faithful and good supervisor. Such a person should not only be educated for this responsibility but also be engaged in continuing education and supervision as a way of maintaining a high quality in the task. Weekly supervisory conversations of not less than an hour in length are the norm. These may take place in one-to-one settings or in small peer or staff groups, preferably both. Whether in individual or multiple-person staff arrangements, the supervisory conversation needs to be kept inviolate from the intrusion of routine operational concerns which can be handled separately.

PEER GROUP

Although there is a great deal of ministry that is necessarily done in isolation from peers (though certainly not from people), there is a critical need for persons in ministry to have a small group of peers among whom reflection or ministry can occur. In multiple-person staff situations this may be simple to arrange. Pastors, however, are often in one-person staff parishes where in-house peer relationships are not possible. Other professionals may also lack natural relationships that can or are unwilling to pursue group supervision. In such cases it is incumbent upon them to seek out nearby peers for supervisory conversation. This is important for the feedback value of the group, as well as for the support and resources that such relationships provide. Although we benefit from a one-to-one supervisory relationship, we maximize the benefits when we include peer supervision.

COVENANT-MAKING

As an agreement, a covenant is contractual. It spells out the terms in which work will be done. I am calling for more than a contract. Pastoral supervision requires covenant-making within its ancient understanding that it is an experience of gift between the covenanted partners, one in which there is "a change of being; a covenanted people is a people changed utterly by the covenant."[8] It is this that makes the supervisory covenant an extension of the ministry of the Christian (Covenant) community. Its creation and fulfillment brings together several "pieces" upon which ministry can proceed. It names the participants, states expectations, defines responsibilities, identifies resources, sets forth an accountability structure, and provides for change. Supervision cannot be effective without it.

FEEDBACK/EVALUATION

Ministry can only be complete when the persons doing it are able to integrate the experiences and insights that emerge out of the ministry for which they are held accountable. Their self-awareness, skill development, theological understanding, and faith commitment are but fragmented pieces of a picture until they put them together into some composite view of who they are, what they do, how they understand faith, and the implications of all this for their spiritual pilgrimage. There are two related processes involved. Feedback is the on-going "mirroring" that occurs as persons who are being supervised meet with their supervisor(s), peer(s), and/or lay committee. Here they receive verbal images of the way they are perceived, get a "reading" on the results of their ministry, and make significant decisions. Evaluation is the periodic formalization of the feedback when the composite picture becomes focused for a point in time. Both are occasions for mutually speaking the truth in love in face-to-face dialogue. The supervisee's self-evaluation is the starting point. If feedback occurs regularly and fully, there will be no surprises in evaluation.

PARTICIPATION OF LAITY

While one may ordinarily refer to the participation of laity in a parish context, the term "laity" here refers more broadly to the persons who, in any particular context, are lay rather than professional—whatever they may be in some other context. The purpose of lay participation is to share the covenant-making and feedback/evaluation processes, facilitate a support system, and serve as liaison between the person being supervised and the context. Some parish and non-parish arrangements call for a committee of persons to do this; where it is not already provided, a lay committee can be created. In either case laity, like the supervisors whose work they extend, should be trained for their responsibilities.

CRITERIA FOR EVALUATING SUPERVISORS

A great deal has been learned from the helping professions about the nature of helping relationships. Each profession has contributed to the theory and practice in this regard, and their experience is translatable into pastoral supervision. Carl Rogers defines a helping relationship as "one in which one of the participants intends that there should come about, in one or both parties, more appreciation of, more expression of, more functional use of the latent resources of the individual."[9]

Building on that idea, it is appropriate to think of supervision as one kind of helping relationship, one that is central to ministry. The question is not whether we will be engaged in supervision in the church but whether we will be committed to excellence in this aspect of ministry. Excellence requires not only the conditions for effectiveness already identified but the presence of certain attitudes, qualities and skills in the persons who do it. The following is such a "working list" developed and used at the Center for Supervisory Studies.[10]

Attitudes
>
> Owns the supervisory role
>
> Comfortable in both one-to-one and group relationships
>
> Vulnerable/willing to take risks
>
> Appreciates ministry as vocation
>
> Open to new insights
>
> Has clear sense of own goals
>
> Open to growth
>
> Seeks supervision for self
>
> Open to diverse persons/life styles
>
> Aware of his/her strengths and weaknesses as a supervisor

Qualities
>
> Authentic
>
> Accurate self-understanding
>
> Person-oriented
>
> Possesses a sustaining faith
>
> Committed to supervision
>
> Sensitive to personal/interpersonal dynamics and behavior
>
> Demonstrates congruity between theory and practice
>
> Sensitive to sexism/racism issues
>
> Sensitive to issues of social justice

Skills
Administration
Able to enter into and maintain a supervisory covenant
Holds supervisee(s) accountable
Faithful to supervisory time
Shares agenda-setting
Exercises/shares authority
Differentiates own needs from those of supervisee(s)
Teaching
Encourages self-directed learning
Assists in theological reflection on meaning of ministry
Helps supervisee(s) identify growing edges
Nourishes wholistic development of supervisee(s)
Is a good model for ministry, including a willingness and ability to
articulate his/her own faith journey
Engages in mutual teaching/learning
Enables supervisee(s) to take responsibility for own lives
Caring
Differentiates between counseling/spiritual direction/supervision
Supports supervisee(s) in strengths and weaknesses
Listens carefully, patiently
Differentiates between own feelings and those of supervisee(s)
Fully present to supervisee(s)
Recognizes and deals openly with feelings (those of the supervisee(s)
and his/her own)
Consultation
Avoids management of supervisee(s) life
Nourishes supervisee(s)' self-supervision
Shares available resources
Available
Offers opinions as options
Skilled in use of the supervisory conversation
Evaluation
Encourages supervisee(s)' self-assessment
Provides honest feedback and evaluation
Makes connections between covenant and evaluation
Seeks evaluation for her/his self
Confronts creatively, constructively

It is one thing to identify criteria, it is another to use them in an acceptable evaluation system. The factors that produce massive resistance to any evaluation procedures have already been described. However, if supervision is to maintain the integrity I am proposing, it must provide ways in which supervisors and supervisory settings can monitor their ministries.

There are specific ways that these criteria can be used to enhance supervisory practice. Of most importance is their use by supervisors to evaluate themselves. Beyond that the criteria can be shared with peers and supervisees as a way of inviting feedback.

At the Center for Supervisory Studies we use them in two ways. At a beginning level we ask participants in our basic course on "The Principles and Practice of Supervision" to evaluate themselves in writing and to engage in a self-peer evaluation process based on these criteria. They are then free to adapt them in whatever supervisory setting they regularly work. At an advanced level, persons who move from the course into our Certification Program engage in an ongoing supervision of their supervision, utilizing these criteria with multiple persons who can give them candid assessment: their supervisor(s), peers who know their work, and supervisees in their work settings. We have found this to be a very creative process.

Growth as a supervisor is not automatic. Even applying criteria for evaluation does not insure supervisory effectiveness. Behind the certification program at CSS is the conviction that the attitudes, qualities, and skills named above can be developed in some persons if not natively present and that they need to be constantly nourished. Certification creates an avenue for supervisors to intentionally and systematically develop these characteristics and to continue in their enhancement. This not only addresses one of the issues arising out of our study reported earlier but suggests a direction for the church if it is serious about the quality of this part of its ministry.

SUMMARY

In presenting the foregoing model and method of supervision, I have worked from a pastoral perspective. It should be evident, however, that the model makes use of the insights from several professional disciplines. It addresses the basic characteristics of supervision described in Chapter III, either reflecting these characteristics or being consistent with them. That is one of the model's strengths; it enables both clergy and laity to utilize the process with equal comfort and competence. The model assumes education in its theory and practice along with ongoing supervision to ensure its quality. In addition, this model takes seriously the lingering issues, also identified earlier, growing out of the study of supervision in other professions. The precise ways of implementing both the model and the method are adaptive to each setting in which they are utilized.[11]

ENDNOTES

1. I refer to Rudolph Ekstein and Robert S. Wallerstein, *The Teaching and Learning of Psychotherapy* (New York: International Universities Press, 1972) and Ronald H. Sunderland, "A Concept of Ministry Which Employs the Supervisory Process Derived from Clinical Pastoral Education," (Unpublished S.T.M. Thesis, Perkins School of Theology, Southern Methodist University, 1968). The dates of the publications may appear confusing; the explanation is that Sunderland used an earlier edition of Ekstein and Wallerstein, but the material referred to is the same.

2. Were this an ordained pastor, the jurisdictional "superintendent" or a consultant might become participants. There are other potential "connections" with the larger community.

3. Thomas W. Klink, "Supervision as a Routine Process in Professional Education in Ministry," *Duke Divinity School Review* 33 (Autumn 1968): 155-73.

4. See Robert Perske, "The Use of the Critical Incident Report," *Journal of Pastoral Care* 20 (September 1966): 156-61. Perske, however, combines the critical incident and verbatim methods.

5. See James D. Glasse, *Putting It Together in the Parish* (Nashville, TN: Abingdon Press, 1972), 86-105, for his model; also Robert A. Evans and Thomas D. Parker, *Christian Theology: A Case Method Approach* (New York: Harper and Row, 1976) for an adaptation of the Harvard Business School model for theological education.

6. I am indebted to the many persons who have participated with me in supervision for refining both the stages and the questions. They grow out of the practice of supervision.

7. The material in this section has been adapted from two papers that I have written: "Models of Supervision," the report of a workshop that I led for ATFE and published in its *Report of Proceedings* of its Fifteenth Biennial Consultation on Theological Field Education, January 10-13, 1979, 132-39, and "Essential Components of a Field Education Program," a working paper presented to the New Field Education Directors' Clinic at the Seventeenth Biennial Consultation of ATFE, San Antonio, Texas, January 12-15, 1983, and published in its *Report of Proceedings*, 17-23. See these sources for their direct application to the supervision of theological students in their field experience.

8. William F. May, "Code and Covenant or Philanthropy and Contract?" *Ethics in Medicine*, ed. Stanley Joel Reiser, Arthur J. Dyck, and William J. Curran, (Cambridge, MA: M.I.T. Press), 69.

9. Carl R. Rogers, *On Becoming a Person* (Boston: Houghton-Mifflin Company, 1970), 40.

10. These criteria have been adapted partly from multiple evaluation materials being used in a variety of supervisory settings and partly from experimentation in my own supervisory work with supervisors who have participated in our program at CSS.

11. For example, the material in this chapter provides the basis for the field education program at United Theological Seminary, Dayton, Ohio. Another school choosing to utilize it would find it adaptable to its own particular needs and setting.

CHAPTER V

LEVELING SOME UNEVEN GROUND: THEOLOGY AND SUPERVISION

It is important to return in the final two chapters to the concerns with which we began, namely, a discussion of the theological dimensions of pastoral supervision. While these concerns have been implicit throughout the book, it is necessary finally to make them as explicit as possible as grounding for the church's ministry of supervision.

I choose to do that in two ways. In this chapter I will present my own theological reflections on supervision which are always in movement. These reflections represent what can happen when we let our experience and heritage (past and present) speak to us. In my case, it moved me to "systematize" my understanding of supervision. In the final chapter I will describe a way of doing theological reflection which can be used by supervisors and supervisees to think theologically about ministry.

TOWARD A THEOLOGY OF SUPERVISION

I want to be clear at the outset about what is meant by "theology." It is understood here as the attempt to interpret and describe human experience in relationship to whatever we understand to be God's activity in the world where human experience occurs.[1] This is seen as a dynamic rather than static discipline, meaning that it is forged daily out of our participation in the world rather than coming to us as a once-for-all set of convictions that have been handed down as "right" for us. This appears to be thoroughly consistent with the way biblical writers theologized and is therefore a worthy model for our use. If there are readers who feel that this is more humanistic than theological, I can only say that, confronted simultaneously with conflicting theological systems and complicated "worldly" decisions, it is not some pronouncement about divine reality that alone must determine how I live but also how I experience God's activity in the arena of my own life. It is in this arena that the religious convictions out of which I live are finally formed. Therefore what is presented here moves **toward** a theology of supervision and makes no claim for being complete or final.

It is necessary that we come to terms with the full impact of this direction of thought, because to suggest a theology of supervision is to break open a path between two critical issues in the church. The first issue is the **role of theology in ministry**. On the one hand, it should go without saying that Christians do their ministry within some theological context. The scandal of the church is that this context is so diverse (and divisive) that there is little common understanding about either what the context is or the resulting ministry should be. I would resist any attempt to codify either one so as to create uniformity of faith and practice; a variety of ministries are a part of Christ's gift to His church. Yet, the effectiveness of Christ's ministry among us is weakened by our failure as Christians to be clear about who we are, what we are about, and for whose purpose we offer our commitment.

In light of our inability to find any unity on a Christian theology of ministry, it may appear presumptuous to suggest a theology of one segment of that ministry. The multiplicity of responsibilities, added to the multiplicity of doctrines among us, fragments the ministry (and ministers) enough already. Must there be, therefore, a separate theology of supervision, and is that different from one's theology of church administration, counseling, preaching, or social change? God forbid. At the same time, if pastoral supervision is as central to ministry as we have already claimed, we would be negligent if we failed to consider the theological insights that emerge out of its practice.

On the other hand, an equally critical issue for the church is the **way in which we go about claiming theological assumptions**. From the beginning of human history people have tried to interpret and describe their experience with both the familiar and the mysterious in their existence. This has involved them in attempts to figure out the nature of divine existence and activity. Of most importance to Christians has been the biblical record which represents the way people of a particular tradition have understood their lives in relationship to what they believed to be revelations of the one true God. Across the years the church, as one expression of that biblical tradition, has produced a multitude of interpreters of the faith who have created numerous theological systems by which their particular interpretations have come to be identified—biblical literalism, ortho-doxy, neo-orthoxy, conservatism, liberalism; or Arminianism, Calvinism, Lutheranism, Wesleyanism; or theologies based upon naturalism, existentialism, demythology, secu-larization, or radicalism. And there are others, all of which have contributed both to our understanding and confusion.

This is not to criticize all such efforts except to say that too many of us have opted out of the theologizing process by letting the most brilliant thinkers or prolific writers (They are not always identical!) do our thinking for us. (To wit, how many pastors I have heard excuse themselves by saying: "I am not a theologian," so . . . !) The result is that we adopt somebody else's system for ourselves—or are blown about among the many winds of doctrine; we become Barthians, or Tillichians, or Bultmannians—or eclectics. In any case, we seek to apply some "authority's" system to our experience—or worse, to other people's experience—as though that finally explains what life and God are all about, only to come up hard against the fact every once in a while that nothing in our adopted system works to explain what we are experiencing. Then we wonder what went wrong.

Supervision, however, as we have seen, is practiced in an arena between action (our doing of ministry) and reflection (our attempt to interpret the meaning of what we have done). In this arena, theology begins not with what somebody says is or ought to be true but with what we are discovering to be true for ourselves. Our action (ministry) is informed by what others believe, but it also raises new and different questions not yet considered or fully explained. These we bring under critical reflective thought (analysis, evaluation) as a way of figuring out answers for ourselves that make sense out of things. Systems of thought belonging to other people's experience (the scriptures, systematic theologies) are not neglected, but rather our own system of thought becomes forged out of our dialogue or encounter with both our experience and that of other theologians.

Thus it is appropriate to speak in pastoral supervision of "doing theology" rather than "applying theology," realizing that both doing and applying are integral to our theologizing. Supervision of ministry is the process that ensures and facilitates the "theological doing." It is my claim that this is the most creative and useful approach to theology for the work of supervision.

Therefore, in suggesting a theology of supervision, care has been exercised to remain faithful to the fundamental principle that experience, not systematic formulae, is the starting point. The theological assumptions outlined here have grown out of the practice of supervision and become a way of interpreting what at least I have found to be true in my own ministry.

SOME SIGNPOSTS ALONG THE WAY

Since the reflections here attempt only to move toward a theology of supervision, the affirmations that follow can perhaps best be viewed as signposts along the way. It is hoped that they will motivate pastoral supervisors, current and potential, to reflect on their own experience and tradition in a manner that will make each one's theology lively, unique, and useful.

INTENTION: RESPONSIBLE LIFE

The first signpost points to the affirmation that **the creative intent for each of us is that we live responsibly**. This is to be done in the existential situation of every person; it has a special meaning for pastoral supervision, because supervision begins with responsibility. The following "slice" of experience with which I have had at least minimal contact serves as an illustration.

While in Great Britain some years ago doing research for this book, I came to know several persons who were seeking to appropriate Jesus' teaching and action concerning responsible life. They identified themselves as Radical Christians. Convinced that Jesus is the one who deserves their commitment, they accepted different ways of expressing it except in their common commitment to responsible action in the world in the name of Christ. One such group was the Ashram Community House located in the inner city of Sheffield, England. There a small group of people lived in community, pooling their incomes and their energies in ministry. The concerns of the poor in their neighborhood became their action agenda. They had signal influence in several critical issues, one being to bring about an alteration in the city's plan to demolish the houses in the area, which would have dislodged people from their homes to make way for modern construction.

The result was renovation of the older but very substantial structures and stability of the neighborhood. One of the original founders of the House, Roy Crowder, describes their presence in that situation as a "Piece of Incarnation" and refers to the process by which they order their life and ministry as "action-reflection."[2] He resists the use of the word "supervision" as a way of accounting for what happens, but it illustrates what I believe occurs when reflection on experience is taken seriously. I suspect the terminology is unimportant.

Those of us engaged in pastoral supervision, whether supervisors or supervisees, share the experience of the Hebrew writers whose reflections on the meaning of life were combined to form the early chapters of the Bible. It is our witness with them that:

1. We are responsible for the natural world; Genesis 1:27-28 declares that God created us in the divine image and gave us dominion over the earth; from the standpoint of a supervisory responsibility, it is an awesome thought that such unbelievable trust could be expressed as to turn control of the earth over to us;

2. We are responsible for ourselves; the entire third chapter of Genesis is an account of "The Fall" or "original sin" of Adam and Eve; in spite of all the excuses and evasions, the story leaves no doubt that we, symbolized here by representative man and woman, are required to make our own decisions and are held accountable for the results; and,

3. We are responsible for each other; in Genesis 4:8-15 the story of Cain and Abel reminds us that we are to "keep"—that is, protect, defend, care for—one another; such concern is required not only on behalf of Abel, the one wronged, but also Cain, the wrongdoer. And in the law by which the Hebrews were directed to order their life there is instruction, later appro-priated by Jesus in his summary of the law: "You shall love your neighbor as yourself" (Lev. 19:18).

It is worth pointing out that these Genesis passages are prime examples of the way the Hebrews engaged in theological reflection on human experience. Hebrew law, which predated these passages, was far-reaching in its ethical demands, though its fulfillment by the masses of people depended heavily on official sanction. It reached its highest verbal expression in the preaching of Amos who is known as the social prophet because of his bold and pointed condemnation of the injustices practiced among the rich ruling class in Israel and his clarion call to "let justice roll down like waters and righteousness like an everflowing stream" (Am. 5:24). Tragically, prophets are not without honor except in their own country; Amos's own people ignored his insightful declarations about the consequences of irresponsibility. We haven't done too well by him since, either, though we enjoy quoting him!

Jesus too was specific in what he had to say about responsible living, and his standards are tough. If we would follow him we are asked to deny ourselves (Mk. 8:34), even to the point of distributing whatever wealth we possess among the poor and living as one of them (Mk. 10:21). The early Christian community in Jerusalem did just that in the days immediately following the resurrection and ascension, selling their posses-sions, distributing them among the needy, and pooling their resources in communal life (Acts 2:44-45); the results of irresponsibility for people who made that commitment were severe (Acts 5:1-11). The Gospel picture of the final judgment describes God's approval going to those who have shared what little or much they have with the sick, naked, hungry, and imprisoned; those who fail to do so reap God's punishment (Mt. 25:31-46). And, in a slightly different vein, Matthew reports Jesus teaching that we must be perfect in our "keeping" by loving and praying even for our enemies (Mt. 5:43-48).

Ministry brings us head-on against these very kinds of responsible situations out of which the ancient biblical historians, the Hebrew prophets, and Jesus himself formed their own "theologies." Supervision provides the opportunity to reflect critically on our ministry in those situations as a way of coming to terms with what they mean for us. It creates a setting in which we can make responsible decisions about ourselves, our ministry, and the world in which we minister—and it presses us to clarity and commitment. Supervision is a microcosm of the world; all the elements of responsibility that the world can throw at us are potentially present, giving us an arena in which to work out our response.

Certainly there is no agreement among Christians about what constitutes an appropriate response to the Gospel. Not many have chosen the radical way, and there are equally sincere persons who in fact see that approach as inappropriate. One point is obvious, however, and the expectations of Scripture are clear: we are charged with responsible oversight of both life and things in a world seen to be under God's authority. Supervision does not presuppose the nature of the response, but it does enable a response to be made. I believe that it is the church's business to make that happen.

ACTUALITY: ESTRANGEMENT VS. RELATIONSHIP

Yet, for all that we have affirmed about living responsibly, the actual condition of human existence is that **we live between estrangement and relationship**. This is our second signpost, and it lifts up the predicament of people in general. Those committed to "living Christ's life among the poor" emphasize one side of the problem, but the poor are not the only alienated persons in society.[3] Estrangement is a universal problem knowing no bounds of social class, though it is interesting that the para/alternative church movement cited above which has succeeded in creating communities of action and support have caught on primarily among the less affluent. This may teach us that the more affluent are particularly vulnerable to the tragedy of estrangement.

There are two almost predictable reactions that occur in our basic CSS course for pastoral supervisors. The participants are normally persons who have been in ministry as pastors or as other professionals for several years. As they engage in the experience of reflecting on one another's acts of ministry as a way of feeling out the supervisory roles, they invariably say either: "I wish I had been able to have this experience when I was in school," or "I wish this experience didn't have to end; it is the most trusting group of people I've ever been in." I have seen persons who felt lonely, isolated, and fearful come to a totally new sense of colleague support as a result of the supervisory experience.

One such pastor came into the course partly because it offered a new experience and partly because it was a way of getting back into a theological atmosphere. (Incidentally, both reasons suggest a certain dissatisfaction with one's present status, but the second particularly points to a potential theological famine among pastors.) Once into the course he discovered that his expectations had been accurate but inadequate. Surrounded by others who had come for similar reasons, he found himself sharing facets of his life that he had not talked about with anyone before. They concerned mostly the loneliness he felt as a pastor without colleagues with whom he could let down his hair in honest conversation. He saw possibilities for ministry in himself that he hadn't felt people needed or wanted, but now at least he could tell somebody about them. Before the course ended he had not only gained a group of colleagues who had an ongoing interest in his ministry, but he had found some new ways of sharing himself as a person and minister with his parishioners who offered him a community of support and encouragement.

A similar story could be told for lay people. Particularly, bridges between lay and clergy have been built as a way of decreasing the sense of estrangement between them. With students the change has been less noticeable because the sense of isolation is not as great, but there are notable exceptions. All of this is to say that, even among those who minister in and through the church, life is lived out between estrangement and relationship.

Reuel Howe suggests that a root problem of our culture is **separation**. In spite of our physical closeness in an urban society, the way in which we organize our lives pulls us apart rather than toward people. We become **alienated** from one another through the strain imposed upon us by the tensions between a desire for intimacy and the need for distance. The result is **loneliness**—the feeling of being isolated even from those near to us. This is particularly true, Howe says, for those who have known love:

> Each of us lives in a lonely place on the far side of the love we have known, and each longs to have those whom we love come and be with us there. Those who would love us are hindered by their own unanswered need of love and therefore cannot reach us in spite of their longing to do so. Likewise do they live on the far side of the love they have known, and they long for us to be with them there; and no matter how we try, we cannot quite reach them because of our self concerns. From the human point of view, this is the great frustration. It is the frustration of being able to love but not being able to love fully; the frustration of being made for love and yet living a relationship which, while it can give much, fails to give all that it promises. Finally, there is the frustration of being unable to accept love, in spite of our great need for it. We cannot accept love because we are too worried about not being loved, which is to say that we do not believe that the love we really need exists.[4]

The Bible confirms this picture of our human dilemma, a condition that Paul Tillich refers to as a state of sin.[5] But it also affirms that beyond estrangement there is relationship. The writers of Ephesians and 1 Peter describe how uniquely true this is for the church. Jesus Christ has made possible a new relationship between people who were once strangers and alien to one another. He has broken down the dividing wall of hostility that kept them separate and brought a new common participation in the community of faith. Whereas once their alienation left them even without hope, they now have a future together, having been reconciled to God and one another in a bond of peace. "So then you are no longer strangers and aliens, but you are citizens with the saints and also members of the household of God ..." (Eph. 2:19). "Once you were not a people but now you are God's people; once you had not received mercy but now you have received mercy" (1 Pet. 2:10).

Reference here is particularly to the fact that the enmity between Jews and Gentiles has been brought to an end by both being fully invited into the new community of faith built upon Jesus Christ. We know from experience that in actual practice the enmity still exists because of our failure to fully enter into the new relationship. And this is precisely my point; we continue tragically to live in estrangement when the doors of relationship are open to us. One of those doors leads us by way of the experience of pastoral supervision where at least some of the dividing walls have been torn down. So says Howe:

> Again, another effect of being separated from one another may be seen in the way we seek out anyone who will listen to us when we need to talk. And if the listeners have ears to hear, they hear people talk mostly about their loneliness and their sense of separation. This is one reason why counselors are in such great demand. A sign of the state of relation in which we live is seen in the fact that only by paying can some of us find people who will listen to us.[6]

Pastoral supervision offers a means of changing that.

CALLING: SERVANTHOOD

This leads to a third signpost to which the signs of supervision point, namely, that **the calling upon the community of faith is to servanthood**. Two observations already made come to focus here. One is that the relationship that supervision makes possible is not created simply for its own sake, as a thing to be indulged in as though it were a security blanket to protect us from the chill winds of the world. The other is that supervision always assumes work (action) as well as learning; there is always a task to be done. Supervision must focus on both.

To illustrate, Philip and Phoebe Anderson, in their discussion of the house church as an alternative for Christian community, write very much in the language of Howe when they describe the way in which the congregation provides a healing relationship for persons in varied states of estrangement. The pattern by which they reflect on their experience together sounds consistent (though not identical) with the process that has been suggested in my own model of supervision. It begins with a description of a "piece" of experience, moves through an analysis of it, and concludes with an attempt to understand it theologically.[7] John Vincent criticizes the Andersons' approach as being too subjective, as lacking the objective corrective of the Gospel.[8] The criticism is valid in terms of the supervisory process also if it indeed becomes arrested at a subjective level and fails to let the Gospel bring both confirmation and judgment. My problem with Vincent's criticism is that he tends to err on the other side to the neglect of the subjective concerns. To repeat, supervision must focus on both.

The temptation to neglect one side or the other is a very real one. It is therefore important to be clear about both what we do and why we do it. It does make a difference whether our ministry is done for our own emotional purposes, for the sake of institutional survival (the other extreme), or for the sake of Christian ministry. Supervision helps sort this out.

Helen was a theological student at the time of the events to be described here. She had come to seminary convinced that she wanted to become a parish pastor—an appropriate goal, except that bound up in her several motivations was a burning desire to prove something to her minister back in the home church who didn't think that women should be pastors. Fortunately, in spite of his opinion, she had made her commitment and enrolled in seminary. The issue did not prove to be a hindrance in her studies until she entered her parish supervised ministry assignment. Then, with the opportunity to reflect on her work, it became clear that her desire to prove herself was interfering with her ability to relate to the people in the parish where she worked—particularly the male supervisor upon whom she had transferred her feelings about the pastor back home. Her native skills, her firm commitment to ministry, and her openness of mind and spirit, however, were among the assets she brought to the occasion. Thus, with the guidance of a skilled supervisor, Jim, who was able to help her identify and work through her motivations, she was able to refine her reasons and direct her energies more constructively. Particularly this meant working out her reasons for being a parish pastor; it meant answering the question of whose purposes she must really serve if she was to minister in Christ's name.

Now what happened here? First of all, pastoral supervision became the process by which she was able, in the midst of doing ministry, to reflect upon both her task and herself in the task; it was the means by which she was able to develop her ability to minister effectively while, at the same time, come to a more appropriate and useful understanding of who she was as a minister (pastoral identity). Second, pastoral supervision became an important arena, though certainly not the only one, in which she forged her response to the Gospel as a Christian; in this case it enabled her to come to terms with her theology of ministry.

I have suggested that this be understood as a call to servanthood. It is a call; Jesus said: "You did not choose me, but I chose you. And I appointed you . . ." (Jn. 15:16). It is a call upon the entire community of faith; Paul wrote: "Now you are the body of Christ and individually members of it. And God has appointed in the church . . . apostles . . . prophets . . . teachers . . . etc." (1 Cor. 12:27-28). It is a call not to "lord" or "exercise authority" over others but to be in the spirit of Jesus who "came not to be served but to serve . . ." (Mk. 10:42-45) and who has bound his service with ours as friends (Jn. 15:15).

It is significant that the three titles often combined and given to Jesus by the church—Prophet, Priest, and Ruler—are all servant roles. We have often interpreted them differently, especially the ruling office, but each of them derive their power not from authority but from servanthood. They are, in fact, supervisory roles, not in the sense of ruling over people but in the sense of enabling them to fulfill their call. Thus, a supervisor who saw himself as a servant could help Helen come to terms with her own servanthood.

There are three central concepts in supervision highlighted in the story about Helen. One is the importance of supervisors having worked their way through the issues of authority and knowing the struggle; the signposts were clearly in view so that Jim could keep Helen's situation focused. The second is the necessity of supervisors being aware and in charge of their own feelings; being temporarily cast in the role of the adversary (Helen's home town minister), Jim could use the occasion not for choosing sides but for mirroring back to Helen the consequences of her displaced anger. The third is that by modeling servanthood in their own ministries, supervisors are able to demonstrate what they point to; Jim's own competent fulfillment of the servant role gave proof of its effectiveness as a style of ministry.

MODEL: JESUS

This suggests the fourth signpost. It is that **Jesus is the model for our practice as Christians in ministry**. This has been stated briefly at points already, but I want to make it obvious now. Christians take their clue from Jesus, and our knowledge of him comes from two sources—the Gospel record and our encounter with him in our own experience. Both sources are experiential and equally important. The Gospels are the record from the past, and they are sufficient for that view; what other people write about him may help or hinder, but what the people who knew him report to us is primary. Therefore, the simple Gospel story in the New Testament is one source from which we get our model for ministry. The other is from our own personal encounter with Jesus. He is the Living Lord of the church who meets us at every turn in daily experience. His living presence as well as his teaching and example confirm and judge our every thought and action. Amid all the theologies that people propose, in the end it is what we do about Jesus as the Christ in our own lives that determines who we are and how we live as Christians.

What this means in the diverse situations in which we find ourselves is another full study in itself, and others have addressed it.[9] My interest here is to put this in the language of supervision, in which we speak frequently of "modeling." The focus in this setting is on supervisors as participants in the ministry they supervise, as persons competent in the professions they represent. Supervisors need to model (exemplify, practice) what they advocate.

I am indebted to Ron Sunderland for his description of Jesus as supervisor. I report here from memory on the basis of remarks that he made, and therefore with the slant of my own understanding of the Gospel record.[10] This impresses me as an excellent way of viewing the supervisor's role. Jesus:

1. Was engaged in the ministry that he invited people to share;
2. Gathered about him a small group of learners (disciples) with whom he shared the tasks of ministry as they were able;
3. Met regularly with the disciples to reflect on their common experience;
4. Filled the multiple roles of teacher, colleague, friend, and confidante with the disciples but always as one who spoke and acted with an authority based on personhood rather than position;
5. Maintained both intimacy and distance with the disciples, participating with them in the celebrations and drudgeries of human existence but frequently withdrawing for times alone;
6. Instructed, corrected, exemplified, chided, loved, expressed anger, supported, challenged, and "stuck by" the ones with whom he had accepted responsibility;
7. Entrusted to his learners the ministry for which he gave even the last breath of his life with confidence in their ability to get on with the task;
8. Finally, gave to those whom he had supervised his full authority to do even greater things than he had been able to do.

That is pastoral supervision at its best!

NEW VARIATIONS ON AN OLD THEME

A useful purpose may be served at this point by taking a page from the world of music. The composer of music seeks and is, in fact, responsible for creating something new when (s)he writes a song or a symphony. There is some ultimate limit to the combination of notes and tunes that is possible, so every new composition is necessarily dependent upon and influenced by what has been written before. Yet each composer's aim is to bring something new into being, something which represents him or her self but which also speaks to other people with kindred emotions. Occasionally this takes the form of a new arrangement of a previously composed tune, where the purpose is not to produce a totally different work but simply to put an already good melody into a musical expression that captures more and varied moods. Some of the greatest moments of musical listening or participation occur in experiencing new variations on old themes.

It is in something of this position that we find ourselves when we describe a theology of supervision. To restate a basic premise of this book, pastoral and supervisory tasks are integral to the church and inseparably related to each other. Though we have usually interpreted it one way or the other, the pastoral office in the New Testament includes **both** the person doing the ministry and the kind of ministry being done. Furthermore, ministry, of which pastoring and supervising are parts, is a calling upon the whole people of God. While we have given lip service to this throughout the church's history, the time is ripe for us to take seriously its full meaning. But, as in Jesus' parable of the bridegroom, no one puts new wine into old wineskins lest the skins burst and the wine be lost. It is necessary to put new wine into fresh skins (Mk. 2:22). I believe that our current experience with pastoral supervision is new wine in fresh skins for the church.

My thought can now be set within the framework of two separated but related passages in Scripture. Jeremiah's work as a prophet took place in the latter days of Judah, beginning about 626 BC. The northern kingdom, Israel, had collapsed nearly a hundred years earlier, and the southern kingdom was in the throes of death—a fate which indeed occurred within Jeremiah's lifetime. In his early years he had seen signs of hope, for King Josiah had ordered a renovation of the temple in order to remove any signs of pagan worship and to restore it as the center of national life. In the process a book of law believed to be Deuteronomy was discovered, and Josiah's reading of it prompted the king to make a covenant with God, in support of which he instituted a massive religious reform throughout the country. Symbols, altars, and priests devoted to pagan gods were destroyed, and the worship of Jehovah was once again proclaimed throughout the land. Jeremiah had invested himself with vigor in support of the reform.

As with previous similar attempts, however, the reform lasted only as long as its leader lived; upon King Josiah's death his sons who succeeded him reversed their father's policies and Judah returned to worshipping Baal. In the face of such a disappointing turn of events, Jeremiah sought an explanation. He concluded that the reform had not gone deep enough; it had removed the visible signs of paganism, but it had not changed the loyalties of the people; it had been superficial, and Judah would pay with its life. But there will come a day, he declared, when Israel and Judah will come of age. When that happens, old excuses or unfaithfulness will no longer work; new responsibilities will be required; a new order based on individual as well as corporate accountability will be initiated, supported by a new theology descriptive of the way God will act in the future toward Israel. All this will come about through a new covenantal relationship between God and the people of Israel.

In those days they shall no longer say: The parents have eaten sour grapes, and the children's teeth are set on edge. But all shall die for their own sins; the teeth of everyone who eats sour grapes shall be set on edge. The days are surely coming, says the Lord, when I will make a new covenant with the house of Israel and the house of Judah. It will not be like the covenant that I made with their ancestors when I took them by the hand to bring them out of the land of Egypt— a covenant that they broke, though I was their husband, says the Lord. But this is the covenant that I will make with the house of Israel after those days, says the Lord: I will put my law within them, and I will write it on their hearts; and I will be their God, and they shall be my people. No longer shall they teach one another or say to each other, "Know the Lord," for they shall all know me, from the least of them to the greatest, says the Lord; for I will forgive their iniquity, and remember their sin no more (Jer. 31:29-34).

Before pursuing this for its meaning for pastoral supervision, it is necessary to introduce a second passage from Paul's writings in the New Testament. In the second epistle to the Christians in Corinth, Paul was under compulsion to establish his personal credentials as an apostle. He had, of course, been instrumental initially in the formation of the Corinthian Church about AD 50. His first epistle to the believers there, written four to six years later, had dealt in straightforward language with some thorny problems that had arisen among them, among the more serious being division and immorality. However, there were members of the group who questioned Paul's authority and therefore his teaching; some even questioned his veracity since he had failed to make a return visit as promised. All of this put his position with them in some jeopardy, so he began his second letter with a somewhat labored appeal that they accept not only his ministry but himself as one commissioned by God to speak for Christ.

. . . we are not peddlers of God's word like so many; but in Christ we speak as persons of sincerity, as persons sent from God and standing in his presence (2 Cor. 2:17).

What had happened was that a small body of people originally responded to Paul's preaching by becoming Christians and gathering together into a congregation. But the pattern of previous life styles, the pressures of the world around them, and the particular cosmopolitan nature of Corinthian culture had proven to be too much for them. Consequently, at least some of them reverted to old ways. As a corrective, Paul issued very clear, strict instructions about how they should order their individual and corporate life. But torn between Paul, occasional other teachers representing themselves as Apostles, and their pagan roots, the Corinthian Christians simply found it difficult to maintain the strict loyalty asked of them. Paul now appealed to them, therefore, on a new level; he speaks of a new basis upon which he and they might recognize each other as persons of faith. It will be with a new inner discipline, productive of a new identity, growing out of a new covenant different from that of the old legalistic covenant that they will mutually recommend Christ to each other and to the world.

Are we beginning to commend ourselves again? Surely we do not need, as some do, letters of recommendation to you or from you, do we? You yourselves are our letter, written on our hearts, to be known and read by all; and you show that you are a letter of Christ, prepared by us, written not with ink but with the Spirit of the living God, not on tablets of stone but on tablets of human hearts. Such is the confidence that we have through Christ toward God. Not that we are competent of ourselves to claim anything as coming from us; our competence is from God, who has made us competent to be ministers of a new covenant, not of letter but of the Spirit; for the letter kills, but the Spirit gives life (2 Cor. 3:1-6).

Now, with this brief background to both Jeremiah's and Paul's thought, I venture to suggest the framework of a theology of pastoral supervision.

SUPERVISION AS COVENANT

The key to both passages is the teaching about the new covenant. The primary dimension in the framework, therefore, is **a covenant committed to life rather than law**. Both Jeremiah and Paul understood from experience the inadequacy of law to bring about personal change and commitment. None of the legal approaches—the Torah, official pronouncements, or their own inspired instructions—had proven capable of maintaining obedience among the people to what was expected of them. It was not that the old covenant with its requirements and restrictions was bad, though Paul did say that the law had been his undoing (Rom. 7:7-11). It was simply ineffective because it was:

1. **Remote**. It was a covenant initiated by God with a nation long since divided, scattered, and almost non-existent; while it expected mutual loyalty, it was viewed by many as removed from and disinterested in human life.
2. **Inherited**. It had been given to the forefathers of the nation and passed down from one generation to another; while the covenant itself provided for rituals by which each individual and generation were expected to make the nation's story their own, it was not "owned" by the masses upon whom it was "imposed."
3. **Exterior**. While disinterest in the covenant was frequently revised in times of crisis, it did not engage the majority of people at the core of their being out of which daily decisions were made; except with those occasional persons for whom it became an internalized and passionate concern, the old covenant did not have great appeal.
4. **Inflexible**. It was an absolute system narrowly limited to the Hebrews; while it was under constant interpretation by the scholars, it was rigid in its application and restrictive in terms of their increasing participation in the family of nations. There was little room in it for change.

The new covenant, on the other hand, was seen as being life-centered rather than law-centered, as inviting people to become active participants rather than passive observers or at best occasional actors in an ancient drama. To be sure, it was seen as being divinely initiated and sustained, as involving mutuality in the sense of the communal nature of life, and, in Jeremiah, highly idealistic; but there are significant differences. The new covenant:

1. **Calls for mutual accountability**. While both individuals and the corporate

body are always affected by the actions of the other, the new covenant puts new responsibility on individual persons so that they can no longer hide within the shadow of the group. In this sense, response to it is self-determinative and subject to human error but redeemable within the Lord's promise. There continues to be mutual accountability, but the new covenant gives both individuals and the community the freedom and obligation to respond to what it makes possible.

2. **Offers personal ownership**. That which once belonged to someone else in another time, that which had been handed down as a tradition as though it were something to be possessed or worn to preserve family history, becomes personal because it resides and works from within; the new covenant is part and parcel of the heart—the very core of being. Therefore it can no longer be ignored or relegated to the irrelevant, because it is an integral part of individual and community "selfhood."

3. **Is spiritually dynamic**. It is "written," not with ink but with the Spirit of God, not on tablets of stone but on human hearts. "Written" is a figure of speech here, for the new covenant consists not of letter but of Spirit. It is not a code to be obeyed but a Living Presence to be celebrated, a direction to be pursued. It does not negate obedience but changes the nature of that to which obedience is given. It comes not as some far-off transcendent and non-repeatable event but as something that happens anew within each particular life over and over. Therefore it is alive with possibilities both for the present and the future.

4. **Gives life**. The written code kills, but the Spirit gives life. Whereas the old covenant was remembered only in ritual, the new covenant is renewable through participation in the Spirit. It is life-giving because it provides freedom by which personality, ideas, and actions can expand to meet the challenge of the world in which the covenant must be expressed. No longer must people rely upon outside regulations; the new covenant empowers them to live better than the law can either prescribe or require. It sees possibilities otherwise neglected, includes persons otherwise excluded, and enables changes otherwise considered impossible.

For Jeremiah all this lay in the future; for Paul it was already in effect through Jesus Christ who brought the new covenant into being and "who has qualified us to be ministers" of it. This is not the place for an exegesis of Paul's more extended thought on this subject in Romans, but one reference is instructive:

> . . . you have died to the law through the body of Christ, so that you may belong to another, to him who has been raised from the dead in order that we may bear fruit for God. While we were living in the flesh, our sinful passions, aroused by the law, were at work in our members to bear fruit for death. But now we are discharged from the law, dead to that which held us captive, so that we are slaves not under the old written code but in the new life of the Spirit (Rom. 7:4-6).

The careful reader will notice how dependent the language of supervision is upon this description of the covenant. When we speak in supervision of "contract" we are on the edge of what the Scriptures refer to as "covenant." It is, in fact, more appropriate to use the biblical term, because the supervisory covenant is a commitment to life and

103

growth. In simple terms, it is a statement of intention, usually written, which binds the supervisor and supervisee in a mutually agreed-upon process to see that particular segments of ministry are done and reflected upon. In this sense it is legalistic; at the same time, it is fulfilled in new covenant terms.

Therefore when I as a supervisor sit with a supervisee to write a learning/serving (supervisory) covenant, there are two essential elements to be negotiated. One is a description of the ministry to be carried out; the other is a statement of the goals for growth (change) which represent the supervisee's expectations of the experience. What makes them covenantal is the fact that these elements are mutually created and accepted. They constitute a commitment for which we are each individually and mutually accountable, as we say to each other: "Here is what we will endeavor to accomplish together." Such accountability is possible because the covenant is ours, "owned" because it has grown out of and is therefore part of our core of being, written on our hearts as well as on paper, committed to bearing fruit for life rather than death. It is dynamic not simply because it is pastoral in nature, meaning that it grows out of our mutual commitment to each other, but because it is Christ's own life in our time and our experience. This makes it renewable as well as changeable as Christ's way becomes more clear through our daily encounters. Thus we can affirm as before, this covenant too is alive with possibilities for both the present and the future.

It is with such an understanding that we refer in supervision to the right to fail, meaning that such a covenant runs the risk of being inadequate by some standards, limited by our lack of vision, or perhaps impossible to fulfill because we expect too much. The covenant may be broken. If this approach to supervision is too much for us to tolerate, then we may prefer the old covenant with its legalism and controls. The church knows a great deal about old covenant patterns that do not really trust people, that support supervisory styles designed to regulate ministry through conformity to standards and requirements deemed right for everyone. My experience is that they have created instead much anger, frustration, mediocrity, and attrition.

The new covenant does not eliminate failure, but it takes seriously the importance of ministers owning what they do and finding forgiveness for what they fail to do under God's assurance that each of us will pay for our own sins but that God will forgive our iniquities and remember our sin no more. My contention is that given this freedom and promise, the supervision of ministry has potential both to renew the minister and to do Christ's work, for it will not permit us to blend into the anonymity of a profession but forces us into the open where we are known for who we really are.

SUPERVISION AS RELATIONSHIP

This understanding of new covenant suggests a second dimension in the theological framework of pastoral supervision. It is that the new covenant makes possible **a new relationship based on experience rather than knowledge.** In Jeremiah this is assured in the Lord's promise to be Israel's and Judah's God as they are called to be God's people. As it stands, this was not a particularly new thought for a Jew. What is significant about it is that the people will participate in this relationship not primarily as something they know about from hearsay or someone's teaching but as a result of their own encounter with God.

Ownership of the covenant comes through experiencing it for oneself in a relationship with the other participant(s), for a covenant always involves at least two parties in relationship. Furthermore, under the new covenant this is no longer a relationship of unequals but one in which the participants meet on common ground. This is at least part of what Paul meant when, writing to another congregation, he again spoke of the new life made possible by Christ: "So you are no longer a slave but a child, and if a child then also an heir, through God" (Gal. 4:7).

With the coming of Jesus Christ, a new relationship with God was made possible, one in which all persons can know God first hand. If Jesus brought the new covenant into being as I have suggested, then he was modeling it for us when he said to his disciples: "I do not call you servants any longer, because the servant does not know what his master is doing; but I have called you friends, because I have made known to you everything that I have heard from my Father" (Jn. 15:15). The message seems clear: the new covenant has made a new and intimate relationship possible, to which each individual's own experience with Christ provides access.

This does not negate our servanthood ministry described earlier, for that is how Jesus related and how we relate to the world; but in our relationship with Christ we are friends, serving as "Christs" in our own time and place. Consider then the deep meaning for each of us when in the Lord's Supper we say to one another: "I received from the Lord what I now deliver to you . . ." (Paraphrased from 1 Cor. 11:23). In that moment both I and the one to whom I deliver or who delivers to me the body and blood of Jesus are in a full and equal relationship with God through Christ.

Again the language of supervision is noticeable, because pastoral supervision relies upon a kind and quality of relationship which both grows out of and legitimizes the covenantal relationship. What we have found in practice is indeed that it is a relationship based on experience rather than knowledge. Relationships among ministers, laity and clergy, are two-sided. As stated earlier, on the one hand we know each other as colleagues, get along on the surface in a friendly way, and appear to the world as reasonably congenial folk. On the other hand, privately we are suspicious, mistrustful, and envious. We are not known for our ability to confide in one another as we teach that others should confide in us. It is difficult for us to relate on a deep, personal level except perhaps within very narrow circles, and we do not find it easy either to submit our person or work to colleagues for evaluation.

Consequently, we resist supervision, even though (perhaps especially because) we have been told it is good for us. We hesitate to reveal too much to the people who have authority to determine where we will minister or how much we will be paid, meaning that superintending personnel have their hands tied to begin with. But we are reluctant as well to spill our guts to somebody who may later become pastor in our place or even our superior. If we are the supervising person we may succumb to institutional pressures for getting on with the work, so that we have little time or energy for the really personal concerns. For all we know and talk about Christian relationship, we have a hard time entering into it; and because we tend to see supervision as authority rather than as relationship, the covenant goes unfulfilled no matter how appropriate and intentional it is.

We are likely to continue in this estrangement until we have the good fortune of experiencing a good supervisory relationship for ourselves. To be accepted as a peer, as a colleague, as one who is trusted and loved and appreciated **as we are** is an exhilarating, redemptive experience. For this relationship is one of equals; the supervisor stands not over us but with us. That does not mean similarity in age, belief, position, life style, or any other category by which we are inclined to divide ourselves. It is a relationship in which two (or more) people seek to do and reflect on ministry as ministers, both (or all) of whom are "called to the one hope of [our] calling" (Eph. 4:4). It is a coming together of persons who seek to be fully known and understood, and who discover in the knowing and understanding that we do not need to be afraid of one another, that the Christ in each of us reaches out to the other in encouragement and healing.

At its best and in its intent, the supervisory relationship is a paradigm of the relationship of Jesus with his disciples of which I spoke above. I have known it for myself; I have seen it in others. Without it, supervision is little more than a professional function; with it, a piece of the Kingdom of God becomes a reality.

SUPERVISION AS INCARNATION

The third and fourth dimensions are more difficult to describe because they lie behind more than within the Scriptural passages under consideration, but the third can be expressed this way: the supervisory covenantal relationship releases **a potential for a new identity**. In Jeremiah this is hinted at when he says that in the new order the people will know the Lord because they will know themselves as forgiven persons (Jer. 31:34). Paul puts this in terms of Christians being known by others on the basis of being themselves letters of recommendation, written on our hearts, to be known and read by all (2 Cor. 3:2). The implication in both is that if the quality of relationship described above does in fact exist, it is reasonable that as participants we will see ourselves and be seen by others in its light. The suggestion here is that we who participate in a covenantal relationship of such significance will have a view of ourselves and our world that is consistent with it. The new covenant therefore releases the potential for a new identity which, as Peter so forcefully discovered during the late watches of the night when Jesus was on trial, cannot be totally hidden even if one tries (Mk. 14:66-72).

I have used the word incarnation to describe identity because it communicates the central fact upon which Christian theology depends. The Incarnation means that in Jesus, God entered into and became one with human experience. Human life has not been the same since; we understand who we are in a totally new way because of what Jesus showed us about our own existence. The early church—that original community of Jesus' followers—was able to have such a transforming impact on history simply because its people had been with Jesus in a significant relationship. I believe that Jesus continues to impact our world only when we who are his followers Incarnate that Word again—make it become flesh and blood in our time and place. That which happened at a particular event in history (Jn. 1:14) must happen over and over again. Incarnation for our day means that this identity must be released among us who call ourselves Christians, that we come to know ourselves as well as to be known by others as Jesus' continuing Presence in the world—to the end that all might come to know him.

I have suggested earlier that the way Jesus enabled a "school of learners" to become the church models a supervisory style. I am now suggesting that supervision is an incarnational experience when it brings a new identity into being. To review briefly, one objective of supervision is to foster professional identity, meaning that it is intended that we come through the supervised experience to identify with the professional role in which we function. We come to think of ourselves as professionals of a certain kind—doctors, social workers, teachers, ministers. In the church we often refer to this as the development of pastoral identity. This assumes as well the achievement of personal identity, that is, a certain amount of self understanding which enables us to be aware of our actions and the motives that lie behind them. These two identities, professional and personal, have proven to be two major foci of professional education.

Supervision is incarnational when it makes possible still another identity having to do with faith, understood here not as a set of beliefs or blind trust but as action-response; to have faith is to act in response to what we accept as being true. It is this, in fact, that most clearly distinguishes pastoral supervision from that of other professions. We bring to pastoral supervision a history of religious experiences, a certain amount of indoctrination, some past as well as current commitments, a limited or extensive body of knowledge as well as impressions about the faith tradition, and a lifetime of both positive and negative encounter with our particular world which influence how we respond to all the rest. All of these have a way of getting confused and intermixed. The way in which they get sorted out and organized into a "system" out of which we can live and minister is all-important. This is the "stuff" of which theology consists—a way of understanding life so that it makes sense and we are freed to act in Christ's name. It is when such an identity comes alive—is incarnated—in us that we can incarnate that word anew in the world. Pastoral supervision that does not focus on this part of identity has missed the point.

Pastoral supervision is the most likely place for this to happen because it occurs at the intersection of action and reflection. But it will happen only if supervisors have found that identity for themselves. It is hard for the blind to lead the blind. This does not mean that pastoral supervisors have all things worked out neatly and fully; we, too, must live at our growing edges. But it does mean that we must find our identity both as Christians and as supervisors—that is, as those who are willing to be "Christ" to one another in the sense that Jesus was to his disciples. Not everyone can, is willing, or is capable of this identity. But where we are, supervision holds the potential for being incarnational.

SUPERVISION AS JUDGMENT AND GRACE

The fourth and final dimension in a theological framework of pastoral supervision is that **supervision reveals and activates both God's judgment and grace**. I put it this way because God always acts to restore in grace those upon whom judgment comes. Thus we see running through Jeremiah's prophetic message a kind of symphonic theme of restoration; Israel and Judah must be chastened because of their sins, but the time coming will be even better than the time past: "I will make an end of all the nations among which I have banished you, but I will not make an end of you!" (Jer. 46:28) "For I will restore health to you, and your wounds I will heal, says the Lord" (Jer. 30:17). So even though they broke the covenant which had been made when God took them by the hand to bring them out of the land of Egypt, they will be offered a new covenant in which their iniquity will no longer be counted against them. There will be grace after judgment.

For Paul the judgment is personal, against "ungodliness and wickedness" among those who "are without excuse" because "what can be known about God is plain to them, because God has shown it to them" (Rom. 1:18-20). Therefore "God gave them up" as having "served the creature rather than the Creator" (Rom. 1:24-25), knowing that God's judgment falls "on those who do such things" (Rom. 2:2). This is the failure of the written code which kills (2 Cor. 3:6). But grace has come in Jesus Christ; though "all have sinned and fall short of the glory of God, they are now justified by his grace as a gift" (Rom. 3:23-24). This is the new covenant which gives life (2 Cor. 3:6). This is the "light" that "shines in the darkness," which the world rejected, but which dwelt among us "full of grace and truth" (Jn. 1:1-14). In the midst of judgment, there will be grace.

The message of the Bible is clear; both judgment and grace are realities of our experience, and they come to us uniquely when we confront Jesus' life and teachings, death and resurrection. He himself both judges and restores us.

It is in these terms that we experience pastoral supervision. We come under judgment every time we bring a piece of our life experience to another person or group for reflection. To share the events of brokenness, division, hostility, failure, doubt, and indecision which mark our ministry—or even those moments of joy and success to be celebrated—is to lay ourselves open to the criticism of our colleagues as well as God. None of us enjoys having our colleagues evaluate a sermon we have preached, a situation we have bungled, or communication that has broken down. That can be frightening, anxiety-producing, intimidating; it is certainly an invitation to judgment.

It can also be challenging, restorative, exhilarating. It becomes this when grace is experienced as well as judgment. We experience grace every time we discover that others have the same problems and questions, whenever we find that we are accepted and loved not only for who we are but because we have been willing to reveal a part of ourselves for others to know and appreciate, each time we are affirmed as a person and minister who is struggling with the key human issues. We come under grace in all those moments when we feel the support and trust of our colleagues who are now able to give themselves to us because we have given ourselves to them.

I have found pastoral supervision to be a tremendously affirming experience. For it to be that, of course, depends upon it being covenantal, relational, and incarnational. All that we have said heretofore comes to fulfillment at this point; what I have described in terms of mutual responsibility, interdependence, and servanthood become expressed here. Grace becomes ours in the trusting relationship of those who, in those uncertain and scary moments when our very being is "on the line," come to us as Christ came to his disciples.

Thus, it is in pastoral supervision that we meet Christ. He is there not only in his Living Presence but also in the supervisor who models him for us. I believe that finally the way we know God is through people; "If you have seen me, you have seen God," Jesus said, to paraphrase John 14:9. I now say, if you have seen a good pastoral supervisor, you have seen Christ alive and at work bringing both judgment and grace into our needy lives.

CONCLUSION

The practice of supervision has forced me to reflect seriously on my experience of God's activity in the world, the record of my faith tradition about God's activity, and the world's way of appropriating or ignoring that activity. My dialogue with these sources of faith have led me to some conclusions about the way supervision can and must occur among people of faith. Upon reflection in supervision, my operative theology has been powerfully influenced—not settled, but refined. It remains a pilgrimage.

One task remains—to describe how I got here in my thinking and what that can teach us about pastoral supervision. That is the point of the final chapter.

ENDNOTES

1. I use the term "human experience" because it carries some common meaning. In Chapter VI, I will be more precise in its use and will substitute the term "lived experience" which needs more definition than is useful here.
2. Roy B. Crowder, "Inner City Incarnation," in *Stirrings: Essays Christian and Radical,* ed. John J. Vincent (London: Epworth Press, 1976), 69-74. For a description of the broader movement through the Urban Theology Unit, see also Vincent's two small books *Alternative Church* (Belfast: Christian Journals Limited, 1976) and *Jesus Thing* (London: Epworth Press, 1973).
3. Vincent, *The Jesus Thing*, 84.
4. Reuel L. Howe, *Man's Need and God's Action* (Greenwich, CT: Seabury Press, 1953), 10.
5. Paul Tillich, *The Shaking of the Foundations* (New York: Scribners, 1948), 155.
6. Howe, *Man's Need*, 12-13.
7. Phillip and Phoebe Anderson, *The House Church* (Nashville, TN: Abingdon Press, 1975), 80-89.
8. Vincent, *Alternative Church*, 32-34.
9. See John J. Vincent, *Secular Christ* (Nashville, TN: Abingdon Press, 1968).
10. Ronald H. Sunderland in a workshop on "Equipping the Laity for Ministry," held November 1-4, 1976 at The Cenacle, Houston, Texas.

CHAPTER VI

TRANSFORMING THE ROUGH PLACES:
A WAY FROM HERE TO THERE

An issue in pastoral supervision that has been lurking in the shadows for years is the role of theological reflection. Some practitioners of the art might say that supervision **is** theological reflection; most would agree that it stands at the heart of the supervisory conversation; many also admit that it is the part of the conversation most easily slighted.

I have already stated that the supervisory conversation should lead to growth in self-awareness, ministering competence, theological understanding, and Christian commitment. Growth in all of these areas is possible only when the conversation is motivated by theological concern and enabled by theologizing skills. In this final chapter I want to expand on Stage 4 of the supervisory conversation outlined in Chapter IV in order to show more fully how theological reflection can take place within that conversation.

Admittedly, there is some confusion around the term "theological reflection." It is a term broadly used to refer to varied processes. In the pages that follow I will briefly review three models of theological reflection as examples of current thinking and practice in order to introduce my own thought. I will then discuss narrative theology as a particular method of theological thinking, particularly the way the use of narrative influences the formation of identity. The chapter will end with the presentation of a narrative model of theological reflection and the way it can be utilized in a typical supervisory case. All of this will build upon the model and theology of supervision already described.

CURRENT MODELS OF THEOLOGICAL REFLECTION

The model of theological reflection that is probably best known in supervisory circles is that of James and Evelyn Whitehead in their book *Method in Ministry*. The value of their work lies partly in the fact that they write both as theologians and as field educators who are familiar with the dynamics of supervision. Working from the understanding that "theological reflection in ministry is the process of bringing to bear in the practical decisions of ministry the resources of the Christian faith," they posit for their model three sources of information relevant to decision making in ministry: Christian Tradition, personal experience, and cultural information.[1]

By **Tradition** they mean the information drawn from Scripture and church history which bears on concrete pastoral concerns. They emphasize the importance of "befriending the Tradition," not in the sense of intellectual mastery of it but of developing intimacy with it so that it is a readily available source. The second source, **experience**, they understand to be the accumulated experience of the individual minister and the community of faith in which the reflection takes place, as shaped by the culture and Tradition. It consists of all the convictions, feelings, ideas, and biases bound up in that accumulation of experience. The third source is **cultural information** arising out of the symbols, mores, and sciences of the culture in which the reflection occurs, including philosophy, politics, social sciences, and other religious traditions.

A similar approach is taken by Patricia Killien and John de Beer in their Four-Source Model of which they say: "As sources for religious education, **Tradition**, **Culture**, **Positions**, and **Action** form a model which functions as a framework for designing methods that connect life and faith and help people do theology in their everyday life."[2] Killien and de Beer define their sources in much the same terms as do the Whiteheads, except that at the point of what the Whiteheads call experience they suggest two sources for reflection: one they call **Position** by which they mean the individual's attitude, convictions, beliefs, and spoken values; the other they call **Action**, meaning the thoughts, feelings, and perspectives associated with action as well as the actions themselves.

The Whitehead model provides a way for both individuals and communal units to engage in theological reflection. The Killien/de Beer model, while used in small group settings, emphasizes individual formation or decision-making. Used primarily with lay persons, it combines biblical study and reflection on experience. Its microscope method is particularly relevant to the supervisory setting because it begins with individual story or "life narrative" and assists the participants in reflecting on their experience through the use of metaphor.[3]

William Close, also a theologian with supervisory experience, joins in confirming my belief that "clergy and lay people are now perceiving increased skill in theological thinking as a personal learning need."[4] This calls, he says, for more than immersion in the thought of "Master theologians," though immersion in one or more of their systems is desirable. Proposing what he calls a "pastoral interventionist" method of doing theology, he writes:

> As long as ministers are content to pursue a clarification of the church's doctrine, or to devise "answers" to existential questions . . . their traditional theological resources will serve them well. Should they, under the pressure of demanding pastoral situations, seek to move beyond understanding what is happening toward an actual intervention in order to effect some changes they will require something more. . . .
>
> Clearly what is called for is a theological method which enables the pastor to move deftly through analysis toward a strategy for a pastoral intervention. Such a method will have to take account of the theological question or issue which is implicitly at stake in the pastoral situation, utilize the theoretical resources of the biblical and theological tradition in such a way as to suggest a course of action, and finally, permit ongoing assessment and adjustment by way of feedback from experience.[5]

There are other responses to the cry for help in theological reflection, more numerous than space permits to review.[6] All of them argue the case for it; some present concrete models of how to do it. Each of them add to our understanding. Probably no model will provide methods fully applicable to every situation. However, there is an area of theological study that is only beginning to be explored in relationship to supervision; I refer to narrative theology. It offers what I believe is a still more promising way to move us from here to there, that is, from supervision as merely a problem-solving or educational or therapeutic activity to supervision as "doing theology"—not to the exclusion of the other values, but providing the framework within which the total supervisory task is carried out.

The promise for theological reflection in narrative theology lies in what Stephen Crites calls the narrative quality of experience—the recognition that "the formal quality of experience through time is inherently narrative."[7] Earlier, in Chapter V, I suggested that theology is an attempt to interpret and describe human experience in relationship to God's activity in the world. Building upon that idea, I understand theological reflection to be a way of thinking about the God/human relationship so as to bring the narratives of human experience and the narratives of God's activity into dialogue with each other. It is this dialogue that makes supervision an essential part of the church's ministry.

NARRATIVE THEOLOGY: A DEFINITION

Recent years have witnessed a revival of interest in narrative or story as a way of understanding and communicating faith.[8] The writings of narrative theologians contain some common threads; a summary of these threads will illuminate my thought.

First, narrative theology is a **method** of theological inquiry that uses story rather than theological proposition as its primary subject. It is not an accident that when we seek to tell who we are, what we believe, where we have been, and where we are going we often do so in the form of stories. This is frequently the only way we have to make sense of past and current experience and to anticipate the future. It is the time-honored method that human beings have used to preserve and communicate what is of primary importance. Narrative theology sees these stories both as the means to communicate faith and as the content of faith. In life we not only need and have stories to describe what life is about, but life **is** story; and the life of faith is a particular story. Human story takes on primary significance when it is understood as part of the Christian story.[9]

Second, narrative theology is a vehicle for **examining religious convictions**. Michael Goldberg says that convictions are "those kinds of persistent beliefs that a person or community holding them cannot easily relinquish without becoming a significantly different person or community."[10] Theological propositions are convictional statements, but narrative theology concentrates on what Sallie TeSelle calls the experience of "coming to belief." By this she means the way in which belief as convictional proposition comes to express itself in faith as lived experience. That happened preeminently, she says, in Jesus, whose story is formative for Christians.[11] Its value lies in its power to shape the content of our own story.

Third, the examination of religious convictions focuses upon **lived experience**. By "lived experience" is meant the broad range of human engagements, "religious" and "secular." It has its origin in both immediate event and in memory. In the case of the latter it may be associated with events stretching back beyond our lifetime but re-told or re-enacted to make them current. An example is the Christian Eucharist which S. W. Sykes calls "public narrative;" it is event-in-memory made current through memorializing so that it becomes my/our event.[12] Narrative theology takes of equal importance the lived experience of the past and present and the convictional statements which arise from it. The task of the theologian, Goldberg says, is to "consciously and continuously strive to keep those statements in intimate contact with the narratives which gave rise to those convictions. . . ."[13]

Fourth, the lived experience upon which narrative theology focuses is that of both **individuals and communities**. It is, to be more accurate, the lived experience of the individual-in-community, because convictions are never arrived at alone. They grow out of interaction with and participation in the group or groups of persons whom we trust to mold our thinking and acting. Every community has its "scripture," its traditions, its collection of myths and legends around which it organizes its life. These elements of community life are appropriated to varying degrees by individuals and made a part of their "convictional system." This is what James McClendon calls a convictional community, that is, a "community of expectations, a community in which character is cultivated."[14] The church is one, but only one, such convictional community. At the same time, each community is shaped by the individuals who make up its "membership." Individual stories are shaped by and, in turn, re-shape the stories of the community.

Fifth, narrative theology begs the question about what constitutes "story." Gabriel Fackre says that there are basically three kinds of story: (1) **canonical story** which focuses upon a body of received literature, primarily Scripture, understood through the use of critical methods of inquiry; (2) **life story**, by which he means the making of new story, the telling of one's own story; and (3) **community story**, the tradition of the church, told in the experiences of the community of faith, including the creedal statements.[15] Other narrative theologians suggest that "story" includes myth, legend, ritual, and symbol from non-Christian sources as well. Of importance to us here is Fackre's emphasis on both the **received and emerging natures of story**.

One final point, then, must be emphasized in this summary of narrative theology. While predominantly Christian language has been used, the need to focus on experience which is not particularly Christian, and to examine the convictions arising from it, is equally important. For example, national holidays (such as Independence Day or Thanksgiving Day) may be equally or more formative for Christians than those associated with the church. The power of cultural experience to shape the convictions out of which we live is strong indeed. Therefore, I want to expand on Fackre's meaning when he speaks of canonical and community story; the narratives and creedal statements by which people live, including Christians, are not all found in the church's liturgy!

To speak in supervisory terms, the task in theological reflection is constantly to hold up for examination the convictional statements and stories by which we and our supervisees live, in light of both the narratives of experience from which they have come and the primary narrative of Christian experience which shapes our lives as persons of faith. "The business of theology," says Goldberg, is to "make us reflect on life."[16] Narrative theology suggests a way to do that.

THE ROLE OF NARRATIVE IN IDENTITY FORMATION

In the previous chapter I spoke of the role that supervision fulfills in the formation of identity. At stake here is my belief that identity formation is a more critical task in supervision than generally assumed. Too frequently supervision gets stuck in skill development, or problem solving, or getting ministry done. Although these are important results, it falls upon supervision to help its participants be clear about who they are so they can become equipped for effective ministry. Without a clear identity, efforts designed to improve skills or to do ministry are like the seeds in Jesus' parable of the sower (Mt. 13:3-9) which fell on unfertile ground; they have no soil in which to grow.

We determine our identity from clues found in many sources: religion, gender, ethnic or national origin, culture, occupation, et cetera. We think and act out of images that take on formative significance for who we are, what we stand for, how we want to be known, and how we are or want to be engaged in the world.[17] James Fowler and Robin Lovin speak of this when they relate "being" to faith and say that "to have faith . . . is to engage all of life in relation to a unifying center of meaning and value."[18]

The task of supervision is to help persons find a sense of wholeness that will enable them to live and minister in consistent, organized, meaningful ways. This is as important for those of us who are supervisors as it is for our supervisees. Our ability to help individuals and communities in their identity formation will depend a great deal upon the clarity with which our own identity has been formed, our ability to keep our identity carefully delineated from that of our supervisees, and our willingness to engage in the identity formation process.

George Stroup says that one of the strengths of narrative theology is that it provides a foundation for reflection on experience, and that such reflection has at its heart a concern for identity. "Questions about Christian identity are at their root questions about Christian faith."[19]

> To understand Christian narrative properly is to be able to reinterpret one's personal identity by means of the biblical texts, history of tradition, and theological doctrines that make up the church's narrative. The real test of Christian understanding is not simply whether someone knows the content of the Christian tradition and can repeat it on demand but whether he or she is able to use Christian faith as it is embodied in the church's narrative to reinterpret personal and social existence.[20]

Building on Stroup's thought, Luke Smith and I have written elsewhere of how narrative can be used to aid the identity formation of both individuals and communities.[21] Our thesis there is that identity is formed out of the interaction of four "systems," all drawn from narrative theology:

1. **Lived experience** — the routine happenings of daily life (often called human experience) and the encounter with ultimate reality (usually called religious experience);
2. **Received Narrative** — the body of Scripture, tradition, doctrine, myth, legend, ritual, and/or symbol which forms the "climate" in which individuals and communities exist;
3. **Emerging Story** — the account we and our communities tell selectively to

communicate what we want others to know about the events, feelings, beliefs, opinions, and memories that we experience; and,

4. **Self-Deception** — the term used to describe the deeply seated tendency that we and our communities have to distort the stories that we tell.

The question for supervision is: How can these "systems" be utilized to create a model of theological reflection that will enhance the supervisory conversation, and how can that conversation aid in the identity formation of its participants? I find the answer in the reference of narrative theologians to autobiography as both a theological resource and method.

DOING THEOLOGY AUTOBIOGRAPHICALLY

In theological reflection, we are enabled to discover (or re-discover) and to "tap" the central or dominant story that finally shapes the story by which we live. Among the many stories which impinge upon us, every person needs what David Burrell and Stanley Hauerwas call "a saving story," that is "a true story" which is "powerful enough to check the endemic tendency toward self-deception, a tendency which inadequate stories cannot help but foster."[22] Without such a saving story we are inclined to simply identify with the multiple roles we fill in life. Our need is to be constituted by a master image that brings wholeness to our lives.

It is this that TeSelle appears to have in mind when she says that our sense of identity is largely determined by the kind of story that we understand ourselves to have been enacting through the events of our careers.[23] Referring to the power of metaphorical language in which the meaning is found within the story though not exhausted by the story, she says that autobiography is one of the narrative forms (the others being parable, poem, and novel) that provides a "source for understanding how language and belief move into a life, how a life can itself be a parable."[24]

Believing comes out of experience, out of one's own story. . . . Neither language nor belief can subsist except in a particular life, and our theologians are unabashedly autobiographical, not because they would boast of where they are in the pilgrimage toward believing but because they know that there is no such thing as a disembodied, abstract theology. . . . "Confessional literature" has been a minor genre in Christian letters, but it ought to be a primary one if the metaphorical method is taken seriously, for where does one start to theologize if not with oneself?[25]

TeSelle outlines four main components of the art of autobiography:

1. **Concern with the self**. Genuine autobiography comes from persons who are pledged to their deepest selves, who "appropriate" their own "self" to create and become who they are.

2. **Dominant point of view**. The most important factor is a dominant vision of self, and each life-incident is an unfolding of that vision according to a "master form."

3. **Harmony between outward events and inward growth**. The unfolding of life must have the "master form" as its determining factor and lead others to feel that they really have "seen" the autobiographer.

4. **Aesthetic and autobiographical knowing**. The knowing that occurs is of the same nature as "knowing" an aesthetic object, not conceptual but a grasping of the feel of life through imagination and being.[26]

What would a theology be like, TeSelle asks, were it to use autobiography as a source? Certainly it would be personal; it would be particular; it would be vocational, parabolic, identity-forming; it would be confessional—which, for most narrative theologians is the purest form of autobiography.

It is instructive to press this idea into the arena of pastoral practice.[27] This is what Eugene King has done when he says that "in the autobiographical evidence of a person's life can be found clues that disclose the convictions which shape and inform experience. The clues are the dominant or controlling images which keep recurring in a person's discourse. The task of the theological biographer . . . is to detect and elaborate the patterns of meaning which those clues disclose."[28]

By "autobiographical evidence" King refers to "diary"—the "first level language" by which one can "come to grips with different experiences close to the moment of their happening." This is the kind of story by which a reader "draws near to the traveler grappling with new terrain, avoiding, backing off, wrestling mastery, being overwhelmed, submitting, hurting, enjoying, and at times 'making friends.'" Autobiography as diary is to be distinguished from "biography" which "never really gets inside the skin of a subject" and from "memoirs" which are "a remembering, looking back over the events and recording them from a vantage point of some later moment in life."[29]

By "clues" King refers to McClendon's idea of dominant or controlling images which both shape a life and reflect its shape to others.[30] King draws upon the life of Dag Hammarskjold as revealed in Hammarskjold's own autobiographical statements. King traces Hammarskjold's struggle with death as the dominant or controlling image. He identifies Hammarskjold's "partners in dialogue" or "story-tellers of human experience and religious faith who answered Hammarskjold's seeking." These partners were biblical and non-biblical, religious and secular; they were the convictional communities which shaped Hammarskjold's convictions, created his images, and formed his character, so that he entered life at a new level of morality and, in turn, helped inform and shape the communities of which he was a part.[31]

King's investigation of Hammarskjold's life leads him to draw some conclusions for pastoral practice:

> A pastor accompanies people in their journey through life; s/he serves them in their search for signposts. Within biblical and Christian faith, that search is for the presence of the living God in the clay of everyday experience. The pastor needs to become a skilled interpreter of the living human documents of his/her community, serving the daily diary of people's experience out of the Judeo-Christian pilgrimage, while having one's own theology remade and challenged by the uniqueness of every individual story.[32]

AUTOBIOGRAPHY AS THEOLOGICAL METHOD

In supervision we take responsibility for accompanying people on a significant part of their life journey: their lived experience in the marketplace, in the work force, in their occupation, and in their religious and vocational pursuits. While it may be assumed that people can leave their convictional communities behind when they enter these arenas, the fact is that they cannot; the job or vocation and its environment simply become one more convictional community shaping and being shaped by each other. So when we supervise someone we are dealing with emerging stories that become focused upon one small but significant slice of any individual's life at a particular moment in time. Together, those several slices of life in those accumulative moments in time become life-forming for the supervisee and the world in which they live.

These emerging stories are autobiographical in the sense that they belong to and are reported by the supervisees out of their recent lived experience. They may be "memoir" or "diary." To the degree that they are memoir they have already become biographical in that they are reported through interpretive eyes, the supervisees' own eyes to be sure, but already subject to the interpretation of memory. To the degree that they are diary (journal), they permit us to enter the supervisees' emerging stories at the vantage point of first-level language—though the conversation begins to take on second-level (interpretive) characteristics simply because we are now looking back and interpreting.

In the supervisory conversation we are "theological autobiographers" whose central task is to assist supervisees to get inside their own story, to become autobiographical once again about their lived experience. We are to help supervisees look theologically at their emerging stories and to find the clues, those dominant and controlling images, that disclose the convictions which shape and inform their stories of experience. Our goal is to help them locate and dialogue with the story-telling partners in their received narrative, to detect and elaborate the patterns of meanings which those partners reveal.

We do this because we know that these patterns of meaning find expression in their life and ministry. By helping them see and understand the patterns of thought and behavior which impact their ministry we are at least creating the conditions in which new images and convictions and character and ministering behavior can be chosen—believing that all behavior of a person of faith is a behavior of ministry. In the process, we ourselves are also prompted and permitted to do the same as participants in the supervisory conversation, and the community of faith is similarly helped if the supervision is complete.

There is a hazard in this in that persons may deceive themselves in their self-told stories by believing and thus reporting, as an evasive tactic, evidence which is not true. The heart of what we do in supervision is to help supervisees become clear about themselves in the context of their ministry. This involves helping them come to terms with the reality around them, to move to authenticity (honesty) of life and work. And, of course, the possibility for self deception and deceptiveness is equally hazardous for the supervisor. This suggests that those of us who supervise must, through our own supervision, take responsibility for having super-vision in relation to both ourselves and our supervisees.

Supervision, from this view, remains biographical in that it usually looks at experience from some point after the ministry being supervised has occurred; the experience is already subject to both the supervisors' and supervisees' interpretations. It becomes autobiographical when it confronts the supervisees (and hopefully the supervisors also) with the opportunity to make inquiry into their own lives, to create new story, to move from memoir to diary in action and reflection. I propose to call it autobiographical because I believe that the crucial role of pastoral supervision is to help its participants do more than reflect on past or future behavior. It is to help us become transformed in the sense of change. Supervision promotes the shaping and forming of both individual(s) and community(s). In the best theological sense, effective supervision leads to ongoing conversion of the heart and mind, and thus of behavior as well.

THEOLOGICAL REFLECTION IN THE NARRATIVE MODE

The foregoing is in itself a narrative description of a model for theological reflection in the narrative mode which I now want to make explicit. It builds upon the model of supervision presented in Chapter IV.

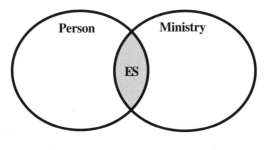

FIGURE 4

When supervisees come for supervision they bring two elements: themselves as **persons** and the **ministry** in which they are engaged. These are equal, interconnected elements. The form in which these elements are presented to us is a "case" (e.g. ministry reflection report, critical incident, verbatim, et cetera). In narrative terms, this case can be called an **emerging story** (ES). It is a narrow slice of a larger story (actually several stories) being offered for reflection, representing "pieces" of both the person and the ministry. It is an emerging story because it takes on new life as a part of the larger story once it is told.

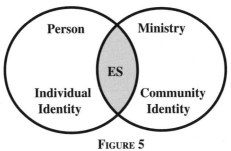

FIGURE 5

There are two primary identities impacting the emerging story when it is brought to us: the **individual identity** of the person (supervisee) and the **community (corporate) identity** of the location in which the supervisee's ministry is being done (e.g., congre-

119

gation). Both identities help shape the emerging story.

Parts of the person's life and the community's life that influence the emerging story may be unrecognized and unstated. Also, there are other communities with which the supervisee is connected that influence the way she/he "knows" her/himself and thus help shape the emerging story (e.g., family, friends, peer groups, school, other congregations, et cetera).

In addition, the supervisor's identity, growing out of a similar variety of personal and community connections impacts the supervisory relationship. Of particular concern is the impact of the common community identity in which both supervisor and supervisee are involved. The emerging story is the point at which those multiple identities meet and interact.

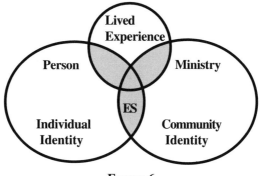

FIGURE 6

There are at least three components to any emerging story that is brought for supervision. One is **lived experience**, that is, all of the experiences of the past that effect what story is selected for telling, how and why it is selected, what is told or not told, and how the event or situation is interpreted. If we listen carefully to the stories that are brought to us for supervision, we will hear a great deal not only about what is currently happening but about what has already happened that is important for the identity of the supervisee.

Of course, the lived experience of the supervisee is primary data, but of equal importance is the lived experience of the community out of which the story arises. Only a small part of the lived experience of either may have been communicated to the other; some has been forgotten or rejected. A still smaller part finds its way explicitly into the emerging story, but that part is important because it points to the larger formative story.

The supervisor's lived experience also becomes activated as the emerging story triggers memories of either a similar or dissimilar nature and influences the way we hear it. Again, that which arises out of the supervisor's and supervisee's common community from which the emerging story comes takes on critical importance.

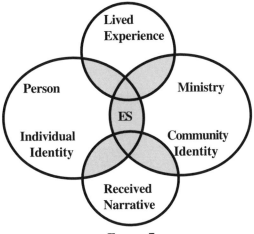

FIGURE 7

A second component of the emerging story is **received narrative**. This is the accumulation of scripture, tradition, myth, legend, ritual, and belief that constitute part of the participant's identities and have informed and shaped the story. Some of the received narrative arises out of the supervisee's identity, only a part of which is consciously recalled or claimed (owned) and of which a still smaller part is expressed in the emerging story.

The same is true for the community; not all of the received narrative which makes up the community's identity is remembered, not all of it is accepted, and only a fragment may have been passed along to the supervisee. However, bits and pieces of the received narrative of both the supervisee and the congregation finds its way into the emerging story.

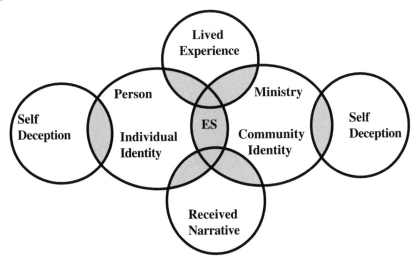

FIGURE 8

Once again, there are other communities of which the supervisee is a part that have their own scripture, tradition, et cetera which impact the emerging story. And, as with lived experience, the supervisor's received narrative also bears its influence as the story unfolds. That is, our understanding of and participation in scripture, tradition, and liturgy combined with our own set of beliefs will bear upon the way the story is told, heard, understood, and interpreted.

The third component of the emerging story, potential if not actual, is self-deception. It represents the fact that in telling the emerging story the supervisee may not tell the entire story or the real story. The story may be distorted—maybe because there is something that the supervisee doesn't know or understand, or maybe because there is something the teller does not want known (or even want to know). One may tell only a half-story or an untruthful story. That may be due to an innocent omission; it may be a deceptive tactic; but it may be a maneuver growing out of the teller's self-deception, having convinced him/herself that the truth is being told.

In forming the emerging story the supervisee decides what story to tell, what to include or exclude, and how to present some particular engagement in the world. In doing so such factors as "How do I see myself as a person?", "What do I want people to now about me?", and "How do I want to be engaged in the world?" will be considered. Thus the student has a choice to make, and the angle of vision taken will determine which choice is made. One alternative is to tell a cover story; this is designed to deceive in order to make oneself look better, to hide error, to defend one's action. It is this alternative that, if chosen consistently across time, can lead to self-deception. The other alternative is to tell a truthful story; this is the way of transformation because it means that the supervisee is open to all the possibilities in the story—the opportunity for learning and growth through weakness as well as strength.

Communities and supervisors may be equally inclined to deceive themselves in the way they tell their own stories or hear the stories that are told to them. Their identities are also at stake in the supervisory relationship.

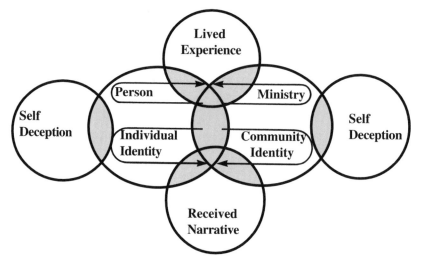

FIGURE 9

122

The task of supervision in this model is to help the supervisee tell and enlarge the emerging story by drawing upon the lived experience and received narrative of her/his own life and the life of the community in which the event occurred. In doing so the supervisee can be helped to become more clear about his/her identity. By knowing her/himself more fully and intimately, the supervisee can be enabled to minister with better insight, intentionality, responsibility, sensitivity, and openness. Thereby the tendency toward self-deception can be checked and/or corrected. In this process, both the supervisor and the communities in which the supervision occur can also be helped to clarify the convictions and patterns by which they live.

A SUPERVISORY CASE STUDY IN THEOLOGICAL REFLECTION

This leads me finally to describe how a narrative model of theological reflection works out in a supervisory situation. The intent here is to suggest some methods for getting us from here to there. To do so I turn to a case briefly in ministry.

THE YOUTH RETREAT

Recently I have been confronted by an incident that has a bearing on the ministry to the youth at the Church. Its scope, however, is much broader than this. The feeling was expressed at a Youth Retreat, but it reflects a much broader segment of the Church. During our Youth Retreat we had a program directed toward getting the people involved to see themselves in a trust relationship toward one another. The thrust of the program led to a spirit of oneness in Christ individually and collectively. This was climaxed by a Communion Service which was planned by the Youth. After the service there was a showing of emotions (tears and embracing). The advisors became very disturbed at this and expressed their feelings. One advisor who was the mother of one of the girls took her aside and told her to "knock it off." The other couple tried to change the atmosphere to one of fun and games.

Upon arriving home there were phone calls to other parents and the conversations implied the retreat was an "emotional fiasco."

In our evaluation meeting at home an outsider was invited to attend the meeting. He was the husband of one of the advisors and a school principal. I was left to understand in no uncertain terms that these youth were too young to show such emotion and the Y.F. should be fun and games.

I talked with the youth at their evaluation meeting concerning their feelings at retreat, and most of them thought that it was one of the high points of their Christian life.

I see my function as a future pastor to minister to the spiritual needs of all the people. I do not want to alienate a group nor do I want to be a recreational director.

The advisors who reacted are good people who need to be recognized, but I find it difficult to be all things to all people.[33]

The supervisory conversation begins with an emerging story brought by a student,

Tom, to his supervisor, Sue, about a youth retreat for which he had taken responsibility as part of his field education placement. The retreat was planned as part of a learning goal that Tom had included in his Learning/Serving Covenant with the congregation to develop resources and skills in ministering to persons through retreats. The youth retreat was his first effort; he had chosen youth for his initial event because he had some experience working with this age group and felt that it was a safe way to start.

Tom had developed the covenant carefully in consultation with Sue and the Teaching Church Committee (the lay supervisory committee chosen to work with Tom and Sue). He had kept Sue and the committee informed during the retreat planning process. Suggestions from those sources had been incorporated into the planning, so all systems looked good as the weekend approached. Tom knew that Sue was aware of all this as he handed her the critical incident report the day before their meeting, but still he found himself reviewing it verbally with her as they began their supervisory conversation.

What can we expect to happen as Tom and Sue confront the event? Certainly, Sue must give Tom an opportunity to let the full story emerge—not just what is written on the paper, but also the bits and pieces of information that Tom selects gradually to move his story through the conversation. Sue must listen closely for the interpretation that Tom puts upon it. She must also be sensitive to Tom's feelings which color the way he views the event and its outcome; many of them are right on the surface in the written report, while others might need help to become expressed. Careful attention to the Information and Evaluation stages (Stages 1 and 2) of the supervisory conversation will guide Tom and Sue through this part of the journey.

Such attention will reveal the issues that are involved. Some of them are:
1. Tom's issues:
   a. His entrapment between youth and adults, between children and parents;
   b. His understanding of the nature of the church, ministry, worship, and religious experience;
   c. His role and authority vis-a-vis the role and authority of advisors, parents, and "experts";
   d. His relationship and ongoing ministry to the congregation (particular individuals as well as the congregation at large);
   e. His personal, professional, and spiritual identity.
2. The youths' issues:
   a. Their integrity as persons whose judgment can be trusted;
   b. Their freedom and right to determine their own program;
   c. Their personhood (identity) as youth in the body of believers;
   d. Their present and future relationship to the church.
3. The congregation's issues (advisors, parents, others):
   a. Their authority;
   b. Their understanding of church, ministry, worship, and religious experience;
   c. Their role as a congregation in ministry to its youth and its leadership, to Tom in particular;
   d. Their pattern of communication in the church;
   e. Their identity as the people of God.

4. Sue's issues:
   a. Her role and authority as pastor/supervisor;
   b. Her understanding of church, ministry, worship, and religious experience;
   c. Her identity as pastor and as supervisor.

This case is pregnant with issues, each of which has multiple facets. Any one of them deserves an entire supervisory conversation. Particularly, the case illustrates how the identities of individuals and communities inevitably influence each other. The immediate concern is a conflict that needs resolution. Once Tom's story of the event, along with his feelings and issues arising out of it, have been articulated ordinary analysis might be useful (Stage 3); that will help move Tom and Sue toward some decision and commitment (Stage 5). But the conversation will fail as pastoral supervision if theologizing (Stage 4) does not take place. There follows some steps which can enable theologizing in preparation for decision-making. These steps assume familiarity with and some competence in all five of the stages of the supervisory conversation outlined on pages 80-82, but they are designed to enlarge and facilitate (not replace) Stage 4.

ENLARGING THE EMERGING STORY

It is vital that Sue see, and help Tom see, the scope of his emerging story and of the several stories that have grown out of the event. They must consider how the stories impinge on each other. That is, it is important that Tom see his emerging story, written and embellished, in relationship to a larger community story being told, not isolated from it. Moreover, Sue must help Tom see that the several versions of the story are not simply due to faulty judgments, or cantankerous whims, or destructive intentions. Those elements may or may not be present, but essentially the stories grow out of other factors more theologically based.

Immediately, Tom's emerging story is the composite of factors which he has chosen to put together into his story of what happened. It will be useful for him to realize what choices have been made in framing the story. Thus Sue must listen carefully to Tom's enlargement of the story as they sit together and to help him inquire into: What theological assumptions lie behind his story? What images, feelings, and opinions helped shape it? What view(s) of ministry influenced him? It will help if together Sue and Tom can build some metaphors which will help enlarge the story. The point is for Sue to help Tom be aware of all the nuances of the story as it continues to emerge in his mind by helping him really hear his presented story in light of the rest of the story.

RECALLING THE LIVED EXPERIENCE

At the heart of the stories emerging from the critical incident are past experiences which have impacted the way the participants respond to this particular experience. So Sue needs to help Tom think and talk about previous religious experiences that relate to the youth retreat. Where and how did they occur? To what important events and places and people are they connected? What makes them important? How have they influenced his life of faith and his understanding of ministry?

It is not only "religious" experiences that are important; Sue must help Tom get in touch with other experiences as well—experiences which support or challenge what he has already discovered about himself which have prompted him to respond as he does to this experience: his upbringing, previous work with youth and adults, and education. The objective is to help Tom move inside his lived experience. He needs not only to know what the experiences are but to claim them as **his** experience, as expressions of who he is. In this way he can begin to understand the relationship between what has happened to him in the past and what is happening to him now.

TAPPING THE RECEIVED NARRATIVE

What Tom has identified as his lived experience is more than raw data, more than a series of events. It is "word made flesh" growing out of his received narrative. Tom lives out of an understanding of life that has been formed out of that which is "sacred" for him. So the supervisory conversation must make it possible for him to tap that "sacred" material. That can be uncertain ground, because what is "sacred" will likely not all have the stamp of the sacramental upon it.

Tom must be helped to locate all the sources of his convictions related to the youth retreat and to lift these convictions up for examination. He needs to distinguish his convictions from his feelings and opinions. So Sue will need to help him recall from Scripture, church tradition, and cultural sources those things which function as "truth" for him. Through this process Tom will have the opportunity to clarify the attitudes and values which impact his story of the youth retreat.

CONNECTING EXPERIENCE, NARRATIVE AND STORY

A critical step in theological reflection comes at the point where lived experience and received narrative meet in emerging story. It is one thing to speak of bringing together the past and present into a meaningful whole in one person's own life. It is another to speak of this for the individual-in-community. In the case of the youth retreat, Tom needs not only to see his story in relationship to a larger community story, but he needs to realize that the community story is a part of **his** story. The congregation's lived experience, and perhaps its received narrative, have already become part of his experience and narrative.

That involves more than simply hearing and appreciating the history of the congregation and what makes these advisors and parents respond the way they do. If Tom is to be part of that congregation as one who ministers within it (and I do not know any ultimately meaningful way to minister from outside a congregation), he must **be** a "member" of the congregation. That does not include necessarily agreeing with or adopting its interpretation of reality; it does include letting its story "in-form" his story in a way that the language, symbols, and rituals of each can become "re-formed" as "their" story within the Christian story.

As pastor/supervisor, Sue is in a strategic position to facilitate that "forming" by inquiring into Tom's understanding of and experience in the church, particularly the local congregation in which the event under consideration occurred. Who is he in relationship to this congregation? Sue may need to provide information of which Tom is not aware. More than that, Sue must help Tom come to terms with the meaning of community and of membership in a community. She must help him decide whether or not he can and is willing to be in a covenant relationship with this congregation that will enable him to incarnate both judgment and grace in his ministry. How does he envision himself ministering to this congregation in this situation?

CHECKING FOR SELF-DECEPTION

It should be obvious that the opportunities for self-deception are ubiquitous. Sue's task as supervisor is to help Tom tell a truthful story; that is the only kind of full and complete story there is. I am referring to the story Tom tells to himself though that is not unconnected from the story he tells to others. When he says that he sees his "function as a future pastor to minister to the spiritual needs of **all** the people," that he does "not want to alienate a group," is he really being honest with himself? He does recognize that it is "difficult to be all things to all people," but how tempted might he be to try that impossible task, and to succumb finally to the pastoral tragedy of telling himself day after month after year that he can do just that?

At this period in his pastoral formation he is raising the right questions: Who am I? Who do I want to be? What shape shall my ministry take? Now is the time to help Tom avow the inconsistencies as well as the hopes, to accept the incongruencies and ambivalences as well as the expectations for coherence as part of his reality. Sue's opportunity as supervisor is to assist Tom in being "truthful" about his life before he gets locked into an impossible pattern of trying to be somebody he cannot be—and, of course, to encourage him to become all that he can be. Truthfulness on Tom's part must, of course, be matched by truthfulness in the congregation; it is equally subject to self-deception. While it is another step in the supervisory process, the congregation, like Tom, must be called to account for its appropriation of its experience and narrative.

"AUTOBIOGRAPHING" THE STORY

A good way to understand what is being suggested here is to consider what it means to become autobiographical about oneself. Of course, autobiography is about oneself. I am suggesting that to be autobiographical is to take responsibility for being who we are. Michael Novak says that "we in part invent who we are."[34] An autobiography represents one's own understanding of oneself—how one wants to be known. It is a way of bringing thought and action into some kind of unity within the framework of a story. One could leave that task to others, to biographers. "Autobiographing" our story means to take responsibility for (a) claiming our past and present, our events and memories, our experience and narrative, as our own, and (b) presenting to others a full, complete, embodied parable (metaphor) that will allow them to know us for who we are. This is the only way we can make the past become truly present and to anticipate a viable future.

It is said of Johann Sebastian Bach that he not only wanted his students to learn how to play other people's music but to write their own.[35] What is called for in the case of the youth retreat is for Sue to help Tom become autobiographical about himself as person, as Christian, and as minister. She can do that by challenging him to "compose" (verbalize) and to live out the "music" that he wants to have heard through his life and ministry.

EXPLORING THE FUTURE

Theological reflection in supervision is never simply an exercise to help us understand something more clearly or to engage in for its own sake. It is done for the purpose of making life decisions. In terms of supervision, I have located it as Stage 4 of the supervisory conversation. In a sense it is not a stage at all but an attitude that we bring to the conversation. Yet, it is a stage in the sense that what comes before and what comes after is also crucial to the conversation.

What I have described as a method to think theologically about a youth retreat must find its completion as Sue helps Tom (a) address the issues growing out of the retreat, (b) formulate plans for ministering to and with the people impacted by the retreat, and (c) make yet another in a series of decisions about his future life and ministry. What finally makes theological reflection such an important stage is its ability to anticipate the future in light of a past that has been remembered and a present that has been attended within the power of the story that informs all stories—God's story. The decisions that Tom makes have the potential to be decisions "birthed" in Christian hope—namely, the conviction that all that is remembered and attended and anticipated is within God's future.[36]

In describing the way a narrative model of theological reflection might work in the youth retreat case, I have concentrated on Tom; the supervisory conversation begins with his emerging story. The immediate purpose of the conversation is to (1) help Tom clarify his self-understanding, his identity, at the point where it "collides" with the congregation's identity,[37] (2) to acquire some skill or insight that he can use to deal with the situation that awaits him when he leaves the conversation, (3) to gain theological perspective so that whatever he does is consistent with pastoral ministry, and (4) to make new ongoing commitments to Christian faith as the empowering principle in his life. In the midst of meeting those supervisory objectives, Sue will model for and with Tom how he can continue to supervise the other participants in the situation. It is important that he (and Sue) extend the process to them; their issues and needs are similar.

Sue can do even more. She has a unique opportunity to teach this way of reflecting theologically to the Teaching Church Committee which, with her, is responsible for Tom's supervision. By helping such a key group of people to reflect this way with Tom, she can begin establishing a network of persons and groups within the congregation to practice theological reflection as an ongoing practice in church and world. It provides a creative means for all Christian persons to reflect on their particular ministry.

CONCLUSION

I have suggested throughout this chapter that theological reflection within the supervisory conversation provides a way of making supervision a transformative event. In a separate article I have written that "the distinctiveness of ministry supervision lies in its transformational nature, its capacity for facilitating the empowerment of persons and institutions in their `journey of development.'"[38] In this chapter now concluding I have spelled out a way for transformation to occur through the use of narrative (emerging story, lived experience, received narrative, and the ever-present inclination toward self-deception). Particularly I have shown how this identity formation can be a transformative process when it takes place within the "autobiographing" of individual and community story.

In this sense supervision is called to be prophetic. I have taken a clue from Isaiah where the prophet was called to announce the coming of God to people and their community in a critical time of their existence (exile and restoration). Using the language of metaphor (poetry) drawn from the people's context, this "minister" considered the way across the desert to the place where God's glory would once again be revealed to God's people. Foreseeing the obstacles (rough places), the prophet was nevertheless called to announce that the crooked places would be made straight, the uneven places would be made level, the way would be prepared for God's arrival among them—not by their efforts but by God's doing.

Supervision accompanies persons and communities through significant times of their development, times that are filled with both obstacles and opportunities. Those times lead into ways that are filled with rough places. The supervisory task is not to prepare the way but to point to the way to what God is already doing to transform the rough places into a highway that can be traveled in the fulfillment of ministry. This is a theological task; to do supervision is to do theology in the midst of daily experience. This is a salvatory process, because it provides a framework for confession and forgiveness; it establishes the conditions in which covenant, relationship, incarnation, judgment, and grace can occur.

Hopefully it has also become clear how this method of doing theological reflection offers an effective way of making responsible decisions within the supervisory relationship. The case of the youth retreat suggests how this can happen not only for an individual but for a "community" as well (the youth group, advisors, parents, supervisory committee, perhaps the entire congregation).

Throughout this chapter I have emphasized the mutual nature of this model. Pastoral supervision is not just for the student (or staff member, or committee chairperson); it is for the whole body of Christ. Thus theological reflection is the task of the entire community of faith. It is the church's way of drawing upon its primary resource to order its life.

ENDNOTES

1. James D. and Evelyn Eaton Whitehead, *Method in Ministry* (New York: Seabury Press, 1980), 1.
2. Patricia O'Connell Killien and John de Beer, "'Everyday Theology': A Model for Religious and Theological Education," *Chicago Studies* 22 (August 1983): 196.
3. See *Manual for Mentors* and *Learning Resource Guide* (Sewanee, TN: Baernwick Center, School of Theology, University of the South).
4. William J. Close, "What Does It Mean To Think Theologically?" *Theological Field Education: A Collection of Key Resources* (N.p.: Association for Theological Field Education, 1979), 2: 75.

5. Ibid., 86-87.

6. The reader is referred to the bibliography for additional resources.

7. Stephen Crites, "The Narrative Quality of Experience," *Journal of the American Academy of Religion* 39 (September 1971): 291.

8. Narrative theologians tend to use the terms "narrative" and "story" interchangeably. I will follow that pattern here when discussing narrative theology, but I will make a distinction between them later in this chapter.

9. Narrative theologians use terms such as the "Christian story," the "story of Jesus," and "The Story" to refer to the narratives which shape Christian life. See Gabriel Fackre, *The Christian Story* (Grand Rapids, MI: William B. Eerdmans Publishing Company, 1984); Sallie McFague TeSelle, "The Experience of Coming to Belief," *Theology Today* 32 (July 1975): 159-65; and Robert McAfee Brown, "My Story and 'The Story,'" *Theology Today* 32 (July 1975): 166-73.

10. Michael Goldberg, *Theology and Narrative: A Critical Introduction* (Nashville, TN: Abingdon Press, 1982), 34. Cf. James William McClendon, Jr. and James M. Smith, *Understanding Religious Convictions* (Notre Dame: University of Notre Dame Press, 1975), 7. McClendon and Smith define conviction as "a persistent belief such that if X (a person or a community) has a conviction, it will not easily be relinquished and it cannot be relinquished without making X a significantly different person (or community) than before."

11. TeSelle, "The Experience," 160. For an elaboration of this idea, see also a larger version of her thesis in her book *Speaking in Parables: A Study in Metaphor and Theology* (Philadelphia: Fortress Press, 1975).

12. S. W. Sykes, "Story and Eucharist," *Interpretation* 37 (October 1983): 365.

13. Goldberg, *Theology*, 35. Cf. James William McClendon, Jr., *Biography as Theology: How Life Stories Can Remake Today's Theology* (Nashville, TN: Abingdon Press, 1974), 178. McClendon says: "Biographical theology need not repudiate and should not ignore the propositional statement of theological doctrine. What it must insist is that this propositional statement be in continual and intimate contact with the lived experience which the propositional doctrine by turns collects, orders, and informs. Without such living contact, theological doctrine readily becomes (in a perjorative sense) objective-- remote from actual Christian life, a set of empty propositions in the confidence that their meaning is exemplified in contemporary Christian experience."

14. McClendon, *Biography*, 22.

15. Gabriel Fackre, "Narrative Theology: An Overview," *Interpretation* 37 (October 1983): 343-50.

16. Goldberg, *Theology*, 94.

17. Kenneth H. Pohly and Luke B. Smith, "The Use of Narrative in Identity Formation: Implications for Supervision," *Spirituality, Ministry and Field Education*, vol. 5 of *Theological Field Education: Key Resources* (N.p.: Association for Theological Field Education, 1986).

18. James Fowler and Robin Lovin, *Trajectories of Faith: Five Life Stories* (Nashville, TN: Abingdon Press, 1980), 19.

19. George W. Stroup, *The Promise of Narrative Theology* (Atlanta, GA: John Knox Press, 1981), 20.

20. Ibid., 96-97.

21. Pohly and Smith, "The Use of Narrative," 131-32.

22. David Burrell and Stanley Hauerwas, "Self-Deception and Autobiography: Theological and Ethical Reflections on Speer's *Inside the Third Reich*," *Journal of Religious Ethics* 2 (Spring 1974): 111.

23. Paraphrase of TeSelle, *Speaking in Parables*, 139. Quotes Stephen Crites, "Myth, Story, History," *Parable, Myth, and Language*, ed. Tony Stoneburner, (Cambridge, MA: The Church Society on College Work, 1968), 68.

24. Ibid., 94.

25. Ibid., 85.

26. Ibid., 151-55.

27. McClendon, *Biography*, 197. McClendon opens the door to this when, near the end of his book, he refers to the autobiographical inquiry of the theologian into her/his own life.

28. Eugene King, "Dag Hammarskjold's Befriending Death: A Case Study in Theological Reflection," *Pastoral Sciences*, Vol. 1 (Ottawa, Ontario: Institute of Pastoral Studies, 1982) 91-112, Cf. Dag Hammarskjold, *Markings* tr. Leif Sjoberg and W. H. Auden (New York: Alfred A. Knopf, 1964), and "Old Creeds for a New World" in *Servant of Peace*, ed. Wilder Foote (New York: Harper and Row, 1963), 23-24. King's use of the term "theological biographer" suggests a way of thinking about "pastoral supervision."

29. Ibid., 94-96.
30. McClendon, *Biography*, 190-91.
31. King, "Dag," 105.
32. Ibid., 96.
33. This critical incident is used with the permission of its author.
34. Michael Novak, *Ascent of the Mountain, Flight of the Dove,* rev. ed. (San Francisco: Harper and Row, 1978), 208.
35. I heard this in a devotional message given for a class in supervision at Andover Newton Theological School on the occasion of Bach's 300th birthday, March 21, 1985. I do not know the original source.
36. Crites, "The Narrative," 298. Discussing the importance of consciousness and memory in relationship to the present and the future, quotes Augustine, *The Confessions*: "Consciousness anticipates and attends and remembers, so that what it anticipates passes through what it attends into what it remembers." (11.28).
37. Stroup says: "The narrative of confession or autobiography emerges from the collision between individuals and their personal identity narratives and the Christian community and its narratives." *Promise*, 91.
38. Kenneth H. Pohly. "The Distinctiveness of Ministry Supervision," *Journal of Supervision and Training in Ministry* 10 (1988): 116. I am indebted to Tjaard G. Hommes for the concept of transformation as empowerment. See his article "Educational Theory Base for Field Education," *Theological Field Education: A Collection of Key Resources* (N.p.: Association for Theological Field Education, 1977), 1: 5.

EPILOGUE

The writing of this book has been an attempt to draw together and to integrate some resources for pastoral supervision which otherwise would remain fragmented and disconnected. Readers may see other connections; the reference notes and the bibliography point to sources which may be pursued for those who are interested.

What began as a standard practice in the early church has received little literary attention until recent years. Even now it tends to be approached in piecemeal fashion, with isolated references to clinical, educational, and parish concerns. This book is an effort to address the question of supervision in its context of the church at large — clergy and laity, 'religious' and 'secular', 'church' and 'world'. It takes the view that the ministry of pastoral supervision occurs wherever and whenever people carry out their supervisory work within its spirit.

One of the excitements in supervision is to witness the way people become empowered in supervision to translate what they have experienced into a way of doing ministry in their own particular contexts. It has been my joy to see this happen for people in a variety of life situations--including the occupational disciplines reviewed in this book.

It is significant that this is one area, among others, in which the Church can join forces with other helping institutions to enable ministry in the world. My experience in an educational setting, where supervision is my 'business', is that we have a great deal to teach each other. While that in itself is not a new insight, we have not usually combined our insights and expertise around supervisory concerns. This book makes the attempt to let the various disciplines of work inform each other--to raise new questions and to offer new possibilities that we tend to miss or avoid within our own circles. It offers an appeal for all supervision to become 'pastoral' in the largest sense of that word.

Thus, I invite supervisors from the many walks of life to join in the dialogue in order that we might learn from each other. I have directed my words to the church in general and theological education in particular as the arena in which my life and work are pursued. If they seem critical at points it is because I am committed to the church universal and to the best of supervisory practice within it; one only criticizes that (those) about which (whom) one cares deeply. I hope my readers get that message as well as the rest of what I have tried to say.

BIBLIOGRAPHY

SUPERVISION

BUSINESS AND INDUSTRY

Allen, Louis A. *Professional Manager's Guide*. 4th ed. Palo Alto, CA: Louis A. Allen Associates, Inc., 1969.

Andrews, Kenneth R. "The Progress of Professional Education for Business." *Theological Education* 5 (Spring 1969): 144-66.

Bennis, Warren G. *Changing Organizations*. New York: McGraw-Hill, 1966.

Bennis, Warren, and Burt Nanus. *Leaders: The Strategies for Taking Charge*. New York: Harper and Row, 1985.

Berne, Eric. *The Structure and Dynamics of Organizations and Groups*. New York: Grove Press, 1963.

Drury, Susanne S. *Assertive Supervision: Building Involved Teamwork*. Champaign, IL: Research Press, 1984.

Dubin, Robert. *Human Relations in Administration*. Englewood Cliffs, NJ: Prentice-Hall, 1961.

Ecker, Paul, John Macrae, Vernon Ouellette, and Charles Telford. *Handbook for Supervisors*. Englewood Cliffs, NJ: Prentice-Hall, 1959.

Eddy, William B., W. Warner Burke, Vladimir A. Dupré, and Oron P. South, eds. *Behavioral Science and the Manager's Role*. Washington, DC: NTL Institute for Applied Behavioral Science, 1969.

Etzioni, Amatai. *Modern Organizations*. Englewood Cliffs, NJ: Prentice-Hall, 1964.

Famularo, J. J. *Supervisors in Action*. New York: McGraw-Hill, 1961.

Gimmell, Gary. "Managing Upward Communication." *Personnel Journal*, February 1970: 107-10.

Hitt, William D. *Management in Action*. Columbus, OH: Battelle Press, 1985.

Katz, Robert L. "Skills of an Effective Administrator." *Harvard Business Review* 33 (January-February 1955): 23-42.

Kindall, Alva F., and James Gotza. "Positive Program for Performance Appraisal," *Harvard Business Review* 41 (November-December 1963): 153-60.

Lateiner, Alfred R. *The Techniques of Supervision*. New London, CT: National Foreman's Institute, 1954.

McGregor, Douglas M. "The Human Side of Enterprise." *Management Review*, November 1957.

———. *The Human Side of Enterprise*. New York: McGraw-Hill, 1960.

Mager, Robert F., and Peter Pike. *Analyzing Performance Problems, or You Really Oughta Wanna.* 2d ed. Belmont, CA: Pittman Learning, 1984.

Maslow, Abraham. *Eupsychian Management: A Journal.* Homewood, IL: Richard D. Irwin, 1965.

Morris, Jud. "How to Motivate." *Manage,* October 1967, 18-24.

Organizational Effectiveness Through the Managerial Process. Cincinnati, OH: Senco Products, Inc., 1974.

Ouchi, William G. *Theory Z.* New York: Avon, 1982.

Ramey, David A. *Empowering Leaders.* Kansas City, MO: Sheed and Ward, 1991.

Reber, Ralph W., and Gloria E. Terry. *Behavioral Insights for Supervision.* Englewood Cliffs, NJ: Prentice-Hall, 1975.

Ready, R. K. *The Administrator's Job.* New York: McGraw-Hill, 1967.

Schein, Edgar H. *Organizational Psychology.* Englewood Cliffs, NJ: Prentice-Hall, 1970.

Taylor, F. W. *Scientific Management.* New York: Harper and Row, 1948.

Weber, Max. *Sociology of Religion.* Translated by Ephraim Fischoff. Boston, MA: Beacon Press, 1963.

Weber. *The Theory of Social and Economic Organization.* Edited by Talcott Parsons. Glencoe, IL: Free Press and Falcon Wings Press, 1947.

EDUCATION

Barnett, Bruce. "Overcoming Obstacles to Peer Coaching for Principles." *Educational Leadership* 47 (May 1990): 62-64.

Brandt, Ronald S., ed. "The Coaching of Teaching." *Symposium in Educational Leadership* 40 (October 1982): 3-59.

———. "The Realities of Supervision." *Symposium in Educational Leadership* 41 (April 1984): 3-27.

———. "Redefining Supervision." *Symposium in Educational Leadership* 46 (May 1989): 2-64.

Borrowman, Merle L. "The Professional Education of Teachers." *Theological Education* 5 (Spring 1969): 222-39.

Cogan, Morris L. *Clinical Supervision.* Boston, MA: Houghton Mifflin, 1973.

Costa, Arthur L., and Robert Garmston. "Supervision for Intelligent Teaching." *Educational Leadership* 42 (February 1985): 70-80.

Deal, Terrence E. "Reframing Reform." *Educational Leadership* 47 (May 1990): 6-12.

Duke, Daniel L. "Setting Goals for Professional Development." *Educational Leadership* 47 (May 1990): 71-75.

Eisner, Elliot W. "The Art and Craft of Teaching." *Educational Leadership* 40 (January 1983): 5-13.

Ellis, Elmer C., Joseph T. Smith, and William Harold Abbott, Jr. "Peer Observation: A Means for Supervisory Acceptance." *Educational Leadership* 36 (March 1979): 423-26.

Evans, Marilyn Crouse. "Metaphor as Method for Teacher Reflection." Unpublished MATS Project for United Theological Seminary, 1989.

Glatthorn, Allan A. *Alternatives in Education*. New York: Dodd, Mead, 1975.

———. *Differentiated Supervision*. Alexandria, VA: Association for Supervision and Curriculum Development, 1984.

Glickman, Carl D. *Developmental Supervision*. Alexandria, VA: Association for Supervision and Curriculum Development, 1981.

———. "Open Accountability for the '90s: Between the Pillars." *Educational Leadership* 47 (April 1990): 38-42.

———. "Supervision and the Rhetoric of Empowerment: Silence or Collision?" *Action in Teacher Education* 10 (1988): 11-15.

———. *Supervision of Instruction: A Developmental Approach*. Boston, MA: Allyn and Bacon, 1990.

Hopfengardner, Jerrold D., and Peggy E. Leahy. "Providing Collegial Support for Experienced Teachers." *Journal of Staff Development* 9 (Spring 1988): 48-50.

———, and Ronald Walker. "Collegial Support: The Case for an Alternative to Principle-Led Supervision of Instruction." *NASSP Bulletin* 21 (April 1984): 35-40.

Mosher, Ralph L., and David E. Purpel. *Supervision: The Reluctant Profession*. Boston, MA: Houghton Mifflin, 1972.

Ornstein, Allan C. "Teachers as Professionals." *Social Science* (Summer 1977): 139-44.

Pickhardt, Carl E. "Supervision and the Power of Help." *Educational Leadership* 38 (April 1981): 530-33.

Reavis, Charles A. "Clinical Supervision: A Review of the Research." *Educational Leadership* 35 (April 1978): 580-84.

Reilkoff, Theresa. "Collegial and Student Oriented Advantages of Supportive Supervision Over Clinical Supervision of Teachers." *NASSP Bulletin* 65 (November 1981): 28-34.

Robinson, Phil C., ed. "Reshaping the Teaching Profession." Symposium in *Educational Leadership* 42 (December 1984/January 1985): 3-59.

Sergiovanni, Thomas J. "Adding Value to Leadership Gets Extraordinary Results." *Educational Leadership* 47 (May 1990): 23-27.

———. "Is Leadership the Next Great Training Robbery?" *Educational Leadership* 36 (March 1979): 388-94.

———, ed. *Supervision of Teaching*. Alexandria, VA: Association for Supervision and Curriculum Development, 1982.

Snyder, Karolyn J. "Clinical Supervision in the 1980s." *Educational Leadership* 38 (April 1981): 521-24.

Unruh, Carl B., and Harold E. Turner. *Supervision for Change and Innovation*. Boston, MA: Houghton Mifflin, 1970.

Williams, Stanley W. *New Dimensions in Supervision*. Scranton, PA: Intext Educational Publishers, 1972.

Wittrock, M. C., ed. *Handbook of Research on Teaching*. 3rd ed. New York: Macmillan, 1986.

PSYCHOTHERAPY

Arlow, Jacob A. "The Supervisory Situation." *Journal of the American Psychoanalytic Association* 11 (July 1963): 576-94.

Augspurger, Richard E., and Roger D. Fallot. "Philosophies of Pastoral Counseling Supervision." Symposium in *Journal of Supervision and Training in Ministry* 8 (1986): 52-131.

Beier, Ernest G. "On Supervision in Psychotherapy." *Psychotherapy: Theory, Research and Practice* 1 (August 1963): 91-95.

Chessick, Richard D. *Why Psychotherapists Fail.* New York: Science House, 1971.

DeBell, Daryl E. "A Critical Digest of the Literature on Psychoanalytic Supervision." *Journal of the American Psychoanalytic Association* 11 (July 1963): 546-75.

Ekstein, Rudolph, and Robert S. Wallerstein. *Teaching and Learning of Psychotherapy.* 2nd ed. New York: International Universities Press, 1972.

Elrick, Harold. "The Clinical Education of the Medical Student." *Journal of Medical Education* 42 (May 1967): 453-59.

Emch, Minna. "The Social Context of Supervision." *International Journal of Psychoanalysis* 36 (1955): 298-306.

Fallot, Roger D. "Metaphor and Change in the Supervision of Psychotherapy and Pastoral Counseling." *Journal of Supervision and Training in Ministry* 6 (1983): 23-32.

———, ed. "Ministries of Individual and Social Transformation: A Symposium." *Journal of Supervision and Training in Ministry* 7 (1984-85): 77-140.

Fleming, Joan, and Therese Benedek. *Psychoanalytic Supervision.* New York: Grune and Stratton, 1966.

Hartung, Bruce M. "Issues in Supervision During a Training Year." *Journal of Pastoral Care* 31 (September 1977): 172-77.

Henry, William E., John H. Sims, and S. Lee Spray. *The Fifth Profession.* San Francisco: Jossey-Bass, 1971.

Hess, Allen K., ed. *Psychotherapy Supervision.* New York: John Wiley & Sons, 1980.

Hogan, Richard A. "Issues and Approaches in Supervision." *Psychotherapy: Theory, Research and Practice* 1 (August 1963): 139-41.

Hoover, Edwin A. "Pastoral Supervision as an Interpersonal Experience." *Journal of Pastoral Care* 31 (September 1977): 164-71.

Karl, John C. "Forming the Inner Cup: The Ministry of Supervision with Pastoral Counselors." *Journal of Supervision and Training in Ministry* 7 (1984-85): 15-36.

Kaslow, Florence W., and Associates. *Issues in Human Services: A Sourcebook for Supervision and Staff Development.* San Francisco: Jossey-Bass, 1972.

———. *Supervision, Consultation, and Staff Training in the Helping Professions.* San Francisco: Jossey-Bass, 1977.

———, ed. *Supervision and Training: Models, Dilemmas, and Challenges.* New York: Haworth Press, 1986.

Kolb, Lawrence C. "Consultation and Psychotherapy." *Current Psychiatric Therapies* 8 (1968): 1-10.

Lewin, Bertram D., and Helen Ross. *Psychoanalytic Education in the United States*. New York: W. W. Norton, 1960.

Meerloo, Joost A. M. "Some Psychological Processes in Supervision of Psychotherapists." *American Journal of Psychotherapy* 6 (July 1952): 467-70.

Mueller, William J., and Bill L. Kell. *Coping with Conflict: Supervising Counselors and Psychotherapists*. New York: Appleton-Century-Crofts, 1972.

Muslin, Hyman L., Alvin G. Burstein, John E. Gedo, and Leo Sadow. "Research on the Supervisory Process." *Archives of General Psychiatry* 14 (April 1967): 427-31.

Rader, Blaine B. "Supervision of Pastoral Psychotherapy." *Journal of Pastoral Care* 31 (September 1977): 178-85.

———. "The Organizational Context of Supervision and Training." *Journal of Supervision and Training in Ministry* 3 (1980): 87-99.

Schuster, Daniel B., John J. Sandt, and Otto F. Thaler. *Clinical Supervision of the Psychiatric Resident*. New York: Brunner/Mazel, 1972.

Tarachow, Sidney. *An Introduction to Psychotherapy*. New York: International Universities Press, 1963.

Tischler, Gary L. "The Beginning Resident and Supervision." *Archives of General Psychiatry* 19 (October 1968): 418-22.

Wise, Carroll A. "The Supervisory Alliance in Pastoral Psychotherapy." *Journal of Pastoral Care* 31 (September 1977): 186-93.

Wolberg, Lewis R. *The Technique of Psychotherapy,* Part II. New York: Grune and Stratton, 1967.

SOCIAL WORK

Appelby, John H., Virginia C. Berkman, Robert T. Blazejack, and Vicki S. Gorter. "A Group Method of Supervision." *Social Work* 3 (July 1958): 18-22.

Austin, Lucille N. "Basic Principles of Supervision." *Social Casework* 33 (December 1952): 411-19.

Barnat, Michael R. "Student Reactions to the First Supervisory Year: Relationships and Resolutions." *Journal of Education for Social Work* 9 (Fall 1973): 3-8.

Berkowitz, Sidney J. "The Administrative Process in Casework Supervision." *Social Casework* 33 (December 1952): 419-23.

Bloom, Leonard, and Cherie Herman. "A Problem of Relationship in Supervision." *Social Casework* 37 (July 1958): 402-06.

Burns, Mary E. "Supervision in Social Work." *Encyclopedia of Social Work* (1965): 785-90.

Dailey, Wilda J., and Virginia P. Hogan. "Brief Recording and Supervision." *Social Casework* 39 (May 1958): 278-82.

Fizdale, Ruth. "Peer-Group Supervision." *Social Casework* 39 (October 1958): 443-50.

Holcomb, Emerson. "An Analysis of the Supervisory Job." *Social Casework* 37 (March 1956): 126-31.

Jones, Betty Lacy, ed. *Current Patterns in Field Instruction in Graduate Social Work Education*. New York: Council on Social Work Education, 1969.

Kadushin, Alfred. *Consultation in Social Work*. New York: Columbia University Press, 1977.

————. *The Social Work Interview*. New York: Columbia University Press, 1972.

————. *Supervision in Social Work*. New York: Columbia University Press, 1976.

————. "Supervisor-Supervisee: A Survey." *Social Work* 19 (May 1974): 288-97.

Leader, Arthur L. "An Agency's View Toward Education for Practice." *Journal of Education for Social Work* 7 (Fall 1971): 27-34.

Levy, Charles S. "The Ethics of Supervision." *Social Work* 18 (March 1973): 14-21.

Mandell, Betty. "The Equality Revolution and Supervision." *Journal of Education for Social Work* 9 (Winter 1973): 43-54.

Munson, Carlton E. "The Concepts of Effectiveness and Efficiency Applied to the Social Work Profession: An Historical Perspective." *Journal of Education for Social Work* 14 (Spring 1978): 90-97.

————. *An Introduction to Clinical Social Work Supervision*. New York: Haworth Press, 1983.

————. "Professional Autonomy and Social Work Supervision." *Journal of Education for Social Work* 12 (Fall 1976): 95-102.

————. "The Uses of Structural Authority and Teaching Models in Social Work Supervision." DSW diss., University of Maryland, 1975. Ann Arbor, MI: University Microfilms International, 1975.

Pettes, Dorothy. "Supervision from Social Work Perspective." Paper presented to the Tenth Biennial Consultation on Field Education, Berkeley, CA, January 15-18, 1969, 36-44.

————. *Supervision in Social Work*. London: George Allen and Unwin, 1967.

Rapaport, Lydia. "Consultation." *Encyclopedia of Social Work* (1965): 214-18.

Scherz, Frances H. "A Concept of Supervision Based on Definitions of Job Responsibility." *Social Casework* 39 (October 1958): 435-43.

Stiles, Evelyn. "Supervision in Perspective." *Social Casework* 44 (January 1963): 19-25.

Watson, Kenneth W. "Differential Supervision." *Social Work* 18 (November 1973): 80-88.

Wilson, Suanna J. *Confidentiality in Social Work*. New York: Free Press, 1978.

CLINICAL PASTORAL EDUCATION

Beech, Lawrence C. "Supervision in Pastoral Care and Counseling: A Prerequisite for Effective Ministry." *Journal of Pastoral Care* 24 (December 1970): 233-39.

Beverly, Urias H. "Blacks in Clinical Pastoral Education." *Journal of Pastoral Care* 36 (September 1982): 203-208.

Boisën, Anton T. "The Period of Beginnings." *Journal of Pastoral Care* 5 (Spring 1951): 13-16.

Bruder, Ernest E. "Training and the Mental Hospital Chaplain." *Journal of Pastoral Care* 11 (Fall 1957): 136-45.

————, and Marian Barb. "A Survey of Ten Years of Clinical Pastoral Training at St. Elizabeth's Hospital." *Journal of Pastoral Care* 10 (Summer 1956): 86-94.

Chilgren, Richard A., and James B. Nelson. "Human Sexuality in Ministry." *Eighth Annual Conference Proceedings*, Association of Clinical Pastoral Education, October 1975, 59-69.

Criswell, Grover E., and James E. Gebhart. "In-Service Clinical Pastoral Education." *Journal of Pastoral Care* 23 (December 1969): 237-40.

Denys, Jozef. "My Understanding of Ministry and Pastoral Supervision in Clinical Pastoral Education." *Pastoral Sciences* 9 (1991): 5-16.

Friesen, John W. "Evaluating Supervised Clinical Pastoral Education: A Pilot Study." *Journal of Pastoral Care* 27 (December 1973): 229-35.

Gerkin, Charles V. "Clinical Pastoral Education and Social Change." *Journal of Pastoral Care* 25 (September 1971): 175-81.

Getman, Clyde J. "CPE Supervisors: Psychologists or Theologians?" *Journal of Pastoral Care* 36 (September 1982): 172-76.

Grant, Gerald. "An Objective Evaluation of an Eleven-Week Supervised Pastoral Education Program." *Journal of Pastoral Care* 29 (December 1975): 254-61.

Hammett, Hugh B. "The Historical Context of the Origins of CPE." *Journal of Pastoral Care* 29 (June 1975): 76-85.

Heminway, Joan E. "Position Paper on CPE Supervision and Learning." *Journal of Pastoral Care* 26 (September 1982): 194-202.

Hiltner, Seward. "Fifty Years of CPE." *Journal of Pastoral Care* 29 (June 1975): 90-98.

Jong, Jan de. "Supervision and Theology in CPE." *Journal of Supervision and Training in Ministry* 1 (1978): 10-16.

Jorjorian, Armin D. "The Meaning and Character of Supervisory Acts." *Journal of Pastoral Care* 25 (September 1971): 148-56.

Klink, Thomas W. "Issues in Learning Through Supervision." *Journal of Pastoral Care* 17 (Summer 1963): 61-72.

————. "Supervision from a Clinical/Pastoral Care Perspective." *Report of Proceedings, Tenth Biennial Consultation on Field Education*, Berkeley, CA, January 15-18, 1969, 17-25.

Lapsley, James N. "Supervision in the Parish and in Clinical Training." Editorial, *Journal of Pastoral Care* 21 (September 1967): 179-80.

LeFevre, Perry. "On Rereading Boisën." *Pastoral Psychology* 19 (September 1968): 5-7.

McCarthy, Marie, and David B. McCurdy, eds. "Supervision and Training as an Ethical Endeavor." Symposium in *Journal of Supervision and Training in Ministry* 12 (1990): 106-229.

Merrill, William R. "Design for Mythic Learning: A New Use of the Tutorial." *Journal of Pastoral Care* 21 (June 1967): 65-77.

Mitchell, Kenneth R., ed. "Foundations of Supervision: The Contributions of Thomas Klink." Symposium in *Journal of Supervision and Training in Ministry* 11 (1989): 151-255.

Oglesby, William B., Jr. "Heritage and Commitment: CPE in the Second Half Century." *Eighth Annual Conference Proceedings*, Association for Clinical Pastoral Education, October 1975, 84-89.

Patton, John H., and John Warkinton. "A Dialogue on Supervision and Consultation." *Journal of Pastoral Care* 25 (September 1971): 165-74.

Peterkin, Judith. "A White Australian Woman's Reflections in Supervising Black Students in America." *Journal of Pastoral Care* 37 (June 1983): 98-102.

Powell, Robert C. *Fifty Years of Learning Through Supervised Encounters with Living Human Documents*. New York: Association for Clinical Pastoral Education, 1975.

St. Clair, Robert J. "Toward a Social Field Theory of Supervision." *Journal of Pastoral Care* 23 (September 1969): 142-52.

Seaton-Johnson, Anthony Wayland, and Craig A. Everett. "An Analysis of Clinical Pastoral Education Supervisors: Their Identities, Roles, and Resources." *Journal of Pastoral Care* 34 (September 1980): 148-58.

Southard, Samuel. "Criteria for Evaluating Supervisors-in-Training." *Journal of Pastoral Care* 17 (Winter 1963): 193-202.

Sunderland, Ronald H. "A Concept of Ministry Which Employs the Supervisory Process Derived from Clinical Pastoral Education." Unpublished S.T.M. thesis, Perkins School of Theology, Southern Methodist University, 1968.

Thomas, John R. "Evaluations of Clinical Pastoral Training and 'Part-Time' Training in a General Hospital." *Journal of Pastoral Care* 12 (Spring 1958): 28-38.

Thornton, Edward E. *Professional Education for Ministry*. Nashville, TN: Abingdon Press, 1970.

Ulanov, Ann Belford. "The Feminine and the World of CPE." *Journal of Pastoral Care* 29 (March 1975): 11-22.

Wise, Carroll A. *Religion in Illness and Health*. New York: Harper, 1942.

FIELD EDUCATION

Auten, David J. "Supervisor's Training Program." *Pastoral Hermeneutics and Ministry*: Vol. 4 of *Theological Field Education: Key Resources*. N.p.: Association for Theological Field Education, 1983, 264-68.

Beiswenger, Donald F. "Differentiating Modes of Supervision in Theological Field Education." *Theological Education* 11 (Autumn 1974): 50-58.

———. "The Presentation Process." *Theological Field Education: A Collection of Key Resources*. N.p.: Association for Theological Field Education, 1977, 1: 139-41.

Bollinger, Richard A. "What is Pastoral Supervision?" *Theological Field Education: A Collection of Key Resources*. N.p.: Association for Theological Field Education, 1977, 1: 53-56.

Dahlstrom, Earl. "Problems of Supervision in the Varieties of Internships." *Report of Proceedings of the Tenth Biennial Consultation on Field Education*, Berkeley, CA, January 15-18, 1969, 58-69.

Elias, Jacob W. "Supervised Ministries in the Free Church Tradition." *Report of the 17th Biennial Meeting of the Association of Professional Educators for Ministry*, Pittsburgh, PA, June 19-21, 1982, 55-67.

Feilding, Charles R. *Education for Ministry*. Dayton, OH: American Association of Theological Schools, 1966.

Gessell, John M. "Clinical Pastoral Training and the Curriculum for Theological Education: A Position Paper." *Journal of Pastoral Care* 22 (September 1968): 168-70.

Gross, Joseph E. "An Analogy of Pastoral Supervision." *Theological Field Education: A Collection of Key Resources*. N.p.: Association for Theological Field Education, 1977, 1: 139-41.

Goodwin, Hilda M. "Dilemmas Confronting the Supervisor in Theological Education." *Theological Education* 5, Suppl. 1 (Summer 1969): 503-08.

Hanley, Denis J. "Professional Supervision of Pastoral Work." *Theological Education* 5, Suppl. 1 (Summer 1969): 497-502.

Howe, Reuel L. "The Nature of Pastoral Supervision." *Theological Field Education: A Collection of Key Resources*. N.p.: Association for Theological Field Education, 1977, 1: 58-64.

Hunt, Richard A., and Craig Emerick. "Measuring Student Performance in Internship Settings." *Theological Field Education: A Collection of Key Resources*. N.p.: Association for Theological Field Education, 1981, 3: 235-38.

Hunter, George I. "Supervision: A Professional Resource and a Service for Ministry." *Theological Field Education: A Collection of Key Resources*. N.p.: Association for Theological Field Education, 1977, 1: 103-16.

———. *Supervision and Education-Formation for Ministry*. Cambridge, MA: Episcopal Divinity School, 1982.

Jordan, Merle R. "Utilizing Helplessness with Supervisees." *Journal of Supervision and Training in Ministry* 2 (1979): 73-81.

Klink, Thomas W. "Supervision as a Routine Process in Professional Education for Ministry." *Duke Divinity School Review* 33 (Autumn 1968): 155-73.

McCarty, Doran C. *The Supervision of Ministry Students*. Atlanta, GA: Board of Home Missions, Southern Baptist Convention, 1978.

———. "Theological Principles for the Supervisory Task." *Theological Field Education: A Collection of Key Resources*. N.p.: Association for Theological Field Education, 1977, 1: 82-85.

Morentz, Paul E. "The Supervision of Supervisors." *Theological Field Education: A Collection of Key Resources*. N.p.: Association for Theological Field Education, 1977, 1: 187-93.

Nace, Robert K. "The Teaching Parish and the Supervising Pastor." *Theological Education* 11 (Summer 1975): 319-28.

Noyce, Gaylord. "Patterns of Evaluation for Ministry Students." *Theological Field Education: A Collection of Key Resources*. N.p.: Association for Theological Field Education, 1981, 3: 229-34.

Oates, Wayne E. "Pastoral Supervision Today." *Pastoral Psychology* 24 (Fall 1975): 17-29.

Pohly, Kenneth H. "Models of Supervision." *Report of Proceedings, Fifteenth Biennial Consultation on Field Education*, ATFE, Washington, DC, January 10-13, 1979, 132-39.

————, and Luke B. Smith. "The Use of Narrative in Identity Formation: Implications for Supervision." *Spirituality, Ministry, and Field Education*, Vol. 5 of *Theological Field Education: Key Resources*. N.p.: Association for Theological Field Education, 1986, 128-46.

Pregnall, William S. "Method of Supervising Case Study." *Theological Field Education: A Collection of Key Resources.* N.p.: Association for Theological Field Education, 1977, 1: 167-68.

————. "Supervision of Theological Students." *Theological Field Education: A Collection of Key Resources.* N.p.: Association for Theological Field Education, 1977, 1: 150-52.

————, and Elizabeth E. Hampton. "Training Field Education Supervisors." *Theological Education* 11 (Summer 1975): 308-14.

Seabright, Russell F. "A Model of Supervision for the Integration of Social Awareness and Ministry Functioning During a Year of Internship in Lutheran Theological Education." Unpublished D.Min. Project for United Theological Seminary, Dayton, Ohio, 1984.

Spafford, William B., Jr. "The Question of Extensive Training." *Journal of Pastoral Care* 7 (Spring 1953): 33-36.

Spencer, Ralph W. "Evaluation in the Context of Field Education." *Occasional Paper* 1, Association for Theological Field Education, Winter 1976.

Steere, David A. "An Experiment in Supervisory Training." *Journal of Pastoral Care* 23 (December 1969): 202-17.

Stewart, Charles William. "Training Pastoral Supervisors for Seminary Field Education." *Journal of Pastoral Care* 25 (March 1971): 24-32.

Supel, Joan. "Supervision and Spiritual Direction." *Theological Field Education: A Collection of Key Resources.* N.p.: Association for Theological Field Education, 1979, 2: 179-88.

Travis, Arthur E., Jr. "Supervision: Some Assumptions." Paper presented to the St. Mary's Seminary Department of Field Education, Institute of Religion, Houston, Texas, April 1974.

Treese, Robert L. "Supervisory Training and Integration." *Theological Field Education: A Collection of Key Resources.* N.p.: Association for Theological Field Education, 1977, 1: 177-86.

Wagenhofer, John. "Authority in the Supervisory Process." *Spirituality, Ministry, and Field Education.* Vol. 5 of *Theological Field Education: Key Resources*. N.p.: Association for Theological Field Education, 1986, 184-90.

Weeks, Susan Conley, and Mary Beth Johnston. "The Development of Ministers: Implications for Supervisory Interventions." *Spirituality, Ministry, and Field Education.* Vol. 5 of *Theological Field Education: Key Resources.* N.p.: Association for Theological Field Education, 1986, 191-209.

White, Ernest, and Gaines Dobbins. "The Supervision of Doctor of Ministry Students." *Spirituality, Ministry, and Field Education.* Vol. 5 of *Theological Field Education: Key Resources*. N.p.: Association for Theological Field Education, 1986, 236-47.

Wise, Carroll H. "The Relationship Between Clinical Training and Field Work Supervision." *Journal of Pastoral Care* 8 (Winter 1954): 89-94.

THE CHURCH AT LARGE

Adams, Henry B. "Consultation: An Alternative to Supervision." *Journal of Pastoral Care* 25 (September 1971): 157-64.

Anderson, Herbert E., Homer W. Ashby, Jr., and David L. Lindberg., eds. "Supervision of Ministry in a Parish Context." Symposium in *Journal of Supervision and Training in Ministry* 10 (1988): 106-231.

Anderson, James D. "Pastoral Support of Clergy-Role Development Within Local Congregations." *Pastoral Psychology* 22 (March 1971): 9-14.

Avery, William O. "Enhancing Supervision Using Fowler's Developmental Theory." *Journal of Supervision and Training in Ministry* 10 (1988): 3-18.

Broholm, Dick, and John Hoffman. *Empowering Laity for Their Full Ministry*. Newton Centre, MA: Center for Ministry of the Laity, Andover Newton Theological School, 1982.

Bailey, Paul C. "From Grief to Greeting: Supervising the Pastor-Parish Relations Committee and Pastor Through Termination and Start Up." Unpublished D.Min. Project for United Theological Seminary, Dayton, Ohio, 1991.

Clinebell, Howard J. "Experiments in Training Laity for Ministry." *Pastoral Psychology* 22 (June 1971): 35-43.

DeWolf, L. Harold. "Needed: All-Round Pastoral Training." *Pastoral Psychology* 20 (March 1969): 7-9.

Glasse, James D. *Profession: Minister*. Nashville, TN: Abingdon Press, 1968.

————. *Putting It Together in the Parish*. Nashville, TN: Abingdon Press, 1972.

Gerlach, Barbara A., and Emily C. Hewitt. "Training Women for Ministry." *Andover Newton Quarterly* 17 (November 1976): 118-24.

Harris, John C. "New Trends in Pastoral Care for Pastors." *Pastoral Psychology* 22 (March 1971): 5-8.

Houts, Donald C. "Consultation Teams: A Supervisory Alternative." *Journal of Supervision and Training in Ministry* 3 (1980): 9-19.

Howe, Reuel. *The Miracle of Dialogue*. Greenwich, CT: Seabury Press, 1963.

Hunter, Rodney J. "Commitment as Psychological Process: Theory and Pastoral Implications." *Pastoral Psychology* 24 (Spring 1976): 190-205.

"Leadership and Servanthood: Episcopacy and District Superintendency in the United Methodist Church." *Daily Christian Advocate*, Advance Edition F, 27 April 1976.

Leslie, Robert C., and Emily Hartshorne Mudd. *Professional Growth for Clergymen*. Nashville, TN: Abingdon Press, 1970.

Lum, Doman. "Training Lay Counselors for Church and Community Mental Health." *Pastoral Psychology* 21 (May 1970): 19-26.

Mahon, Robert. "An Example of the Use of Professional Development Groups in Support of New Ministers." *Pastoral Psychology* 22 (March 1971): 31-38.

Nelson, James D. "United Methodist Heritage." *Spiritual Formation Resources Packet* (Section I, Paper C). Nashville, TN: Division of Ordained Ministry, Board of Higher Education and Ministry, The United Methodist Church, 1982.

Newbigin, Lesslie. *The Household of God*. London: SCM Press, 1953.

Oates, Wayne E. *The Christian Pastor*. Rev. ed. Philadelphia: Westminster Press, 1964.

"Pastoral Supervision--A Ministry of the Church." Editorial, *Journal of Pastoral Care* 25 (September 1971): 145-46.

Peck, George, and John S. Hoffman, eds. *The Laity in Ministry*. Valley Forge, PA: Judson Press, 1984.

Pohly, Kenneth Holt. *The Contextual Model as an Option for the Church's Educational Work*. Monograph 4. Nashville, TN: Board of Discipleship of the United Methodist Church, 1974.

Ramsden, William E. "Pastoral Care as a Function of the Church." *Pastoral Psychology* 22 (February 1971): 56-59.

Sims, Bennett J. "Continuing Education as a Peer Support Experience in the Dynamics of Change." *Pastoral Psychology* 22 (March 1971): 39-43.

Sims, Edward R. "W.E.C.A.--A Response to Passivity and Isolation Among Parish Pastors." *Pastoral Psychology* 22 (March 1971): 44-49.

Spencer, Ralph W. "Daring to Risk Supervision." *Christian Ministry* 7 (January 1976): 9-13.

Taylor, David M., ed. *We Were Brought Together*. Report of the National Conference of Australian Churches. Sydney: Australian Council for the World Council of Churches, 1960.

Vandecreek, Larry, and Jerry Royer. "Education for Interdisciplinary Teamwork." *Journal of Pastoral Care* 24 (September 1975): 176-84.

Van Wagner, Charles A., II, "Supervision of Lay Pastoral Care." *Journal of Pastoral Care* 31 (September 1977): 158-63.

NARRATIVE THEOLOGY

BASIC SOURCES

Brown, Robert McAfee. "My Story and The Story." *Theology Today* 32 (July 1975): 166-73.

Crites, Stephen. "The Narrative Quality of Experience." *Journal of the American Academy of Religion* 39 (September 1971): 291-311.

Crossan, John Dominic. *The Dark Interval: Towards a Theology of Story*. Niles, IL: Argus Communications, 1975.

Dunne, John S. *A Search for God in Time and Memory*. London: Macmillan, Paperback Edition, 1970 (1969, 1967).

Fackre, Gabriel. "Narrative Theology: An Overview." *Interpretation* 37 (October 1983): 340-52.

Goldberg, Michael. *Theology and Narrative: A Critical Introduction*. Nashville, TN: Abingdon Press, 1982.

McClendon, James William, and James M. Smith. *Understanding Religious Convictions*. Notre Dame: Notre Dame University Press, 1975.

McFague, Sallie. *Metaphorical Theology: Models of God in Religious Language*. Philadelphia: Fortress Press, 1982.

Navone, John, and Thomas Cooper. *Tellers of the Word*. New York: Le Jacq Publishing, 1981.

Niebuhr, H. Richard. *The Meaning of Revelation*. New York: Macmillan, 1941. (Especially Chap. 2: "The Story of Our Life.")

Scholes, Robert, and Robert Kellogg. *The Nature of Narrative*. New York: Oxford University Press, 1966.

Stroup, George W. "A Bibliographical Critique." *Theology Today* 32 (July 1975): 133-43.

———. *The Promise of Narrative Theology*. Atlanta, GA: John Knox Press, 1981.

TeSelle, Sallie McFague. "The Experience of Coming to Belief." *Theology Today* 32 (July 1975): 159-65.

———. "Parable, Metaphor, and Theology." *Journal of the American Academy of Religion* 42 (December 1974): 630-45.

Wicker, Brian. *The Story Shaped World*. Notre Dame, IN: Notre Dame University Press, 1975.

Wiggins, James B., ed. *Religion as Story*. New York: Harper and Row, 1975.

Wilder, Amos. "Story and Story World." *Interpretation* 37 (October 1983): 353-64.

PRIME EXAMPLES

Alter, Robert. *The Art of Biblical Narrative*. New York: Basic Books, 1981.

Buechner, Frederick. *A Room Called Remember*. San Francisco: Harper & Row, 1984. (Chap. 5: "The Two Stories," 46-56.)

———. *Now and Then*. New York: Harper & Row, 1983.

———. *The Sacred Journey*. New York: Harper & Row, 1982.

Close, Henry T. "Metaphor in Pastoral Care." *Journal of Pastoral Care* 38 (December 1984): 298-305.

Estess, Ted L. "The Inenarrable Contraption: Reflections on the Metaphor of Story." *Journal of the American Academy of Religion* 42 (September 1974): 415-34.

Fowler, James W., and Robin W. Lovin. *Trajectories in Faith: Five Life Stories*. Nashville, TN: Abingdon Press, 1980.

Frazier, Richard T. "The Use of One's Story in C.P.E." *Journal of Supervision and Training in Ministry* 1 (Winter 1978): 17-25.

Jensen, Mark. "Some Implications of Narrative Theology for Ministry to Cancer Patients." *Journal of Pastoral Care* 38 (September 1984): 216-25.

Jensen, Richard A. *Telling the Story*. Minneapolis, MN: Augsburg, 1980.

Keen, Sam, and Anne Valley Fox. *Telling Your Story*. Garden City, NJ: Doubleday, 1973.

Krieg, Robert. "Narrative and Field Education." *Theological Field Education: A Collection of Key Resources*. N.p.: Association for Theological Field Education, 1981, 3: 95-98.

McClendon, James William, Jr. *Biography as Theology: How Life Stories Can Remake Today's Theology*. Nashville, TN: Abingdon Press, 1974.

Orr, Dick, and David L. Barrett. *Bible Journeys*. Valley Forge, PA: Judson, 1980.

Summers, Thomas A. "Story Day in C.P.E." *Journal of Supervision and Training in Ministry* 4 (1981): 37-48.

Sykes, S. W. "Story and Eucharist." *Interpretation* 37 (October 1983): 365-76.

SPECIAL ISSUES

Burrell, David, and Stanley Hauerwas. "Self-Deception and Autobiography: Theological and Ethical Reflections on Speer's Inside the Third Reich." *Journal of Religious Ethics* 2 (Spring 1974): 99-117.

Christ, Carol. *Diving Deep and Surfacing*. Boston: Beacon Press, 1980.

Cone, James H. "The Story Context of Black Theology." *Theology Today* 32 (July 1975): 144-50.

Fingarette, Herbert. *Self-Deception*. New York: Humanities Press, 1969.

————. *Self in Transformation*. New York: Basic Books, 1963.

Harnad, David B. *Images for Self Recognition*. New York: Seabury Press, 1977.

Hauerwas, Stanley. "Causistry as a Narrative Art." *Interpretation* 37 (October 1983): 377-88.

————. *Truthfulness and Tragedy*. Notre Dame: Notre Dame Press, 1977.

————. *Vision and Virtue: Essays in Christian Ethical Reflection*. Notre Dame: Fides Publishers, 1974.

Metz, Johann Baptist. *Faith in History and Society*. New York: Seabury Press, 1980.

Pascal, Roy. *Design and Truth in Autobiography*. Cambridge, MA: Harvard University Press, 1960.

Roth, Robert P. *Story and Reality*. Grand Rapids, MI: Eerdmans, 1973.

TeSelle, Sallie McFague. *Speaking in Parables: A Study in Metaphor and Theology*. Philadelphia: Fortress Press, 1975.

Thiemann, Ronald F. "Piety, Narrative, and Christian Identity." *Word and World* 3 (Spring 1983): 148-59.

Trible, Phyllis. *God and the Rhetoric of Sexuality*. Philadelphia: Fortress Press, 1978.

Wink, Walter. *The Bible in Human Transformation*. Philadelphia: Fortress Press, 1973.

GENERAL SOURCES

Barr, James. *The Scope and Authority of the Bible*. Philadelphia: Westminster Press, 1980. (See Chap. 1, "Story and History in Biblical Theology," 1-17.)

Fackre, Gabriel. *The Christian Story: A Narrative Interpretation of Basic Christian Doctrine*. Grand Rapids, MI: Eerdmans, 1978.

Frei, Hans W. *The Eclipse of Biblical Narrative: A Study of Eighteenth and Nineteenth Century Hermeneutics*. New Haven, CT: Yale University Press, 1974.

Fuller, Reginald H., and Pheme Perkins. *Who is Christ? Gospel Christology and Contemporary Faith*. Philadelphia: Fortress Press, 1983. (See Chap. 6, "Mark as Narrative Christology".)

Harnad, David B. *Faith and Virtue*. Philadelphia: Pilgrim Press, 1973.

Keen, Sam, and James Fowler. *Life Maps*. Waco, TX: Word Books, 1978.

Kerr, Hugh T. "What's the Story?" *Theology Today* 32 (July 1975): 129-32.

Kort, Wesley. *Narrative Elements and Religious Meanings*. Philadelphia: Fortress Press, 1975.

McClendon, James William, Jr. "More on Narrative." *Theology Today* 40 (April 1983): 49-53.

Novak, Michael. *Ascent of the Mountain, Flight of the Dove*. San Francisco: Harper and Row, 1978. (Especially Chap. 2, 43-87.)

Tracy, David. *The Analogical Imagination*. New York: Crossroad, 1981.

Via, Dan O., Jr. "Religion and Story: Of Time and Reality." *Journal of Religion* 56 (October 1976): 392-99.

Wiggins, James B. "Re-imaging Psycho-History." *Theology Today* 32 (July 1975): 151-58.

Wilder, Amos. *Jesus Parables and the War of Myths*. Philadelphia: Fortress Press, 1982. (See Chap. 1, "The World Story," 45-69.)

Woelfel, James. "Frederick Buechner: The Novelist as Theologian." *Theology Today* 40 (October 1983): 273-91.

———. "Religious Studies and Life Stories." *Theology Today* 39 (April 1982): 7-16.

Wright, George Ernest. *God Who Acts: Biblical Theology as Recital*. London: SCM Press, 1952.

THEOLOGICAL REFLECTION

THEORETICAL PERSPECTIVES

Bennett, G. Willis. "Religious Experience and the American Religious Scene." *Theological Field Education: A Collection of Key Resources*. N.p.: Association for Theological Field Education, 1981, 3: 43-47.

Caldwell, Charles F. "Towards a Definition of Pastoral Theology." *Theological Field Education: A Collection of Key Resources*. N.p.: Association for Theological Field Education, 1979, 2: 13-19.

Carroll, Jackson W. *Ministry as Reflective Practice*. Washington, DC: Alban Institute, 1986.

Cooke, Bernard. "The Current State of Theological Reflection." *Theological Field Education: A Collection of Key Resources*. N.p.: Association for Theological Field Education, 1981, 3: 73-78.

Durkin, Mary G. "Pluralism and Church Reform: Pastoral Theology Looks to the Future." *Toward Vatican III*, ed. David Tracy, Hans Kung, and Johann Metz, (Concilium and Seabury Press, 1978), 179-87.

Farley, Edward. "Phenomenology and Pastoral Care." *Theological Field Education: A Collection of Key Resources*. N.p.: Association for Theological Field Education, 1979, 2: 37-54.

———. *Theologia*. Philadelphia: Fortress Press, 1983.

Frazer, Ian M. "Theology by the People." *Ministerial Formation: Programme on Theological Education*. 28 (October 1984): 3-10.

Garibaldi, Ronald, and Daniel Novotny. *The Art of Theological Reflection*. University Press of America, 1987.

Haarsma, Frans. "Religious Experience in Practical Theology." *Theological Field Education: A Collection of Key Resources*. N.p.: Association for Theological Field Education, 1981, 3: 49-56.

———. "Theoretical Problems in Practical Theology." *Theological Field Education:*

A Collection of Key Resources. N.p.: Association for Theological Field Education, 1979, 2: 27-36.

Holmes, Urban T. "An Outline of An Intentional Theory of Ministry." *Theological Field Education: A Collection of Key Resources.* N.p.: Association for Theological Field Education, 1979, 2: 131-143. Reprint from *St. Luke's Journal of Theology* 20, no. 2 (March 1977).

———. *The Future Shape of Ministry.* New York: Seabury Press, 1971.

Hommes, Tjaard G. "Theological Reflection and Ministry." *Theological Field Education: A Collection of Key Resources.* N.p.: Association for Theological Field Education, 1979, 2: 1-10.

———. "The Minister as Theologian." *Theological Field Education: A Collection of Key Resources.* N.p.: Association for Theological Field Education, 1979, 2: 21-26.

Hug, James S. *Tracing the Spirit: Communities, Social Action, and Theological Reflection.* (Woodstock Theology Series) New York: Paulist Press, 1983.

Jancoski, Loretta. "Developmental Psychologies and Religious Experience." *Theological Field Education: A Collection of Key Resources.* N.p.: Association for Theological Field Education, 1981, 3: 33-41.

Kinast, Robert L. "Theological Reflection in Ministry Preparation." *Spirituality, Ministry, and Field Education.* Vol. 5 of *Theological Field Education: Key Resources.* N.p.: Association for Theological Field Education, 1987, 115-27.

King, Eugene. "Religious Experience and Theological Reflection." *Theological Field Education: A Collection of Key Resources.* N.p.: Association for Theological Field Education, 1981, 3: 63-71.

———. "Tasks and Skills of the Theologian in Pastoral Studies." *Spirituality, Ministry, and Field Education.* Vol. 5 of *Theological Field Education: Key Resources.* N.p.: Association for Theological Field Education, 1987, 104-14.

McCarty, Doran. "Religious Experience as a Methodological Problem for Theology." *Theological Field Education: A Collection of Key Resources.* N.p.: Association for Theological Field Education, 1981, 3: 25-31.

McDonnell, Kilian. "I Believe That I Might Experience." *Theological Field Education: A Collection of Key Resources.* N.p.: Association for Theological Field Education, 1981, 3: 79-89. Reprint from *Continuum*, 5. no. 4 (1968).

Moore, Robert, and Jack Seymour. "Practical Hermeneutics and Religious Leadership: Implication for Theological Education." *Pastoral Hermeneutics and Ministry.* Vol. 4 of *Theological Field Education: Key Resources.* N.p.: Association for Theological Field Education, 1983, 105-19.

O'Connell, Lawrence J. "Pastoral Theology: Janus of the Theological Enterprise." *Theological Field Education: A Collection of Key Resources.* N.p.: Association for Theological Field Education, 1979, 2: 55-61.

———. "The Evolving Notion of Experience: A Preface to Understanding Religious Experience." *Theological Field Education: A Collection of Key Resources.* N.p.: Association for Theological Field Education, 1981, 3: 11-23.

———. "Theological Reflection and Ministerial Identity." *Theological Field Education: A Collection of Key Resources.* N.p.: Association for Theological Field Education, 1979, 2: 165-69.

Richardson, Robert L., Jr. "Religious Experience and the New Testament." *Theological Field Education: A Collection of Key Resources.* N.p.: Association for Theological Field Education, 1981, 3: 57-62.

Shelp, Earl E., and Ronald H. Sunderland. *The Pastor as Theologian.* New York: Pilgrim Press, 1988.

Taylor, Michael H. "Theology by the People of God." *Ministerial Formation: Programme on Theological Education.* 28 (October 1984): 11-18.

Thiemann, Ronald F. "Making Theology Central in Theological Education." *Christian Century* 4-11 February 1987, 106-108.

MODELS/METHODS

Ames, Stephen A. H. "Theological Reflection: Purposes, Pathways, Choices." Unpublished paper, 1983.

Arnott, Robert J. "Theological Methodology for Pastors and Congregations." *Pastoral Hermeneutics and Ministry.* Vol. 4 of *Theological Field Education: Key Resources.* N.p.: Association for Theological Field Education, 1983, 242-52.

Asquith, Glenn H. "The Case Study Method of Anton T. Boisen." *Journal of Pastoral Care* 34 (June 1980): 84-94.

Brusatti, Louis T. "Theological Reflection and Erickson's Developmental Framework." *Theological Field Education: A Collection of Key Resources.* N.p.: Association for Theological Field Education, 1979, 2: 151-64.

Close, William J. "Methodologies in Distinguishing Human Experiences, Religious Experience and Faith Existence." *Theological Field Education: A Collection of Key Resources.* N.p.: Association for Theological Field Education, 1981, 3: 99-108.

———. "What Does It Mean to Think Theologically?" *Theological Field Education: A Collection of Key Resources.* N.p.: Association for Theological Field Education, 1979, 2: 75-88.

Collins, Raymond F. *Models of Theological Reflection.* Lanham, MD: University Press of America, 1984.

Conlon, James A. "Theological Reflection and Social Analysis." *Spirituality, Ministry, and Field Education.* Vol. 5 of *Theological Field Education: Key Resources.* N.p.: Association for Theological Field Education, 1987, 169-74.

Education for Ministry. A Manual for Mentors. Sewanee, TN: Baernwick Center, University of the South, 1984.

Garibaldi, Ronald J. "Pastoral Hermeneutics and Pastoral Identity." *Pastoral Hermeneutics and Ministry.* Vol. 4 of *Theological Field Education: Key Resources.* N.p.: Association for Theological Field Education, 1983, 195-201.

Killien, Patricia O'Connell, and John de Beer. "'Everyday' Theology: A Model for Religious and Theological Education." *Chicago Studies* 22 (August 1983): 191-206.

Kinast, Robert L. "A Process Model of Theological Reflection." *Journal of Pastoral Care* 37 (June 1983): 144-55.

King, Eugene. "Dag Hammerskjold's Befriending Death: A Case Study in Theological

Reflection." *Pastoral Sciences* 1 (1982): 91-112.

————. "Towards a Method of Theological Reflection on Experience in Ministry." *Pastoral Sciences* 2 (1983): 33-57.

Kinsler, F. Ross. *Ministry by the People*. Maryknoll, NY: Orbis Books, 1983.

Lonergan, Bernard. *Method in Theology*. New York: Herder and Herder, 1972. (New York: Seabury, 1979).

McKenna, Thomas F. "Academic or Pastoral Theology: A False Dilemma." *Theological Field Education: A Collection of Key Resources*. N.p.: Association for Theological Field Education, 1979, 2: 145-49. Reprint from *Priest*. 34: 10-14 (January 1978).

Miller, William A., ed. "A Report on the Symposium: 'CPE as a Model for Theology and Praxis in Lutheran Theological Education.'" *SPC Journal* 10 (1988): 4-18.

O'Shea, Ann. "The Emmaus Story: A Model for Pastoral Supervision." *Journal of Supervision and Training in Ministry* 9 (1987): 29-34.

Poling, James. "Hermeneutics of Ministry Events." *Pastoral Hermeneutics and Ministry*. Vol. 4 of *Theological Field Education: Key Resources*. N.p.: Association for Theological Field Education, 1983, 187-94.

Rahtjen, Bruce D., Bryce Kramer, and Ken Mitchell. *A Workbook in Experiential Theology*. Kansas City, MO: Associates in Experiential Theology, 1977.

Ricoeur, Paul. "The Model of the Text: Meaningful Action Considered as a Text." *Social Research* 38 (Autumn 1971): 529-62.

Shea, John. "Doing Ministerial Theology: A Skills Approach." *Toward Vatican III*, ed. David Tracy, Hans Kung, and Johann Metz. New York: Seabury, 1978, 188-95. Also, *Theological Field Education: A Collection of Key Resources*. N.p.: Association for Theological Field Education, 1979, 2: 123-30.

Trutter, Carl B. "Theologizing in Field Education." *Theological Field Education: A Collection of Key Resources*. N.p.: Association for Theological Field Education, 1977, 1: 157-64.

Whitehead, James. "Theological Reflection in Pastoral Theology." *Theological Field Education: A Collection of Key Resources*. N.p.: Association for Theological Field Education, 1977, 1: 118-22.

————, and Evelyn Eaton. *Method in Ministry: Theological Reflection and Christian Ministry*. New York: Seabury, 1980.

Wingeier, Douglas E. *Working Out Your Own Beliefs*. Nashville, TN: Abingdon Press, 1980.

SUPERVISION AS THEOLOGICAL METHOD

Anderson, Herbert E. "The Spirituality of Learning to Care." *Journal of Supervision and Training in Ministry* 4 (1982): 21-35.

Baldwin, George, and Paul Maves. "Phenomenological Reflections: The Focus of the Supervisory Conference." *Theological Field Education: A Collection of Key Resources*. N.p.: Association for Theological Field Education, 1977, 1: 146-49.

Bergland, James W. "Field Education as Locus for Theological Reflection." *Theological Education* 5 (Summer 1969): 338-45.

Bickel, Arthur O. "Theology/Spirituality Seminars." *Journal of Supervision and Training in Ministry* 2 (Winter 1979): 30-39.

Burbank, Beth, and Gerald Cowing Johnson, eds. "Story Theology and Ministry Supervision." *Journal of Supervision and Training in Ministry* 9 (1987): 130-236.

Close, William J. "The Learning Covenant as Institutionalized Functional Theology." *Theological Field Education: A Collection of Key Resources.* N.p.: Association for Theological Field Education, 1979, 2: 173-77.

Gerkin, Charles V. "Power and Powerlessness in Clinical Pastoral Education." *Journal of Pastoral Care* 34 (June 1980): 114-24.

Harris, J. Edward C. "Supervision: A Biblical Metaphor." *Journal of Supervision and Training in Ministry* 2 (Winter 1979): 86-93.

Hommes, Tjaard G. "Supervision as Theologial Method." *Theological Field Education: A Collection of Key Resources.* N.p.: Association for Theological Field Education, 1977, 1: 86-93.

Hoover, Edwin A. "The Distinction Between Adequate and Excellent Supervision: A Wholistic Perspective." *Journal of Pastoral Care* 34 (September 1980): 190-96.

Kenny, Dennis E. "Clinical Pastoral Education--Exploring Covenants with God." *Journal of Pastoral Care* 34 (June 1980): 109-13.

Krieg, Robert A. "Theological Models and Pastoral Practice." *Pastoral Hermeneutics and Ministry.* Vol. 4 of *Theological Field Education: Key Resources.* N.p.: Association for Theological Field Education, 1983, 120-27.

McCarty, Doran. "Theological Principles for the Supervisory Task." *Theological Field Education: A Collection of Key Resources.* N.p.: Association for Theological Field Education, 1977, 1: 82-93.

Myler, David C. "Resistance to Clinical Learning: Four Biblical Types." *Journal of Supervision and Training in Ministry* 2 (Winter 1979): 60-72.

Nouwen, Henri J. M. "Case-Recording in Pastoral Education." *Theological Field Education: A Collection of Key Resources.* N.p.: Association for Theological Field Education, 1977, 1: 123-31.

Patton, John. "Clinical Hermeneutics: Soft Focus in Pastoral Counseling and Theology" *Pastoral Hermeneutics and Ministry.* Vol. 4 of *Theological Field Education: Key Resources.* N.p.: Association for Theological Field Education, 1983, 89-104.

Richard, Lucien. "The Existing Malaise in the Theologizing of Field Experience." *Theological Education* 9 (Autumn 1972): 67-70.

Woodruff, C. Roy. "Theological Reflection in the Supervisory Process." *Journal of Pastoral Care* 34 (September 1980): 197-203.

GENERAL SOURCES

Anderson, Philip and Phoebe. *The House Church*. Nashville, TN: Abingdon Press, 1975.

Browning, Don. "Analogy, Symbol, and Pastoral Theology in Tillich's Thought." *Pastoral Psychology* 19 (February 1968): 41-54.

Horn, Chevis F. "A Theology of Counseling." *Pastoral Psychology* 19 (November 1968): 29-34.

Houts, Donald C. "Sensitivity, Theology, and Change: Pastoral Care in the Corinthian Letters." *Pastoral Psychology* 20 (April 1969): 28-34.

Howe, Reuel L. *Man's Need and God's Action*. Greenwich, CT: Seabury Press, 1953.

Jernigan, Homer L. "Bringing Together Psychology and Theology: Reflections on Ministry to the Bereaved." *Journal of Pastoral Care* 30 (June 1976): 88-102.

Mitchell, Kenneth R. "Paul Tillich's Contributions to Pastoral Care and Counseling." *Pastoral Psychology* 19 (February 1968): 24-32.

Nouwen, Henri J. M. "Anton T. Boisen and Theology Through Living Human Documents." *Pastoral Psychology* 19 (September 1968): 49-63.

Oglesby, William B., Jr. *The New Shape of Pastoral Theology*. New York: Abingdon Press, 1969.

Tillich, Paul. *The Shaking of the Foundations*. New York: Scribners, 1948.

————. *Systematic Theology*, Vol. 1. Chicago: University of Chicago Press, 1950.

Vincent, John J., ed. *Stirrings*. London: Epworth Press, 1976.

EXPERIENTIAL LEARNING IN MINISTRY OF SUPERVISION

THEORY AND PRACTICE

Baldwin, George W., and Paul B. Maves. "Creating a Model for Field Education." *Theological Education* 11 (Summer 1975): 265-68.

Barrick, William E. "The Function of Field Education Within the Seminary Curriculum: Major Trends and Priorities." *Theological Field Education: A Collection of Key Resources*. N.p.: Association for Theological Field Education, 1979, 2: 189-96.

Becker, Russell J. "The Place of the Parish in Theological Education." *Journal of Pastoral Care* 21 (September 1967): 163-70.

Beisswenger, Donald F. "The Integration of Field Education into the Curriculum." *Report of Proceedings, Tenth Biennial Consultation on Field Education*, Berkeley, CA, January 15-18, 1969, 8-12.

————. "Locating Clinical or Field Based Learning Within Theological Education." *Theological Field Education: A Collection of Key Resources*. N.p.: Association for Theological Field Education, 1977, 1: 12-17.

Bennett, F. Russell. "Simulation/Game and Field Education." *Theological Field Education: A Collection of Key Resources*. N.p.: Association for Theological Field Education, 1981, 3: 253-57.

Bloede, Louis W. "The Intern Year." *Theological Field Education: A Collection of Key Resources*. N.p.: Association for Theological Field Education, 1981, 3: 239-43.

Clark, Linda, and Lynn Rhodes. "Feminism and Field Education." *Theological Field Education: A Collection of Key Resources*. N.p.: Association for Theological Field Education, 1981, 3: 209-12.

Close, William J. "Pastoral Hermeneutics and Field Education." *Pastoral Hermeneutics and Ministry*. Vol. 4 of *Theological Field Education: Key Resources*. N.p.: Association for Theological Field Education, 1983, 172-85.

————. "A Theory Base for Theological Field Education." *Spirituality, Ministry, and*

Field Education. Vol. 5 of *Theological Field Education: Key Resources.* N.p.: Association for Theological Field Education, 1986, 147-59.

Drake, Patricia G., ed. *Building Stronger Lay Committees.* Washington, DC: Alban Institute, 1983.

Fletcher, John C., and Tilden H. Edwards, Jr. "Inter-Met: On-the-Job Theological Education." *Pastoral Psychology* 22 (March 1971): 21-30.

Gilmore, Martha. "Covenant Partners in Learning: Lay Committees/Theological Student." *Report of the 17th Biennial Meeting of the Association of Professional Education for Ministry,* Pittsburgh, PA, June 1982, 55-57.

Hallman, Julieanne. "The Development of and Implications for Teaching Parish Committee as an Integral and Vital Partner in Field Education." Ann Arbor, MI: University Microfilms, 1980. Unpublished D.Min. Project for Andover Newton Theological School.

Handspicker, M. B. "Religious Experience and the Case Study Method." *Theological Field Education: A Collection of Key Resources.* N.p.: Association for Theological Field Education, 1981, 3: 167-71.

Hefferman, William P. "Self-Reflective Process in a Pastoral Field Training Program." *Theological Education* 5, Suppl. 1 (Summer 1969): 436-44.

Hewitt, C. M. Kempton. "Field Education for Hispanic Ministry." *Theological Field Education: A Collection of Key Resources.* N.p.: Association for Theological Field Education, 1981, 3: 205-07.

Hommes, Tjaard G. "Educational Theory Base for Field Education." *Theological Field Education: A Collection of Key Resources.* N.p.: Association for Theological Field Education, 1977, 1: 2-11.

Hunter, George I., Jr. "Theological Field Education: An Ecumenical Experience." *Andover Newton Quarterly* 17 (November 1976): 118-224.

Johnson, John R., Jr. "Clinical Pastoral Education and Student Changes in Role Perception." *Journal of Pastoral Care* 21 (September 1967): 129-46.

Kale, William Arthur. "Field Work at Duke: Its Educational Significance." *Duke Divinity School Review* 33 (Autumn 1968): 141-50.

Kemper, Robert G. *The New Shape of Ministry: Taking Accountability Seriously.* Nashville, TN: Abingdon Press, 1979.

Lloyd, Barton M. "Key Issues in the Personal Preparation of Clergy." *Theological Education* 5, Suppl. 1 (Summer 1969): 420-35.

Lowndes, Robert S. "Theological Education and Field Education." *Theological Education* 5, Suppl. 1 (Summer 1969): 445-54.

McDanile, Charlotte. "Christian Praxis: A Conceptual Model for Field Education." *Theological Field Education: A Collection of Key Resources.* N.p.: Association for Theological Field Education, 1981, 3: 245-51.

Murphy, David M. "Integration of Field Education Into the Curriculum." *Theological Education* 11 (Summer 1975): 285-94.

O'Rourke, David K. "Dissimilar Field Placements in the Pastoral Training Seminar." *Theological Education* 5, Suppl. 1 (Summer 1969): 455-63.

———. "Double Messages in Seminary Training." *Theological Education* 5, Suppl. 1 (Summer 1969): 411-19.

Pohly, Kenneth Holt. "The Clinical Method in Theological Education." Ann Arbor, MI: University Microfilms. Unpublished D.Min. Diss. for Vanderbilt University, Nashville, TN, 1969.

————. "Essential Components of a Field Education Program." *Report of Proceedings, Seventeenth Biennial Consultation on Field Education*, ATFE, San Antonio, TX, January 12-15, 1983, 17-23.

Pregnall, William S. "An Assessment of Lay Committee in Theological Field. *Theological Field Education: A Collection of Key Resources.* N.p.: Association for Theological Field Education, 1981, 3: 223-27.

Schores, Daniel M. "Trends and Issues in Field Education." *Report of Proceedings, Tenth Biennial Consultation on Field Education*, Berkeley, CA, January 15-18, 1969, 13-16.

Seymour, Jack L. "Placement Design: Defining the Context for Field Education." *Theological Field Education: A Collection of Key Resources.* N.p.: Association for Theological Field Education, 1981, 3: 215-21.

Strommen, Merton. "CPE and Readiness for Ministry." *Eighth Annual Conference Proceedings*. Association for Clinical Pastoral Education, October 1975, 50-58.

Telfer, Walter A., and Meredith B. Handspicker. "Teaching Parishes -- Partners in Theological Education." *Andover Newton Quarterly* 17 (November 1976): 108-17.

Way, Peggy. "New Directions in Theological Education." *Eighth Annual Conference Proceedings*. Association for Clinical Pastoral Education, October 1975, 33-49.

Whitehead, James D., and Evelyn E. Whitehead. "Educational Models in Field Education." *Theological Education* 11 (Summer 1975): 269-78.

Zimmerman, Jervis S. "The Relevance of Clinical Pastoral Training to Field Education." *Journal of Pastoral Care* 22 (March 1968): 1-6.

THEOLOGICAL FOUNDATIONS

Aden, LeRoy. "Faith and the Developmental Cycle." *Pastoral Psychology* 24 (Spring 1976): 215-30.

Clebsch, William A., and Charles R. Jaekle. *Pastoral Care in Historical Perspective.* Englewood Cliffs, NJ: Prentice-Hall, 1964.

DeVries, Robert C. "Religious Experience in the Reformed Tradition and Its Implications for Field Education." *Theological Field Education: A Collection of Key Resources.* N.p.: Association for Theological Field Education, 1981, 3: 199-203.

Egan, Maureen. "Religious Experience in the Roman Catholic Tradition and Its Significance for Field Education." *Theological Field Education: A Collection of Key Resources.* N.p.: Association for Theological Field Education, 1981, 3: 179-85.

Farley, Edward. "Symposium: The Reform of Theological Education as a Theological Task." *Journal of Supervision and Training in Ministry* 4 (1981): 81-134.

Fowler, James W. *Stages of Faith*. New York: Harper and Row, 1981.

Hall, Charles E., Jr. "Some Contributions of Anton Boisen (1876-1965) to Understanding Psychiatry and Religion." *Pastoral Psychology* 19 (September 1968): 40-48.

Hommes, Tjaard G. "Experiential Learning and Theological Tradition." *Theological Field Education: A Collection of Key Resources.* N.p.: Association for Theological Field Education, 1977, 1: 132-38.

———. "Religious Experience in Field Education and Pastoral Theology." *Theological Field Education: A Collection of Key Resources.* N.p.: Association for Theological Field Education, 1981, 3: 1-7.

Lake, Frank. *Clinical Theology.* London: Darton Longman and Todd, 1966.

Lambourne, R. A. "The Theological Strategy of a British Pastoral Training Course." *Journal of Pastoral Care* 24 (December 1970): 227-32.

Lewis, G. Douglas, ed. *Explorations in Ministry.* New York: IDOC, North America, 1971.

McNeill, John T. *History of the Cure of Souls.* New York: Harper, 1951.

Neibuhr, H. Richard. *The Purpose of the Church and Its Ministry.* New York: Harper and Row, 1956.

O'Connell, Lawrence J. "Fowler, Faith Development, and Theological Education." *Pastoral Hermeneuticsand Ministry.* Vol. 4 of *Theological Field Education: Key Resources.* N.p.: Association for Theological Field Education, 1983, 128-39.

Paetzel, Richard W. "Religious Experience in the Free Church Tradition and Its Implications for Field Education." *Theological Field Education: A Collection of Key Resources.* N.p.: Association for Theological Field Education, 1981, 3: 187-91.

Patsavos, Lewis J. "Field Education in an Orthodox Theological Curriculum." *Pastoral Hermeneutics and Ministry.* Vol. 4 of *Theological Field Education: Key Resources.* N.p.: Association for Theological Field Education, 1983, 289-94.

Schnackenburg, Rudolf. *The Church in the New Testament.* London: Burns and Oates, 1974.

Snyder, Ross. "The Boisen Heritage in Theological Education." *Pastoral Psychology* 19 (September 1968): 9-13, 64-65, 139-144.

Stendahl, Krister. "Formation in Theological Education." *Theological Field Education: A Collection of Key Resources.* N.p.: Association for Theological Field Education, 1977, 1: 94-102.

Stewart, Charles William. *Person and Profession.* Nashville, TN: Abingdon Press, 1974.

Vincent, John J. *Alternative Church.* Belfast: Christian Journals Limited, 1976.

———. *The Jesus Thing.* London: Epworth Press, 1973.

———. *Secular Christ.* Nashville, TN: Abingdon Press, 1968.

Westphal, Bruce M. "Religious Experience in the Lutheran Tradition and Its Implications for Field Ecducation." *Theological Field Education: A Collection of Key Resources.* N.p.: Association for Theological Field Education, 1981, 3: 199-203.

SPECIAL ISSUES

Adix, James. "Pastoral Authority: A Survival Issue." *Journal of Supervision and Training in Ministry* 2 (1979): 5-11.

Aist, Clark, S. "Professional Certification in the Clinical Pastoral Field." *Journal of*

Supervision and Training in Ministry 3 (1980): 101-05.

Beck, James R. "The Pastoral Dimension of Supervision: A Study in Identification and Rapprochment." *Journal of Supervision and Training in Ministry* 9 (1987): 18-28.

Beisswenger, Donald F. "Evaluation in Theological Field Education." *Spirituality, Ministry, and Field Education.* Vol. 5 of *Theological Field Education: Key Resources.* N.p.: Association for Theological Field Education, 1987, 221-35.

Bogia, B. Preston. "Supervision and Stress." *Journal of Supervision and Training in Ministry* 5 (1982): 55-60.

Carp, Al. "Supervision from Peace Corps Perspective." In *Report of Proceedings, Tenth Biennial Consultation on Field Education*, ATFE, Berkeley, CA, 1969, 30-33.

Cavers, David F. "Legal Education in Times of Change." *Theological Education* 5 (Spring 1969): 170-92.

Ciampa, Ralph C. "God-Talk in Pastoral Care." *Journal of Pastoral Care* 30 (March 1976): 27-34.

Conlon, James A. "Social Injustice and Field Education." *Pastoral Hermeneutics and Ministry.* Vol. 4 of *Theological Field Education: Key Resources.* N.p.: Association for Theological Field Education, 1983, 270-74.

Dawson, Caroline. "Foundations for Change: A Proposed Agenda for Theological Field Education." *Spirituality, Ministry, and Field Education.* Vol. 5 of *Theological Field Education: Key Resources.* N.p.: Association for Theological Field Education, 1987, 210-20.

Gibb, Jack R. "Is Help Helpful?" *Theological Field Education: A Collection of Key Resources.* N.p.: Association for Theological Field Education, 1977, 1: 142-45.

Gibbons, James L., Myron C. Madden, Robert A. Preston, and John I. Smith, eds. "Symposium on the Certification Process." *Journal of Supervision and Training in Ministry* 3 (1980): 107-33.

Gustafson, James M. "Theological Education as Professional Education." *Theological Education* 5 (Spring 1969): 243-61.

Hughes, Everett C. "Are the Clergy a Profession?" *Theological Education* 5 (Spring 1969): 287-92.

Keith-Lucas, Alan. *Giving and Taking Help.* Chapel Hill, NC: University of North Carolina Press, 1972.

Lee, Peter V. "The American Medical School: A Case Study in Professional Education." *Theological Education* 5 (Spring 1969): 197-214.

McKenzie, John L. *Authority in the Church.* London: Geoffrey Chapman, 1966.

Mayse, Marilyn, and Paula Jeanne Teague. "Women Supervised by Men." *Journal of Supervision and Training in Ministry* 9 (1987): 35-41.

Mauney, J. Luther, Jr. "Analysis of a Supervisory Impasse." *Journal of Supervision and Training in Ministry* 3 (1980): 21-28.

Meadows-Rogers, Arabella. "Women in Field Education." *Theological Education* 9 (Summer 1975): 301-07.

Moore, Robert L., and Janet A. MacKenzie, eds. "Gender Issues and Supervision: A Symposium." *Journal of Supervision and Training in Ministry* 6 (1983): 137-215.

Perske, Robert. "The Use of the Critical Incident Report." *Journal of Pastoral Care* 20 (September 1966): 156-61.

Rafford, Robert L. "Andragogy and Supervision." *Journal of Supervision and Training in Ministry* 5 (1982): 69-75.

Reed, Kenneth E. "Pastoral Relationships to Community Agencies." *Pastoral Psychology* 20 (September 1969): 43-49.

Rhodes, Lynn, and Shelley Finson. "Women in Ministry: Implications for Field Education Practice." *Spirituality, Ministry, and Field Education.* Vol. 5 of *Theological Field Education: Key Resources.* N.p.: Association for Theological Field Education, 1987, 164-68.

Rowatt, G. Wade. "What Does ACPE Expect of Ministry?" *Journal of Pastoral Care* 36 (September 1982): 147-59.

Seabright, Russell. "Cultural Anthropology as Resource to Theological Field Education." *Spirituality, Ministry, and Field Education.* Vol. 5 of *Theological Field Education: Key Resources.* N.p.: Association for Theological Field Education, 1987, 175-82.

Schuller, David S., and Merton P. Strommen. *The Expectations of Ministry: The View of Clinical Pastoral Education.* Dayton, OH: Association of Theological Schools and Association for Clinical Pastoral Education, 1981.

Summers, Thomas A. "Pastoral Certification From a Developmental Perspective." *Journal of Supervision and Training in Ministry* 3 (1980): 73-85.

Switzer, David K. "The Minister as Pastor and Person." *Pastoral Psychology* 24 (Fall 1975): 52-64.

Wingeier, Douglas E. "The Supervision of Doctor of Ministry Candidates." *Journal of Supervision and Training in Ministry* 9 (1987): 5-17.

OTHER BIBLIOGRAPHIC RESOURCES

For additional books and articles on field education and related issues of spirituality and supervision see the bibliographies in *Theological Field Education: A Collection of Key Resources*, N.p.: Association for Theological Field Education, 1977-1983, vols. 1-4.

INDEX

J

K

L

M

N

O

WHALEPRINTS ™

Production Notes

Design and Artwork
      Cover design by Karen Ingle of Penny, Ohlmann, Neiman, Inc.,
      Dayton, Ohio

Type
      Display type: Penny, Ohlmann, Neiman, Inc.
      Text types: Times Roman
      Typesetting: Marti Anderson, United Theological Seminary, Dayton,
      Ohio

Printing and Binding
      Cover: Printed on Springhill C1S 10 point coated one side
      Text: Printed on acid-free 70 pound Cougar Natural
      Printing and Binding by Hammer Graphics, Inc., Piqua, Ohio